Weak and Strong States in Asia–Pacific Societies

Edited by Peter Dauvergne

Allen & Unwin in association with the
Department of International Relations
Research School of Pacific and Asian Studies
Australian National University, Canberra, ACT

First published in 1998.

Allen & Unwin Australia Pty Ltd.
9 Atchison St, St Leonards, NSW 2065, Australia.

Department of International Relations, RSPAS,
Australian National University, Canberra ACT 0200, Australia.

National Library of Australia
Cataloguing-in-Publication entry:

Weak and Strong States in Asia–Pacific Societies.

ISBN 1 86373 983 1.

1. Asia, Southeastern – Politics and government – 1945– .
2. Asia, Southeastern – Social conditions – 20th century.
3. Melanesia – Politics and government – 20th century.
4. Melanesia – Social conditions – 20th century. I. Dauvergne, Peter.
II. Australian National University. Dept. of International Relations
(Series: Studies in world affairs; no. 18).

320.1

Unless otherwise stated, publications of the Department of International Relations are presented without endorsement as contributions to the public record and debate. Authors are responsible for their own analyses and conclusions.

Table of Contents

Notes on Contributors

Harold Crouch is a Senior Fellow in the Political and Social Change Department, Research School of Pacific and Asian Studies, Australian National University, Canberra, Australia. He is the author of *Government and Society in Malaysia* (Ithaca, NY: Cornell University Press, 1996) and *The Army and Politics in Indonesia* (Ithaca, NY: Cornell University Press, 1988).

Peter Dauvergne is a Research Fellow in the Department of International Relations, Research School of Pacific and Asian Studies, Australian National University. He is the author of *Shadows in the Forest: Japan and the Politics of Timber in Southeast Asia* (Cambridge, MA: The MIT Press, 1997).

Sinclair Dinnen is a Postdoctoral Fellow in the Political and Social Change Department, Research School of Pacific and Asian Studies, Australian National University. He was formerly head of the Crime Studies Division at the National Research Institute in Port Moresby; he has also lectured at the Law Faculty of the University of Papua New Guinea. He is co-editor (with Ron May and Anthony Regan) of *Challenging the State—The Sandline Affair in Papua New Guinea* (Canberra: National Centre for Development Studies and Department of Political and Social Change, Research School of Pacific and Asian Studies, Australian National University, 1997).

Ben Kerkvliet is Professor and Head of the Department of Political and Social Change, Research School of Pacific and Asian Studies, Australian National University. He is the author of *Everyday Politics in the Philippines: Class and Status Relations in a Central Luzon Village* (Berkeley: University of California Press, 1990) and co-editor (with Doug J. Porter) of *Vietnam's Rural Transformation* (Boulder, CO: Westview Press, and Singapore: Institute of Southeast Asian Studies, 1995).

Peter Larmour is the Director of Graduate Studies in Development Administration at the National Centre for Development Studies, Research School of Pacific and Asian Studies, Australian National University. His most recent publications include, 'Models of Governance and Public Administration', *International Review of Administrative Sciences* 63(3): 383–94, and 'Corruption and Governance in the South Pacific', *Pacific Studies*, forthcoming.

Stephanie Lawson is Professor of International Relations (Asia–Pacific), School of Economic and Social Studies, University of East Anglia,

Norwich, United Kingdom. She is the author of *Tradition versus Democracy in the South Pacific: Fiji, Tonga, and Western Samoa* (New York: Cambridge University Press, 1996) and editor of *The New Agenda for Global Security:* Cooperating for Peace *and Beyond* (Sydney: Allen & Unwin, in association with the Department of International Relations, Research School of Pacific and Asian Studies, The Australian National University, 1995).

Ron May is Senior Fellow in the Department of Political and Social Change, Research School of Pacific and Asian Studies, Australian National University. He is a former director of the Institute of Applied Social and Economic Research, Papua New Guinea. His publications include *The Changing Role of the Military in Papua New Guinea*, Canberra Papers on Strategy and Defence No. 101 (Canberra: Strategic and Defence Studies Centre, Research School of Pacific Studies, Australian National University, 1993) and the co-edited (with F. Nemenzo), *The Philippines After Marcos* (London: Croom Helm, 1985).

Joel S. Migdal is Robert F. Philip Professor of International Studies at the Henry M. Jackson School of International Studies, University of Washington, Seattle. Recent publications are, 'Studying the State', in Mark Irving Lichbach and Alan S. Zuckerman, eds, *Comparative Politics. Rationality, Culture and Structure* (Cambridge/New York: Cambridge University Press, 1997) and Baruch Kimmerling and Joel S. Migdal, *Palestinians: The Making of a People* (Cambridge, MA: Harvard University Press, 1994).

Acknowledgements

This volume is based on the papers presented at the Workshop on Weak and Strong States in Melanesia and Southeast Asia, Research School of Pacific and Asian Studies, the Australian National University, 12–14 August 1997. This workshop was funded by the State, Society and Governance in Melanesia Project (in the Research School of Pacific and Asian Studies, the Australian National University). This project is supported by the Commonwealth Department of Foreign Affairs and Trade and the Australian Aid Agency (AusAID).

I am thankful for the constructive comments on this book by my colleagues Tony Regan and Greg Fry, as well as the anonymous reviewers. I also appreciate Robin Ward's untiring research, copy-editing, and preparation of the index, as well as Lynne Payne's work preparing the manuscript and Mary-Louise Hickey's final copy-edit. Finally, I am most grateful to the contributors to this book, who vigorously discussed these ideas at our workshop, promptly supplied drafts, and enthusiastically made revisions.

1 Weak States, Strong States: A State-in-Society Perspective

PETER DAUVERGNE[1]

What is a strong state? When is a state weak? Many political scientists use the terms 'strong' and 'weak' states—sometimes precisely, but more often with only a hazy sense of what they mean. This book advances our understanding of the concepts of strong and weak states within a state-in-society approach. This approach views a state as one organisation within a societal arena where groups and individuals contest rules and norms. The authors build in particular on the theoretical ideas of Joel Migdal, especially his book *Strong Societies and Weak States: State–Society Relations and State Capabilities in the Third World* (1988), and his co-edited book with Atul Kohli and Vivienne Shue, *State Power and Social Forces: Domination and Transformation in the Third World* (1994). They do not revisit the historical development of a state-in-society approach, which is already well covered in *State Power and Social Forces*. The empirical chapters focus on a number of states in Southeast Asia and the South Pacific, areas that contain a rich variety of states and societies, from the apparently strong states of Singapore, Indonesia, and Vietnam to the seemingly weak states of the Philippines, Papua New Guinea, Vanuatu, and the Solomon Islands. This is ideal ground for studying the inherent strengths and weaknesses of states as well as the analytical advantages and disadvantages of using the concepts of strong and weak states.

The authors in this book move beyond a simple dichotomy of weak and strong states. They do not assume that the concepts of strong and

---

1   An earlier version of this article appeared as 'Weak and Strong States in the Societies of the Asia–Pacific,' in *Pacific Economic Bulletin* 13, no. 1 (June 1998) 129–36. I am grateful to the editor of *Pacific Economic Bulletin* for permission to draw on this article.

weak states are necessarily useful labels or straightforward terms. Instead, they vigorously challenge these concepts, pointing out limitations, and suggesting parameters for their use. Each author has viewed states as part of their societies, although specific definitions—such as capacity, autonomy, legitimacy, effectiveness, weak, and strong—are left up to individual authors. Generally the authors define a state as a multifaceted organisation with a legitimate monopoly over the use of violence. This organisation consists of an executive, legislature, bureaucracy, courts, police, armed forces, and, when applicable, schools and public companies. States attempt to develop and impose uniform rules and norms within their societies. Embedding the analysis in this perspective simultaneously adds a deeper and more sophisticated understanding of the concepts of weak and strong states as well as a state-in-society approach.

As in other state-in-society analyses, the authors disaggregate states and assume that internal tensions and competition among state sections significantly shape state policies, actions, and capacity. In this view, states generally aim to preserve legitimacy and order, in part by raising revenue, resisting internal and external threats, coordinating state agencies, and controlling or responding to societal pressures. They are not, however, monolithic organisations: state output is a result of struggles among state sections and with relevant non-state organisations. For this reason, the authors in this book are not primarily concerned with the extent of state autonomy and instead focus on how states are woven into their society. They also see states and societies in constant flux, each continually altered by the structure and actions of the other.

Definitions of state strength vary somewhat, although most writers accept that it involves, at least in part, the willingness and ability of a state to maintain social control, ensure societal compliance with official laws, act decisively, make effective policies, preserve stability and cohesion, encourage societal participation in state institutions, provide basic services, manage and control the national economy, and retain legitimacy. Strength or weakness is seen as arising from how all levels of the state interact with various social groups. The particular features of a country— such as its political system, military and police, bureaucracy, pre-colonial, colonial, and post-colonial histories, economic structure, cultural traditions, and relative position in the regional and international systems— shape the extent of state control over social groups and the extent that social forces reshape, reinforce, or undermine state strength. Ties to social forces can be a key source of state strength; but they can also be a decisive source of weakness. In this view state strength is more than just organisational cohesion, coordination, centralisation, or financial capacity— although of course all of these may help maintain a state's ability to impose rules and norms.

Staying within the boundaries of a state-in-society approach, while still encouraging a range of questions and specific definitions, allows four related themes to emerge from the chapters in this book.

- States often labelled as weak can be remarkably resilient, allowing them to stay intact despite poor services, internal disorder, and financial mismanagement.

- Even states that analysts consider some of the world's strongest are not immutably strong, and in some areas and sectors they can be remarkably weak.

- A dynamic view of state strength and weakness is essential—one that accepts the multiple dimensions of strength and weakness, the importance of perspective, and continual change over time.

- A state-in-society approach provides a more refined understanding of state strengths and weaknesses than treating states and societies as dichotomous and undifferentiated, or as mere products of the dominant social group.

Together these themes, which are expanded below, provide a useful guide for further research on weak and strong states—one that will hopefully help avoid some of the more simplistic analyses and conclusions that have surrounded many previous discussions.

Weak States and Hidden Strengths

After the collapse of the Berlin Wall in 1989, an increasing number of analysts started to paint a picture of vulnerable and frail states—of states on the verge of disintegrating, imploding, or breaking apart. The end of the Soviet Union seemed to confirm these predictions. Yet most states have survived and a world of Lebanons has not occurred. Since then, it has become increasingly clear that even the weakest states contain areas of strength—strengths that allow them to survive despite inefficient and ineffective services, and internal disorder and random violence. Within certain societal, regional, and international contexts, some of the world's weakest administrative states—ones that often have low administrative capacity, poor services, ineffective financial managers and tax collectors, and inefficient and wasteful officials—can be remarkably resilient.

International factors, and organisational, allocational, and coercive characteristics partly explain the resilience and cohesion of states. Global institutions, international law, and the international society of states legitimise and reinforce state agencies and structures. The globalisation of capital, international financial organisations, and bilateral and multilateral aid provide crucial funds for many weak administrative states. For example, aid accounts for over fifteen per cent of Gross Domestic Product in Papua New Guinea, over twenty per cent in the Solomon Islands, and over 30 per cent in Vanuatu (Larmour:chapter 5). Some states are also held together in part by state members effectively allocating goods and services to support allies and appeal to the rational self-interest of opponents. These states may be inefficient and wasteful; but this inefficiency is often crucial to maintain the loyalty of key societal groups. The stability of some states is also partly explained by the tendency of people to maximise gains and minimise risks. And states with strong coercive arms at their core can, at least for awhile, prevent their own collapse (Migdal:chapter 2).

But these factors alone cannot explain the resilience and cohesion of many states. An important factor is that most states now have unquestioned meaning in peoples' lives. For most people, states are more than just a source of services and material goods. They are also more than just an effective nest for patron–client units. This shared meaning has developed through the creation of law, public rituals, and informal interaction that constitutes and reconstitutes public space. Together, these factors can naturalise the state. In such cases, most people simply cannot imagine life without the state, in the same way they cannot imagine life without oceans and mountains. Even when a state becomes inefficient and corrupt, people generally imagine new leaders rather than a new organisational structure (Migdal:chapter 2).

Of course, not all states are naturalised—for instance, diverse, fragmented, and relatively new states like the Solomon Islands. These states are not, however, inevitably unstable and ready to collapse. Other factors can reinforce cohesion in these states, such as leaders responding to societal demands and pressures through personal networks that provide particularistic benefits. Less commonly, and somewhat paradoxically, weak administrative states may also remain intact in part because people expect little from the state and do not depend on the state for their survival. In the Solomon Islands, for example, the subsistence and semi-subsistence economies support about 85 per cent of the population. Although to some extent people rely on the state for roads, schools, medical clinics, and administrative support, most people, especially outside of the capital of Honiara, can easily survive without the state. Moreover, because non-state organisations—such as the church, land owners, and big men—provide many typical state services, and because the services that the state does provide have been poor for so long, people expect little from the state. Inadequate state services do not, therefore, undermine state legitimacy in the Solomon Islands in the same way as in countries where societal members expect high quality state services. Low levels of education, a weak sense of collective national consciousness, and fragmented and relatively small identity groups (such as kin, tribes, language, and islands groups) further dilute any internal desire or moves to overthrow the state (Kabutaulaka and Dauvergne 1997).

The apparent resilience of weak administrative states may also in part be a result of analysts exaggerating actual weaknesses, perhaps because they perceive state–society interactions as part of a process of disintegration rather than as a natural process of mutual transformation. In Papua New Guinea, for example, many commentators have predicted that the post-colonial state will collapse. There are certainly signs of internal disorder and violence, growing economic hardship and disparity, and social disintegration. The state is unable to handle new and serious social and legal problems like gang crime (known as *raskolism*). Internal conflicts, deteriorating government services, and the increasing disillusionment with politics are also worrying signs. Of equal, if not greater concern, is the increasing tendency of the state to resort to coercion to control violent social groups. Upon close examination, however, the cumulative impact of these problems is unlikely to cause the state to disintegrate. Compared to the colonial state, some sections of the post-colonial state have certainly become weaker. Others, however, such as the Ombudsman Commission and the superior courts, remain effective and strong. Moreover, the state is strong in terms of its control over, and distribution of, material rewards. Bilateral and multilateral aid, international organisations, and the integration of the economy into international markets also bolster the state from internal forces of disintegration. In short, the imminent collapse of the Papua New Guinea state is unlikely, in part because analysts have exaggerated the problem, in part because of the innate strengths of some sections of the state, in part because of the resilience of older forms of social order, and in part because of its integration into the international community. Rather than the total collapse of the state, as the state and society transform each other, a new order appears to be emerging in post-colonial Papua New Guinea, a highly contested order that is increasingly blurring the lines between the state and social forces (Dinnen:chapter 3).

Comparing Papua New Guinea with the Philippines further refines our understanding of how state–society relations shape state capabilities and cohesion. Generally, scholars consider these states weak. Yet, while the society of Papua New Guinea is generally seen as weak, Philippine society is viewed as strong. In Papua New Guinea, labour and non-governmental organisations have little influence, and political parties do not have mass followings. Churches play an important role in shaping social life, but have little political clout. In the Philippines, powerful patron–client networks, a plethora of non-governmental organisations, an influential Roman Catholic church, a politicised academic community, and strong leftist groups create a vibrant and often confrontational civil society. Despite these societal differences, in both countries compliance with state laws is low while societal participation is relatively high. Yet legitimation appears to be higher in Papua New Guinea. This is partly explained by the frequent turnover of political leaders, the absence of deep social cleavages, and the social expectation that national politicians deliver material benefits to constituents in Papua New Guinea. At different points in time, many people in Papua New Guinea may be indifferent to the state—or perhaps see the state as largely irrelevant to their everyday lives. But generally, most people feel the state is essential for providing basic public goods and services. Societal reactions to the Philippine and Papua New

Guinea states are consistent with recent constitutional reforms and proposals to limit state powers in the Philippines and enhance state powers in Papua New Guinea (May:chapter 4).

Recognising the recent construction of states and societies, such as those in Melanesia, also provides a more balanced assessment of strength and weakness. Pre-colonial Melanesia was effectively stateless, ruled by big men, elders, and chiefs. Colonial powers constructed Melanesian states, imposing a centralised bureaucratic authority. These states then played a key role in constructing larger overarching societies. Prior to colonial states, people generally lived in small, often incoherent, groups defined more in terms of relationships than identities. Colonial states invented traditions and delineated boundaries. Melanesian states and societies, then, are both relatively new. Weak post-colonial states with tenuous control over post-colonial societies are in many ways a natural outgrowth of this history, and assessing these states against an ideal of a centralised state and a wider society could well be misleading (Larmour:chapter 5).

Strong States and Innate Weakness

Just as weak states contain hidden strengths, seemingly strong states often contain striking weaknesses. One reason this occurs is that the source of state strength can also be a critical weakness—such as relying heavily on patronage to appease opponents and maintain support. The structure of the state, and the way that leaders have manipulated the state apparatus, can also contribute to underlying weaknesses. For example, over the last 30 years Indonesian President Soeharto centralised control and eliminated opposition, in part through repression, strict laws, political manœuvres, and economic management, but also in part through prudent distribution of patronage. This route to a strong state—at least in terms of dominating society—has left Indonesia exceptionally vulnerable. Corruption is out of control. Policy implementation is often dismal as state officials ignore rules in exchange for personal gain. Despite Soeharto's resignation as president in May 1998, his children and allies remain at the centre of monopolistic conglomerates, bad bank loans, and extravagant financial schemes. The sharp depreciation of the rupiah and the ensuing economic upheaval in the second half of 1997 exposed the inherent limitations of the Indonesian economy. The source of much of Indonesia's current economic woes is the vast patronage network that underpins the political system. Indonesia's indecisive and evasive response to the economic crisis was a natural outgrowth of this patrimonial state. Only intense pressure from the International Monetary Fund and virtual economic collapse finally pushed the state to announce far-reaching reforms in early 1998 (Crouch:chapter 6).

Indonesia's weakness, however, extends beyond policy failures and mismanagement. The military, which is still at the core of the political order, is fragmented and could destabilise a transition to a new political regime. Recent riots and political demonstrations indicate that popular societal anger can quickly bubble to the surface. Soeharto's resignation and President B.J. Habibie's promise of political reforms had relieved some of the pressure by the end of May 1998. But societal anger could well grow stronger, especially if unemployment and prices continue to rise in the wake of the 1997–98 economic crash. It is even conceivable that societal pressures, along with internal state struggles for control of state patronage, could crumble this previously strong state, suddenly making it one of the weakest in the Southeast Asian region (Crouch:chapter 6; Dauvergne:chapter 8).

Systemic and structural weaknesses such as those in Indonesia, then, could cause otherwise strong states to shatter in a crisis. But a crisis is not necessary to reveal weaknesses in strong states. Most states tend to be much stronger in the capital city and urban areas than in the outer regions. State control over societal rules and norms is much higher in Jakarta, Manila, Port Moresby, and Honiara than in the far flung islands of Kalimantan, Mindanao, Bougainville, and Choiseul. State services—such as transportation, communication, medical, and administrative—also tend to be far superior in the capitals. And the sense that states are a natural part of the landscape is stronger in urban areas where far more people attend the theatre of the state.

Most states also tend to be particularly weak when challenging traditional practices. States often face considerable hurdles trying to eliminate, for example, swidden farming, traditional marriage practices, land tenure, or patron–client exchanges (again, especially when these occur far from the centres of power). States face even greater problems confronting powerful business interests, especially when they are linked to political, military, and bureaucratic leaders. These problems are compounded even further when state policies or actions undercut corporate profits. Business resistance can be so resolute that states which are generally strong can have little capacity to act in a particular area or sector. In Indonesia, for example, loggers and plywood processors, protected and aided by webs of state officials, routinely evade environmental and tax rules, and ignore efforts by sections of the state to reform the industry (Dauvergne:chapter 8).

Misreading the sources of state strength can obscure innate weaknesses. For example, to some extent cultural features, such as deference to authority and respect for elders, can reinforce state strengths. Yet, in the case of Singapore, pointing to culture as a source of state strength masks important weaknesses. In many respects, Singapore is undeniably one of the world's strongest states. The state dominates social groups. There is relatively little government corruption, and compliance with legislation is strong. The standard of living and educational levels are high. It is safe, clean, and everything runs on time. The government has even managed a peaceful and effective leadership transition from Lee Kuan Yew to Goh Chok Tong. Part of this control arises from élite manipulation of culture. Elites use Confucianism to facilitate obedience and conformity. Confucianism also helps to justify the rejection of norms that underpin modern democratic politics, especially the principles behind an active and relevant political opposition. Yet Confucianism has no more cultural resonance in Singapore than many Western democratic ideas. It is instead a tool of the People's Action Party to maintain control in a system that only superficially resembles a democracy. Arguing that Confucianism explains why people conform and obey is therefore misleading, especially since this conceals the mechanisms of political control over social forces. The focus on Confucianism also obscures a critical weakness of the Singapore state: low or manipulated societal participation in state institutions that undercuts state legitimacy. Mystical Confucian values do not explain the passive obedience of many Singaporeans; far more important are the great personal risks of opposition, risks that do not seem worth it in a state that provides so many material benefits (Lawson:chapter 7).

Dimensions and Continuums of Strength and Weakness

The preceding themes point to different dimensions, sources, and kinds of state strength and weakness. It is therefore critical to define the elements of 'strength' and 'weakness' carefully and recognise the difficulties of making broad generalisations. A state may be strong internationally and weak domestically. It may have strong coercive powers and the organisational capacity to maintain control; yet it may have low technical and organisational capacity in other areas. It may overwhelm non-state organisations under one regime (defined as the current power holders) yet collapse during the transition to a new one. It may have a high level of legitimacy or a strong moral claim yet have little control over dissidents or insurgents. Or it may dominate the formulation of policies yet have little ability to implement them. It is therefore essential to take a dynamic view of state strength and weakness—to accept that state strength varies across sectors, dimensions, and time, as social forces that oppose or support state goals change, as the determination of state leaders to impose state rules fluctuates, and as different sections of the state undermine official policies (Dinnen:chapter 3; Dauvergne:chapter 8; Kerkvliet:chapter 9). It is also important to recognise the importance of perspective. A state action that one segment of society considers strong (perhaps urban élite), another segment (perhaps rural villagers) could well see as a sign of weakness. A state action may therefore simultaneously increase legitimacy in some segments of society and decrease it in others, which in turn simultaneously increases state strength in some areas and decreases it in others. A state action or inaction that some segments of society perceive as a sign of weakness may also increase overall legitimacy, and therefore strength, of the state (Kerkvliet:chapter 9).

To maintain a dynamic view, it is best to conceive of strength and weakness in terms of a process. A state retreat or concession at a particular point in time may not demonstrate weakness. It could even be a sign of strength if it is part of a process that eventually leads to the state attaining its objective. Conceiving of states in this way also accepts that a strength at one point in time may become a weakness later (or vice versa). No state is all strong or weak. Sometimes their actions fall on the strong end of a continuum, sometimes on the weak end, although most states tend to cluster on one end of the continuum. Conceiving of states in this way also avoids the pitfall of defining states like Vietnam, Singapore, and Indonesia as strong, or the Philippines, the Solomon Islands, and Papua New Guinea as weak, without careful qualifiers. It also helps one understand and navigate the contradictory evidence that surrounds states like Vietnam, which some analysts label as strong while others label it as weak (Kerkvliet:chapter 9).

Shifts along strong–weak continuums tend to occur in response to the extent of state determination (comprising the attitudes and commitment of state members), the extent to which societal forces have 'colonised' the state, and the level of societal concern and resistance. State capacity to make and impose rules tends to decrease as the level of state determination weakens and as societal opposition increases. The intensity and effectiveness of societal resistance is linked to the relative power of the social group and the extent to which this social group perceives state policies or actions as a threat (especially a threat to profits). Conversely, state capacity tends to rise when societal resistance declines, when powerful segments of society align themselves with the state, and when state determination is high. This is a key reason why states that generally overwhelm non-state organisations can be strikingly weak in particular areas and at particular points in times. It also helps explain why generally weak states can at times exhibit remarkable strength (Dauvergne:chapter 8).

Advantages of a State-in-Society Approach

This book demonstrates the analytical value of a state-in-society approach for analysing state policies, actions, strengths, and weaknesses. Valuable insights are gained by examining how pre-colonial, colonial, and post-colonial histories have transformed state–society relations and how these transformations have in turn shaped state strength and weakness. Further insights are gained by accepting that states and societies are not stagnant entities but undergo constant transformations. Disaggregating states also reveals internal tensions and disputes that shape particular state strengths. States are not unitary actors and sections of states often work at cross-purposes, undercutting control and stalemating action. These sections sometimes work more closely with non-state organisations than with other sections of the state. Because of the multiple ways that state sections and societal groups interact, all states are both strong and weak, depending on the dimension, sector, and time. As a state deals with various tasks it is also clear that the specific components of strength and weakness vary. By focusing on how states are woven into society—and how each continually reshapes the other—the authors are able to move beyond facile assessments of state strengths and weaknesses and ask probing questions about why so many inefficient and ineffective states stay intact, why apparently strong states are sometimes surprisingly weak, and why seemingly weak states can be remarkably resilient.

2 Why Do So Many States Stay Intact?

JOEL S. MIGDAL[1]

On the face of it, it is puzzling that more states do not simply fall apart. Why do their components not fly off in a thousand different directions? It has happened to some in recent years: Lebanon, Yugoslavia, Somalia, Ethiopia, Liberia, Zaire, even the vaunted Soviet Union. Why not to others? What can account for the staying power of so many state organisations, most with tens of thousands of workers toiling in hundreds of different agencies with countless sets of varying procedures, goals, interests, pressures, and incentives? All these are scattered across variegated territories with diverse populations. The potential for inter-agency turmoil, mad grabs for scarce resources, forces pulling in different directions, contestation of internalised global forces, and conflicting priorities seems endless—and all that in an organisation harbouring the feasibility for inflicting tremendous violence.

Surveying European expansion across five centuries, Strang (1991) found remarkable ability of non-European political entities—at least those he classified as sovereign—to survive. He found only eleven that went from sovereign to dependent status between 1415 and 1987, and fifteen non-European polities that merged or underwent dissolution. What is striking about the last half of the twentieth century is how many states have been created—unprecedented numbers in the annals of world history—and how few have disappeared, dissolved, or imploded.

1   I would like to thank the following friends for their careful and critical reading of an earlier draft of this article: Michael Barnett, James Caporaso, Gregg Crane, Catherine Dauvergne, Peter Dauvergne, Christine Ingebritsen, Resat Kasaba, Pnina Lahav, Kenneth Lawson, Tom Lewis, and Klaus Schlichte. I would also like to thank Aaron Hudson for his invaluable research assistance.

In fact, during the years of the Cold War, one is hard-pressed to point to more than a handful of cases of states vanishing or falling apart— perhaps Pakistan and Nigeria for a spell, certainly Lebanon, and then some odd instances such as Egypt, Syria, and the United Arab Republic. At the same time, social scientists wrote volumes on how frail so many states have been. They used terms such as quasi-state or soft state or weak state to indicate the vulnerability of many political entities, both to outside forces and to organised domestic groups.[2] Does not state weakness also indicate a fragility that would lead many to shatter irrevocably?

The disintegration of vast empires after World War I and World War II coupled with the powerful idea of self-determination led to a prolife- ration of new states, many extremely weak in terms of internal coherence and their ability to effect public policy that could change people's behaviour in intended ways. In the two decades following World War II alone, the number of states more than tripled. Indeed, the middle of the twentieth century became the heyday for states.

Now, at the impending dawn of the twenty-first century, we live in the age of the state as survivor. New political forms, led by the European Union and powerful non-governmental organisations, loom on the horizon. Book after book has appeared describing how the state's sails have been trimmed (Camilleri and Falk 1992; Duchacek, Latouche and Stevenson 1988; Dunn, ed. 1995; Erfani 1995; Gottlieb 1993; Ingebritsen 1998; Katzenstein, ed. 1997; Keller and Rothchild 1996; Kuehls 1996; Lyons and Mastanduno, eds 1995; Offe 1996; Shapiro and Alker 1996). Others have predicted its imminent demise with such chilling phrases as 'the Lebanisation of the world' (Guehenno 1995:35; Ohmae 1995). The state is increasingly portrayed as the crippled Leviathan, whose life- support system might give way at any time. But reports of its near-death seem decidedly premature—state weakness has not meant state collapse.

The next two sections review several reasons offered by scholars for states' staying intact. The first involves the role of forces from the inter- national environment, which become internalised domestically in both states and societies. The second draws from organisation theory and its emphasis on the trade between states and their subjects: loyalty and sup- port in exchange for selective access to public goods. A third reason focuses on a variant of exchange, where the state serves as an umbrella and money tree for diverse patron–client ties.

While these factors help in understanding some of the elements that fend off disintegrative forces, they do not explain enough. The main argument of the chapter in the last part is that certain areas of state–society interaction can create meaning for people in society, and that meaning, in turn, can naturalise the state. Naturalisation means that people consider the state as natural as the landscape around them; they cannot imagine heir lives without it. If that belief is widespread, it provides a powerful

---

2   Jackson, Migdal, Myrdal.

antidote to disintegrative forces, even in the face of continued weakness in delivering goods, effecting policy, and gaining efficiency.

The latter part of the chapter will explore three overlapping areas where meaning and practice are created—the generation of law in society, the use of public ritual in a context in which politics is seen as theatre, and the constitution and continuing reconstitution of public space. Theory is not yet at the point where it can specify under what conditions meaning is created in these three areas leading to a bolstered state, and where the opposite happens. But it is important at this point to explore these areas of state–society relations in order to understand their underlying relationship to state cohesion and disintegration.

A Global Environment Empowering States

What can one draw from those writing on states as to why more of them do not fall to the countless centrifugal forces within them and within their population? For most writers, the question did not arise at all or was brushed aside (Jackson and Rosberg 1982; Rosenau 1988; and Strang 1991 are clear exceptions). As Rosenau aptly put it, the literature gives the impression that 'the state is to politics what the hidden hand is (à la Adam Smith) to economics' (1988:14). Many ignored the question of state stability by themselves naturalising it in their writings. By the early nineteenth century, they argued, states had become 'the sole constitutive elements of the international system at the exclusion of others' (Spruyt 1994:3). As the normative and juridical way to organise governance—in fact, as nearly the only successful way the twentieth century has seen to establish rule—the state came to seem as much a part of the landscape as mountains and rivers. While some types of literature, especially Marxist writing, did predict the withering away of the state, the stability of states, including Communist states from 1950 on, gave little reason to question their presence or their future.

International law and the international society of states consecrated its form and worked to preserve, not only the society of states as a whole, but frequently individual states as well. Indeed, Jackson and Rosberg (1982) maintain that if we were to take another criterion besides the juridical existence of states, such as whether states effectively control all of their territory, we could count many more of them as having failed to remain intact. They write that 'one cannot explain the persistence of some "states" by using a concept of the state that does not give sufficient attention to the [international] juridical properties of statehood' (1982:4). Jackson (1990) referred to the international conditions that sustained states as 'negative sovereignty'.

While a few scholars investigated how international conditions propped up states, most simply took the state's continued existence for granted. In addition, the bedrock assumptions of International Relations theory reinforced the idea of the inviolability of the state. Models emphasised its rationality, thereby assuming its integrity and coherence (Cederman 1997:29). International Relations thinkers dealt with states almost exclusively as independent variables, rather than dependent ones (Cederman 1997:213). While these writers were reacting against pluralist approaches, systems theory, and Marxist notions, they too—like those they reacted against—simplified the state, treating its complex internal workings as unproblematic.

Realist theorists tended to ignore the internal dynamics of states that might tear them apart and looked, instead, to the configuration of states to explain state stability. The rationality of states, realists argued, frequently leads stronger ones to support weaker ones in an effort to prevent another stronger state from achieving world domination (Waltz 1979). But Strang (1991) has demonstrated that realist theories cannot account for the state stability that he found across five centuries. At the same time that realist and neo-realist theories gripped International Relations, comparativists in Political Science and Sociology made many similar assumptions in their efforts 'to bring the state back in' (Evans, Reuschemeyer and Skocpol, eds 1985).

Starting with the collapse of the Berlin Wall, however, it became increasingly difficult to think of states as inviolable. Words like 'dissolution', 'anarchy', and 'collapse' (Cederman 1997; Kaplan 1997; Schlichte 1997) crept into titles of works on states. Constructivists and those using norms-based approaches began to question the old assumptions of International Relations theory (Wendt 1995; Barnett 1998; Katzenstein, ed. 1996; Klotz 1995; Finnemore 1996), and 'state-in-society' displaced the notion of a totally autonomous, sovereign-ruling authority (Migdal, Kohli and Shue, eds 1994; Evans 1995). In the post-Cold War era when state weakness more often has led to state disintegration into a number of new states (for example, Ethiopia, the Soviet Union, Yugoslavia) or to a collapse of the state's ability to provide even the minimum of personal security (for example, Lebanon, 1975–90; Somalia and Liberia in the 1990s), and in a period in which scholars have given prominence to the internal complexity of the state, the question of why some states fall apart and others stay together has become both more urgent and more accessible.

During the Cold War, the neo-realist argument goes, the very structure of world politics propped up teetering states. Superpower competition resulted in bountiful resources for states even in remote parts of the globe, high incentives for their parts to hang together, and relief for them from much of their traditional role in defending borders against outside attack. Now, with the end of the Cold War and the increased intensity of economic globalisation, the buzz is that the state is at the end of its rope. State weakness, in the absence of the old international props, might now translate directly into state collapse.

The termination of the Cold War, indeed, has brought an increase in the collapse of some states, as in East Africa—enough to spur thinking about why they dissolve (Kaplan 1997; Schlichte 1997; Cederman 1997). But the vast majority, even ones that seemed to be little more than propped up artefacts of East–West competition, have remained intact and, for the moment, seem in no threat of disintegration even when public funds have been squandered and public policies largely ignored.

Part of the reason for the relative stability of the state is that the international factors supporting and sustaining states did not all disappear with the end of the Cold War. Embassies and ambassadors, the United Nations and the World Bank, foreign aid and international agencies—all implicitly or explicitly have designated the state as the proper representation of the people in a given space. As strong economic and environmental factors have been making the state's boundaries quite porous, we have had a countervailing set of international regimes that have encouraged, sustained, and legitimated states as the proper form of rule (Finnemore 1996:2–3; Klotz 1995:24). As Strang argues, the stability of states can be explained, in large part, 'by the cultural constitution of the Western state system as a community of mutual recognition' (1991:162).

It is very rare indeed that international organisations and procedures have not promoted the state as the interlocutor of populations. One recent exception to the rule has been the restrictions placed by the United Nations on the Iraqi state in respect to its Kurdish population following the Gulf War. But that is a true rarity. More common is a case such as that portrayed in Kabutaulaka and Dauvergne's article (1997) on the Solomon Islands. There, a state whose administrative capacity is as low as one could imagine gains succour from a host of international organisations and nearby foreign governments.

International institutions, such as the UN, not only have consecrated the state as the normatively appropriate way to organise rule over people, they also have empowered it by helping shape what it does and how it is constituted. International agencies have made all sorts of assumptions about how the state should occupy itself. It is expected not only to protect its population but to improve people's material lives, ensure their dignity, organise many of their activities, rectify the condition of women and children and indigenous peoples, and much more.

In other words, fairly rigid normative expectations envelop the state. And while these norms bind it, at the same time they empower it. It must undertake tasks that even a century ago were the marks of only a few or none at all—educate youth in public schools, protect the environment, regulate the labour market, and so on. Even where states have failed miserably to put children in classrooms or affect workers' everyday conditions, they still have built huge state agencies assigned to education and labour. All states, whether they regularly succeed in implementing international norms or not, have constructed a sprawling state bureaucracy devoted to social issues, a fearsome security apparatus, and an extensive court system. These are now imperatives for all states, even if just to appear to tackle these sorts of issues. Even weak states have gained international legitimacy, not to speak of an extensive bureaucracy, as they have gone through the motions of putting international norms into practice domestically.

Numerous state bureaux, from agricultural extension to child welfare, have plugged into international agencies. Those international connections have made related state agencies in different countries look remarkably similar, even if their effectiveness differs substantially from state to state. Membership in an international organisation, such as the World Health Organisation, has shaped states' data collection (in fact, it has demanded data collection as a central activity), procedures, base of knowledge, and approaches to their subject of concern. The effect, at least on the surface, has been a world-wide homogenisation of practices, norms, and technical expertise. Little states, big states, they all look remarkably alike, even if some are much more effective than others in putting these international norms to work in the domestic environment.

And their leaders have made the same sorts of claims of territoriality, sovereignty, autonomy, and independence. They issue similar calls for the obedience of their populations and for governing the minutiæ of personal life—demanding taxes, regulating sexual relations, putting limits on parents' authority. And they consist of bureaux and agencies that look notably alike from one side of the globe to the other. In short, globalisation has deepened and strengthened practices that enhance the state's role as much as it has generated practices that bypass the state.

But no matter how developed international norms have been about the proper form and practices for governance or how blustery leaders have been about the inviolability of their states, international support and claims for sovereignty cannot alone explain how and why states stay intact. A focus on global factors should not obscure the overriding importance of the make-up of the state and its relation to those it claims to rule. It also should not make us less aware of those global forces that weaken the state nor hide how superficial the integration of international norms and practices may be. Internalised international institutions may mean very different things in different domestic environments.

Even the direct propping up of states by neighbours or world powers and by international agencies through foreign aid, technical assistance, and military support goes only part of the way towards explaining the remarkable resiliency of so many states. So many states are shot through with corruption, inefficiency, and incapacity to put international intentions into practice with their own populations that we cannot rely only on the elaboration of international norms and the proffering of international support to explain how states stave off their own collapse.

The Organisational Imperatives of the State

Organisational theorists have given some sense of why any organisations, including states, remain intact. But their approaches are only partially satisfying. To some extent that is because some writing on organisations assumes their integrity. For some, a kind of functionalist undertone seeps into discussions on organisation: human beings have goals, wishes, and hopes; organisations exist as ways people connect to each other to realise those ends. In other words, organisations exist simply because people have a need for them. Ahrne (1994:5) writes: 'In the beginning there is organization. The basic human experience is belonging and dependence.'[3] Different pressures and opportunities that units of the organisation encounter may have divisive effects, but its leaders at the top of the hierarchy of authority and control formulate strategic responses and adjust organisational structure to meet the challenges (Hannan and Freeman 1977:961–2). This process is what organisational theorists have called adaptation.

Because state organisations deal with fundamental needs, such as personal security, there is a temptation to say that they are there because people need them to be. But this formulation tells us very little about why state organisations are the dominant mode to fill these needs—why not some other type of organisation?—or why some of these organisations may fail and others not.

To be fair, sociologists have recognised the possibility (perhaps even probability) that organisations will fail. Stinchcombe (1965) got the ball rolling by proposing that young organisations are more likely to die than old ones. In the case of states, however, Stinchcombe's analysis runs into difficulties; young states have fared remarkably well over the last four decades. Hannan and Freeman, arguing that organisations' inertia diminishes the chances for successful adaptation, maintain that different environments 'select' organisations that fit the specific local conditions well and cause ones that are ill-suited to the environment to fail (Hannan and Freeman 1977). Their thinking leads to the notion that organisations necessarily look quite different from one environment to another (Singh, Tucker and House 1994) but, again in the case of states, one has trouble explaining why states the world over look so similar, at least at the

---

3   In another book, Ahrne notes the belief that functionalist thinking dominates organisational theory. 'According to Alexander the antifunctionalist movement has won a total victory. But the presumed functionalist organization theory is still alive. The fact that much of the organization theory Burrell and Morgan regarded as functionalist has survived the downfall of functionalist social theory seems to indicate that organization theory has a life of its own' (Ahrne 1990:30). Ahrne goes on to argue that organisation theory 'has liberated itself from paradigmatic dependencies [like functionalism]' (1990:31). I have my doubts.

superficial level of an organisational chart (the actual functioning of bureaux differs markedly from state to state).

More recently, Ahrne has simply pointed to what organisations have to do to avoid failure.

> Positions have to be fitted together into a working unit in order to counteract centrifugal forces. Even if the fit between positions is rarely perfect, centripetal forces are developed to balance the influence from the surrounding social landscape (Ahrne 1994:104).

In other words, organisational dissolution is always a real possibility; only those that develop countervailing means to offset pressures towards collapse will survive and succeed. But this fashioning of the issue is somewhat unsettling in its use of the passive voice ('centripetal forces are developed'). Who is developing them and how? Why do they succeed and others not?

Too often, these questions have been glossed over in organisational theories, many of which now use an agency-structure approach in reference to public or collective goods (including Ahrne 1994, which also surveys others using an agency–structure approach). This approach maintains that organisations' centripetal forces derive from their owner-ship or control of such goods. By making individuals' access to these goods or resources dependent on membership in, or affiliation with, the organisation—or, what is even more important, on the performance of obligations to the organisation by fulfilling prescribed roles—centrifugal forces leading to dissolution or disaffection are kept at bay.

In other words, a simple trade takes place: individuals submit to the control of their personal behaviour by paying dues, undertaking tasks, and taking orders (all of which act to keep the organisation together) in exchange for access to resources, such as personal security, admission to the health club, and wages. To be sure, this approach still leaves holes in our understanding of who organises, why organisations take the form they do, and why only some organisations overcome the problems of inertia that threaten the delivery of goods to individuals. But it goes a long way towards helping understand organisational integrity, including the cohe-sion of states. As Ahrne writes: 'Incentives and persuasion are centripetal forces in any organization contributing to the upkeep of authority' (1994:111).

While states are subject to the same logic as other organisations in terms of maintaining themselves by being the gateway to collective goods, they also form a special kind of organisation in this regard. Note Krasner's understanding:

> With regard to both breadth and depth, sovereign states have become increasingly formidable institutions. They influence the self-image of those individuals within their territory through the concept of citizenship, as well as by exercising control, to one degree or another, over powerful instruments of socialization. With regard to breadth, states are the most

densely linked institutions in the contemporary world. Change the nature of states and virtually everything else in human society would also have to be changed. Hence, even though environmental incentives have dramatically changed since the establishment of the state system in the seventeenth century, there is little reason to believe that it will be easy to replace sovereign states with some alternative structure for organizing human political life (1988:76).

States are, indeed, complex organisations that often reach deeply and widely into everyday life. As organisations, they include individuals who are actually part of the organisation (officials) and those outside the organisation subject to its control. And the latter are divided between those with a distinctive affiliation—citizenship—and those, such as tourists or resident aliens, without that status. The multiple levels of bargains that any state has with all these different sorts of individuals, while in some ways diffusing its risks, also demand unusual complexity in providing different, sometimes contradictory, products to different groups. States that fail in their side of the basic bargain with those inside the organisation (for example, by not paying soldiers or bureaucrats), or very different sorts of arrangements with citizens (for example, by closing channels to influence officials or leaving the door open to immigration that might affect citizens adversely) or with other residents (for example, by not providing adequate security or by closing the door to immigration that might allow family reunions) are likely to face very serious centrifugal pressures.

States may be more subject than many other sorts of organisations to coming apart at the seams simply because there are so many seams. Their sheer complexity, Offe (1996:63) indicates, eats away at their organisational integrity. He quotes Dieter Grimm's phrase on the 'decomposition of state power by increase of functions' and notes:

> ...the state's claim to rational decision-making suffers from the fact that
> multiplication of the responsibilities is accompanied by a corresponding
> increase in instances, authorities, and administrative agents. This results in
> an internal pluralization and fragmentation of departmental perspectives
> within the administration, an escalation of the respective rivalries, and, on
> the whole, an increasing unpredictability of the resulting long-term and
> 'synergetic' effects of individual policies which are nearly impossible to
> coordinate.

In sum, organisational theorists have given some sound reasons why organisations remain intact, particularly how the provision of selective access to collective goods creates strong centripetal forces. But their approaches still leave one wondering why organisations look as they do, why they do not take different forms, and why other basic bargains might not lead to the replacement of existing structures. While the motivation of individuals has been clearly portrayed—they are rational bargain hunters looking to make the best choices they can to fulfil their wishes—the structure itself, its form and function, has stayed somewhat murky. These questions are amplified when one turns to states, where the multiple-level bargains in which they engage pose additional challenges of maintaining loyalty and where their utter complexity adds to already strong centrifugal tendencies. In short, many states have demonstrated abiding weakness—gross inefficiencies in maintaining bargains with a large and complex population. If it is organisational coherence that keeps states intact, why do the many states that demonstrate incoherence continue to exist?

Historical institutionalists have tried to grapple with some of these questions. Their arguments have gone beyond the rationality that underlies the organisational bargain—individuals' access to collective goods in exchange for fulfilling obligations. Centripetal forces stem too, they have emphasised, from routine. In other words, scholars using this approach have favoured looking at habit in any given situation more than utility maximisation. Koelble (1995:233) notes:

> When making decisions, individuals do not ask the question 'how do I maximize my interests in this situation?' but instead 'what is the appropriate response to this situation given my position and responsibilities?'. In the majority of situations, rules and procedures (that is, institutions) are clearly established, and individuals follow routines. They follow well-worn paths and do what they think is expected of them.

Historical institutionalists, then, have acknowledged the calculation of individuals, but they have emphasised that this sort of individual reckoning cannot be understood in a disembodied way. It takes place within a context, within the confines of rules and procedures of the organisation. Moreover, after a while, individuals do not bother with the demanding course of rationally processing every possible choice that they encounter. Instead, their behaviour becomes routinised within the possibilities that existing organisations afford. Individuals do not need to be presented with the best possible choice by organisations in each instance for them to fulfil their obligations, because they are not always maximising their utility. In most cases, they opt simply to 'satisfice' (March and Olsen 1989).

To be sure, this approach takes the pressure off organisations. States (and other organisations) remain intact even when they cannot put together the best choices for individuals, even when coordination and synergy among policies are low. In these instances, one can imagine even weak and inefficient state organisations continuing to exist. The habit of obeying and fulfilling other obligations adds important centripetal energy to combat disintegrative tendencies. Individuals are reluctant to whimsically abandon their states.

But the focus continues to be on the individual navigating his or her way through a labyrinth of state agencies and bureaux. Little attention is paid to the internal make-up of the organisation itself. And the individual here is a strangely passive being. He or she has become a creature of habit, and there are all too few signs of any affective tie to the organisations that fill needs or fulfil wishes.

We are left in the end with individuals who are either relentlessly rational or maddeningly passive. Little heed has been taken of Edelman's caution of a generation ago:

> To explain political behavior as a response to fairly stable individual wants, reasoning, attitudes, and empirically based perceptions is... simplistic and misleading. Adequate explanation must focus on the complex element that intervenes between the environment and the behavior of human beings: creation and change in common meanings through symbolic apprehension in groups of people of interests, pressures, threats, and possibilities (1971:2).

Inefficient States Keep On Going

Organisational and international factors tell us about the nuts and bolts that hold parts of the state together as well as the global props that help sustain it. But they only skim the surface of how its population affects the state's cohesion. That factor is dealt with mainly by theorising about material distributive issues. A key tenet of organisational theory is that organisations (here, states) maintain themselves by eliciting maximally efficient conduct from members, and they do that by most effectively distributing public goods selectively. The conclusion would be that the most efficient organisations in this regard would have the best chances of survival.

But, as Meyer and Zucker (1989:47) have shown, 'maximally efficient conduct is often not attained' and organisations continue to exist. States are prime examples of often inefficient organisations, sometimes highly inefficient, that keep on going. Kerkvliet's piece in this volume portrays a Philippine state repeatedly failing to implement its own agrarian reform laws. But it remains intact and, indeed, is seen as strong in several respects even by those waiting for reform. The remarkable survival of what at first blush seem like pitifully weak states demands explanations that explore issues beyond efficiency and material distribution and, as Kerkvliet suggests, more nuanced understandings of what 'weak' and 'strong' entail.

One possibility suggested in some of the Asia–Pacific cases is that states may survive as a result of odd bargains in which elements of the state participate. These bargains are between patrons and their clients. At times the patrons inhabit state offices and, at times, not. In either case, elements of the state provide cover for these exchanges. In addition, its administrative apparatus does not interfere too much with existing bargains between patrons and clients. It is in these bargains that meaningful exchanges of material goods and compliance are actually made. There is little Weberian rationality in the provision of services here nor organisation theory's maximal efficiency. Instead, the state's stability rests in good part on its integration into a web of strongman–follower ties.

While grossly inefficient in their own ability as coherent actors to provide security and material benefits to the population, states may provide a secure framework for numerous, disjointed patron–client bargains to flourish. The state, despite its weakness in providing the kinds of services demanded by international norms—security from crime, defence of human rights, development, protection of the environment—may continue to exist by being propped up by other powerful organisations or figures. It is often in the interest of the patrons to sustain the state because of the flow of international resources through the state (which they can appropriate) and because of the fig leaf international legitimacy can provide for their activities.

For the clients of, say, the Solomon Islands, the state seems to carry very little meaning in their everyday lives. Inefficiencies abound. As Kabutaulaka and Dauvergne (1997) point out, while the capital city is in a state of disintegration, state officials sit idly in their offices. It is patrons, for better or for worse, to whom the population must look for any sort of help. Remarkably, the authors point out, the state remains unchallenged. Part of the reason may be the low saliency that the state has in people's minds and how little it affects their daily lives. It may not be worth rebelling against. Certainly, too, international props and quick state responses to pressure points have served the Solomon Island political leaders well.

Still, one must wonder about long-term stability. International agents pour in sums that are not insubstantial in local terms to the state, making it a highly valued prize. As long as there is effective collusion among the patrons, inside and outside the state, on the distribution of those sums, the state remains intact. But that collusion of patrons seems quite fragile in its own right, as Somalia, Lebanon, Rwanda, and other cases have demonstrated.

If the Solomon Islands is an example of a fairly stable state, at least to date, that is extremely weak, some of the Southeast Asian states analysed in this volume show much more robustness. Part of the ability of states, such as Indonesia, to remain intact stems from their well developed and effective coercive arms, using violence to lower the risk of opposition to them. For some of these states, patron–client ties are important, as well, and the relationship of the state to these ties can be a stabilising factor. But coercion alone cannot keep a state intact (for example, Iran under the Shah, or the USSR) and some states' weakness does not derive from their relationships to powerful patrons. For example, the enduring weaknesses of the Indonesian state, as Crouch demonstrates in his chapter in this volume, derive more from its own internal structure than from giving way to strong patrons, and its ability to survive, even prosper, has not been seriously questioned even in the tumultuous events of 1998, which ousted President Soeharto after 33 years of rule. How, then, can we explain states' survival even in the face of enduring weakness and even when ties to extra-state distributional methods (that is, patrons) are not determining?

Constituting the State

A crucial but hard-to-get-at factor in the ability of the state, even a relatively weak state, to stay intact is its place in the meaning people generate about the world around them and their place in it. When states become naturalised—where their dissolution or disappearance becomes unimaginable to their subjects because of their longevity, provision of crucial goods and services, and other factors—they have a much greater chance of counteracting their own inefficiency and ineffectiveness. By no means is a hegemonic idea, such as the state's indispensability, a guarantee of the state's indefinite predominance—hegemonic ideas do falter in the course of history. But where such ideas reign, the state holds a hedge against some failures. In these instances, inefficiency in distributional questions and other aspects of policy implementation need not necessarily lead weak states down the plank.

Many states, including many relatively weak ones, have a deep impact on the structure of society and people's sense of meaning about themselves. At the same time, the structure of society and the meaning people generate in it affect the state and its chances for survival. State and society are in a mutually constitutive relationship. Its centrality in people's lives, its relationship to ongoing conflicts in society, people's expressive relationship to it, all depend on its cohesion. And, simultaneously, these elements of state–society relations shape the form, content, and ultimately the viability of the state.

To understand why states do not fall apart means somehow getting at this doubly transformative process—at how society acts upon the cohesion and form of the state at the same time that the state acts upon the thinking and acting of people, as well as where they find meaning. We can analyse a number of different areas to get at the mutually transformative state–society relations. In the following pages, I look at three of these, which can be fruitful in understanding the resiliency of many states. The three are law, public rituals, and informal behaviour in the public sphere.

Law

While its meaning seems quite straightforward at first glance, 'the word "law" itself is always a primary object of contention' (Cover 1995a:174), but it is in the interest of the state to present the law as if no such contention existed. In its raw form, law involves compelling people to behave in certain ways, but the institution of law implies a sense of justice and rightness that legitimates and obscures the process of forcing others to submit to a particular will. State leaders, especially, have had a very strong interest in presenting their idea of law as if no other meanings of it existed or mattered. They have wanted people to believe that there is no law other than state law and that people's sense of what is just and right finds expression in that law. The legitimacy of the state and its ability to gain people's obedience have depended upon it. Again, Cover:

> There is not automatic legitimation of an institution by calling it or what it produces 'law', but the label is a move, the staking out of a position in the complex social game of legitimation. The jurisprudential inquiry into the question 'what is law' is an engagement at one remove in the struggle over what is legitimate (Cover 1995a:175).

How do states successfully stake out a position in which their law becomes a strong legitimating factor in their rule, giving people a sense that the existence of justice and rightness depend upon the existence of the state and that their world would be topsy-turvy without it? To answer that question, I believe, we must move beyond some of the conventional understandings to a more pluralistic notion of law.

State law has traditionally been thought of in two ways. The first emphasises social control. States have adopted laws as an efficient and predictable means to set the limits and parameters for behaviour in the territory they have claimed to rule, and they have backed up their prescriptions with the use and threat of tremendous violence. This sort of control has been directed both at those outside the organisation (citizens, aliens, tourists) as well as those staffing the state. In this view, then, law is a tool of the state to regulate and direct behaviour, both for controlling the population of a territory and for its own internal control.

The second meaning of law is one that involves self-limitation by states through the creation of, or at least respect for, individual and property rights. Here, it has been liberal states, in particular, that have advocated the notion of inalienable property and human rights, inviolable powers and privileges for individuals. Law here, according to liberal political thought, has involved states' creation of islands of action for individuals, especially in the context of a capitalist society, that cannot be constrained or regulated by the sorts of restrictive law found in the first category, law as social control.

Both these notions of law stress the centrality of the state. It legislates and executes and adjudicates. It creates laws and implements them. The handful of states in the common law tradition do look outside the state organisation itself for the basis of law, valorising the origins of laws in practical everyday transactions and custom, but even in these cases it is state legislative bodies and judiciaries that formalise and validate codes of action. States stand at the centre of self-limiting laws as well as ones geared towards social control; it is the state organisation that determines, or at least codifies, what rights individuals have. The awesome force of the state—its police and judges and jails and executioners—stands behind its edicts.

To be sure, scholars and jurists have recognised that actual practice has not always conformed to state law. It has been contravened by outright criminality, of course, but also by customary law or social convention. Still, the essence of power in this state-centred view of law lies in the narrowness of the gap between state-imposed codes and social practice and in the acceptance by society of state law as the proper and just form of rule. This perspective on law, it seems to me, takes as unproblematic why people should obey the law when there is little or no threat of state violence. In other words, what makes the law seem legitimate in their eyes beyond the big stick it wields?

Cover's comments about the conflicts over who gets to make law imply an alternative standpoint to the state-centred one, that of legal pluralism. It stresses the existence of multiple sets of laws in society, including those opposed to the state, others not controlled by the state but not necessarily in opposition to it, and still others complementary to state law. Some of these may be formal codes, such as Islamic law; others may be long standing but much less formal, such as the law of the manor in feudal societies; and still other sets may be loose, recently generated sets of norms. This last sort of law—'although "law" may be too lofty or lowly a term to describe it' (Finkel 1995:2)—consists of what various groups of people in society think is just and use as their guide to proper behaviour.

In this alternative view, the notion of state law as singular is nothing more than a state-professed ideology seeking to enhance power and legitimacy. In fact, state law stews in a cauldron with numerous other sets of law—some friendly, some not (Galanter 1981). This alternative perspective also notes that these other sets of laws and practices invariably have an effect on state law. Finkel (1995:1) characterised the differences between the state-centred and the legal–pluralist perspectives in this regard as 'should the law [read, state law] follow the path laid by community sentiment [read, other sorts of law], or should the community follow the path the law has laid?' In the legal pluralist view, state law often follows the path set by non-state forms of law.

The notion that state law has been or should be deeply affected by these other sets of law has not been universally accepted, by any means. The mainstream of legal theory has long held that governmental law, the official pronouncements of the state, constitutes the do's and don't's for society, and not the opposite. In this view, 'people outside the institutions and offices of the "legal system" receive rather than generate legal authority' (Brigham 1996:6–7). Through its rules and rights, law does shape and structure society—'law creates and maintains hierarchy and dominance in society' (Susan Burgess quoted in Brigham 1996:ix). But it is important to understand, too, how that society shapes and reshapes state law.

If Cover is right that law is a powerful legitimating force—and I think that he is—then the ability of states to remain intact rests in part on their relationship to these other sets of law. The ability of other categories of law to subvert, strengthen, or transform state law has a deep impact on the chances for the state to hold together and be effective. Much of what law—state and others—does is delineate a universe of meaning for people: what is acceptable and what not, what is right and what wrong. Law is not just setting out what to do and what not to do, it is asserting what is right to do and what is wrong. When state law successfully creates a broadly shared meaning—what Durkheim would call social solidarity— it enhances the conditions for its own survival. Broad social solidarity reinforces the cohesion of the state. State law in such cases is taken by the population as a delineation of right from wrong. It becomes a critical process that 'coalesce[s] groups with diverse concerns into a single political force and that infuse[s] individual participants with the intense affect that comes from defense of one's identity' (Edelman 1971:12). But where state law sits uneasily with other sets of law in the society, it undermines its own ability to give people that sense of meaning in their lives and gain the legitimacy it desperately needs.

Legal scholars and social scientists still know very little about how different sets of laws interact. They also have little sense of how the transformation of state law through the interaction with other forms of law may help create a broadly shared sense of meaning for a population, including legitimacy that can enhance the state's cohesion. What I can suggest here is that state law has been deeply affected by other sets of law, especially by what various groups of people in society have thought is just and have used as their guide to behaviour. Friedman (1990) demonstrated how remarkably United States law was transformed from the nineteenth to the twentieth century as a result of people's changing understanding of themselves and what proper behaviour should therefore be. Indeed, he goes so far as to say that the very meaning of the individual (or, better, individualism) changed, and that has led to a very different legal system from that of a century ago.

In any society significant social change brings with it a proliferation of sets of laws, of legal meanings. Those new legal meanings may turn into texts of resistance, as Cover (1995b:150) calls them, threatening the cohesion of the state. But where state law has been transformed by these other sets of law, where it has created the conditions for melding diverse sets of law generated in society, it has put states in a position to benefit from renewed, broadly shared meaning in society. In other words, social changes in elements of the public and the generation of new non-state forms of law among these publics can transform the make-up of the state (here, in legal terms), the very way the state is constituted. And the state, in turn, can transform society through its application of new law as well as by synthesising different sets of societal law that may be at odds with one another. Where such a double transformation takes place, states come to be associated among those publics with what is right, gaining key legitimacy from that shared sense of meaning.

In the colonial context, where we might have expected the clashes of different sets of laws to be severe, we can find cases of transformation with unexpected results. The imperial powers' law interacted with previous ways of doing things in complex ways. Gulbrandsen (1996), for example, wrote about a people and an area, the Northern Tswana of the then Bechuanaland Protectorate, in which effective pre-colonial legislative and judicial bodies interacted with the newly-imposed British law during the first half of the twentieth century. The result of the interaction, perhaps surprisingly, was the strengthening of the pre-existing bodies, giving the society 'considerable potential to counteract the penetration of European categories and valuations' (Gulbrandsen 1996:127).

For the Tswana the maintenance of a system of law counteracting Britain's attempts to impose a singular, hegemonic law had interesting results. For one, their distinctive strong law 'kept the British willing to retain the Protectorate in the face of the continuous pressure for annexation to the apartheid regime of South Africa' (152). It also prompted the British rulers increasingly to absorb Tswana leaders into the domain of state laws and institutions. Despite their inability to do what they had set out to do, that is, create a British legal system, the colonial rulers found themselves gaining legitimacy from the changes society imposed upon them.

Chanock (1985) uncovered a different African pattern. In his case, the attempt to impose British law had the unintended effect of actually creating *de novo* an African customary law. 'For the perceptions of the traditional order arise from current concerns and are necessary to current conditions' (Chanock 1985:8). Chanock notes that the interaction of colonial state law with this new customary law (which the British pretended had prefigured colonialism) had, and continues to have, complementary effects.

For the colonisation of Africa by Western legal forms and institutions continues under the aegis of the growing legal profession, which in other circumstances, has been among the most verbally ardent of the opponents of colonialism. This process, however, is partly being legitimated by its presentation as a development of a customary law which is essentially African, a recapturing of a pre-colonial dynamic (Chanock 1985:238).

Outside of colonial situations, too, states have had to rely on, respond to, and contend with other systems of law extant in society. In nineteenth century Russia, the state had serious difficulties in providing some overall shared meaning for the society through law. Social changes that produced an active urban middle class pushed legal reformers at the end of the century to introduce 'modern' codes derived from Western Europe, particularly France. Key principles of the new systems of law conflicted with the law of the manor for serfs and patriarchal law for women. The clash of varying sets of laws raised important questions. Were women and serfs (or former serfs) to be understood as rights-possessing individuals subject to state law or as subject to the authority of fathers and husbands?

Could the Russian state afford to assert legal authority over aspects of life formerly ruled by males in families and lords of the manor and still maintain sufficient social stability?

As Engelstein (1988) shows, the interaction of these varying sets of laws raised immediate and practical dilemmas. How would the state treat 'public women' (prostitutes) who were not subject to the authority of husbands or fathers? What would the role of the police be, guarding the morals implied by the other sets of law or treating women as rights-bearing individuals (which implied a whole different sense of what is right)? The state appeared confused, moving back and forth on the implementation of the new codes and unable to develop a coherent system of meaning across its vast territories. State law certainly was transformed but not in a direction that successfully incorporated and integrated the other sets of legal meanings in society. Increasingly, the Russian state found it difficult to generate a law that could produce broadly shared meaning in society, and its legitimacy and ultimate cohesion suffered as a result.

Scholars have only begun to scratch the surface on how different sets of law have affected each other. They cannot generalise about when state law has been successfully transformed in the interaction to reflect key changes in society and to generate a shared meaning for society. But if scholars are to get a handle on how and why states hold together (and others do not), and on what kind of institutional adaptation that takes, they would be well advised to study the law as a key meeting point of state and society. The increasing autonomy of judicial institutions from other branches of the state in countries around the world (for example, Newberg 1995; Osiel 1995; Shapiro and Stone 1994) may speak to the way law serves as a means for society to transform the state even where state bureaucratic, legislative, and executive institutions seem inflexible and impenetrable to popular influence. The interaction of various forms of law, the transformation of state law, and the emerging role of the judiciary may help explain both the adaptability of state organisations and the importance of the state in providing central meaning in people's lives.

Public ritual

Sociologists have observed that organisations often persist despite regularly falling short of doing what they are supposed to do. '[W]e are surrounded by organizations whose failure to achieve their proclaimed goals is neither temporary nor aberrant, but chronic and structurally determined' (DiMaggio 1989:9). States are among those that regularly fall short of passing efficiency tests, some failing abysmally. Their failures are hard to hide; they range from failure to supply security, as evidenced in crime, to the inability to deliver on their end of material bargains, such as not paying soldiers or bureaucrats. One way states have overcome their gross inefficiencies and grave difficulties in meeting central goals has been to gain loyalty and support other than through efficient allocation of public goods; state leaders have garnered backing by re-contextualising the relationship between state officials and citizens beyond simply ruler-and-ruled through the use of public ritual.

Meyer and Rowan (1977) argue that the survival prospects of organisations increase when they successfully adopt ceremonies that express institutional rules functioning as powerful myths. These ceremonies may conflict head on with the goals of efficiency; that is, organisations 'dramatically reflect the myths of their institutional environments instead of the demands of their work activities' (Meyer and Rowan 1977:341). In the case of states, this means that state organisations adopt ceremonies that appeal to the particularities of their population over procedures that maximise their efficiency. They 'incorporate elements which are legitimated externally, rather than in terms of efficiency' (Meyer and Rowan 1977:348). Expensive coronations, which can drain resources needed to achieve stated goals, for example, may affirm moral values by which many in society live and identify states with those values in people's minds; they are acts of 'national communion' (Shils 1975:139).

Ritual and ceremony:[4] it is impossible to conjure up states without thinking about them, from the grand entrance of judges into courtrooms to military parades. State practice from the age of kings to the era of republics has been suffused with elaborate ritual. Ceremonies have had the effect of forging unity, whether of the king's physical body with the body politic or of scattered individuals into a unified carrier of sovereignty supporting a particular state organisation (see Durkheim 1915:427). 'The central authority of an orderly society, whether it be secular or ecclesiastical', wrote Shils, 'is acknowledged to be the avenue of communication with the realm of the sacred values' (1975:151). Rituals and ceremonies connect the sacred to the notion of the nation and the mundane institutions of the state. States and societies both shape, and are shaped by, rituals and the beliefs they support.

Ritual and ceremony resonate with a theatrical ring. It is not surprising that theatre and politics seem to have a twinned existence, mimicking each other and spilling over into each other's domains (Combs 1980). Huet (1982) opens her book on the French Revolution with the culmination of the trial of Louis XVI, that moment when the representatives of the people, one by one, stepped forward to pronounce on the question of 'what penalty shall be inflicted?' Huet (1982:3) writes:

> ...we are indeed within the register of the theater: the material organization, the public, the state, the loges, the ushers, the galleries. The distribution of elements: that noisy, frivolous, enthusiastic theater-going crowd of which Diderot was so fond, and the more sober representatives

---

4 'Ritual is a stereotyped, symbolically concentrated expression of beliefs and sentiments regarding ultimate things' (Shils 1975:154). Also, see his discussion on p. 155 of the term 'ceremonial'.

of the people, loudly declaiming a sentence the repetitiveness of which brought out its force. The text was in dialogue form, as in the theater; however, in this instance the dialogue went beyond the theatrical and bore within it, amid the tumult and the levity of the auditorium, a force that was truly revolutionary.

This last sentence is almost a disclaimer of what was said earlier. Huet (1982:4) follows it by noting: 'This theater was not theater, of course; under the exterior signs of a frivolous scene almost familiar in its frightening levity, History was unfolding.' But the temptation is strong to make what happens into theatre or, as in the case of Hunt's *The Family Romance of the French Revolution* (1992), into a scripted story. In both works, the symbolic relationship of politics to a play or novel gives the gory events of the moment a shared and enduring meaning among the people. And, as the French Revolution vividly portrayed, the society can choreograph events as well as be choreographed by them. Hunt (1992:xiv) puts it this way: 'I use the term *family romance(s)* in order to suggest that much of this imaginative effort [that is, the people's reconfiguring their relationship to political authority] went on below the surface, as it were, of conscious political discourse.'

The connection between politics and theatre has been made repeatedly by observers, from Cicero to Hobbes to Burke. Edmund Burke, for example, saw close links between the two, approving the use of drama in the case of the British monarchy and regarding it with horror in the case of France's revolutionaries (Burke 1969; White 1994; Hindson and Gray 1988). One way commonly used to understand the relationship between theatre and politics is to see how spectacles have been used by politicians to enhance their power. By creating spectacles, as in the theatre, in which the public participates, state officials have sought to inscribe its laws within the spectator's mind, 'not as foreign but as inherent, self-imposed, "moral"' (Bryson 1991:3; Edelman 1988).

Geertz (1980) also suggests an association between the state and theatre, between ritual and power, one that may not always be instru-mental.[5] His case came from the nineteenth-century Balinese state, Negara. Power in this instance was not foremost on the mind of political rulers. Indeed, they showed indifference to actual governing, hesitancy in regulating people's everyday actions, and lack of interest in territorial sovereignty. Their attention pointed 'toward spectacle, toward ceremony, toward the public dramatisation of the ruling obsessions of Balinese culture: social inequality and status pride. It was a theatre state in which the kings and princes were the impresarios, the priests the directors, and the peasants the supporting cast, stage crew, and audience...Power served pomp, not pomp power' (Geertz 1980:13).

---

5   This part of the chapter is adapted from Migdal (1997).

In this view the court-and-capital,

...is not just the nucleus, the engine, or the pivot of the state, it is the
state...It is a statement of a controlling political idea—namely, that by the
mere act of providing a model, a paragon, a faultless image of civilized
existence, the court shapes the world around it into at least a rough
approximation of its own excellence' (Geertz 1980:13).

In his study, Geertz deals with the threat of state dissolution directly.
He sees a constant threat from the disintegrative forces of the 'power
system composed as it was of dozens of independent, semi-independent,
and quarter-independent rulers' (Geertz 1980:19). But what underlies the
staging of politics, the 'controlling political idea' (or what we might label
the master narrative) is a strong counterforce to the disintegrative elements. Master narratives 'operate as the unchallenged first principles of a
political order, making any given hierarchy appear natural and just to
rulers and ruled' (Wilentz 1985:4).

Participation in the Balinese ritualised theatre forged a sense of unity
among those participating as well as an awareness that such unity was
maintained, in great part, by the existence of the theatre state. Have not
politics and public ritual been related in similar ways in our time?
Especially in an age where technology makes both the manipulation and
dissemination of dramatic politics possible on a huge stage, theatrical
images suffuse our current-day politics. The small box of television, in
particular, transforms the complexity and ambiguity of politics into a
moral tale with a readily understandable content and lesson. Edelman
(1988:40) noted that 'in the age of mass communications dramaturgy has
become more central and the pattern it assumes more banal'. Staged
drama are constructions that 'offer answers to troubling questions. They
tell what conditions are healthy or threatening and who are responsible for
success and misfortune' (Edelman 1988:120).

All the elaborate ceremonies that state leaders employ—from inaugu-
rations to press conferences—might not be simply means towards an end.
They might, as in the Balinese case, be ends in themselves, an expression
of a simultaneous unity among people (all are part of the production) and
an order in which some command and others obey (different roles in the
production). The state's officials play a leading role in people's minds in
forging and maintaining that master narrative, the underlying dramatic
unity, and in holding positions of authority.

Of course, such theatre does not guarantee the state's survival.
Particularly in conditions of rapid social and political change, when
notions of where political authority properly lies are in flux, old dramatic
representations may lose their hold. Such a crumbling of the old drama
has been commented on in the case of France's *ancien régime* (Bryson
1991; Hunt 1992; Huet 1982). But these authors, too, note the importance
in the midst of the French Revolution of scripting a new dramatic
representation of unity and authority.

Still, both in the instances of the French Revolution and the Balinese state, those who use the theatrical metaphor present it as a tool used by states to mould and energise society. We can think of this line of thinking as the impresario theory of politics. This metaphor of theatre implies an impresario or producer as one who puts together the production; in the case of politics, the producer is the supreme leadership of the state.[6] We can counterpoise to that impresario model, a collective one. Here the state is not totally free to cast people however it wants; elaborate staging alone will not save any state. The will of the actors, the reaction of the audience, even the attitudes of the stagehands, all count heavily in the eventual success or failure of the production, and all good producers take account of them in staging their spectacle. The state is not only responsive to the society, it is changed by the nature of the population and its beliefs.

Warding off the disintegrative forces pulling at the state involves creating a unity among some or all of the people, as the impresario model implies, and having the state shape itself to key beliefs in society, as the collective model suggests. It is a unity in which the ruled see their roles as tied in to those of friends and strangers around them, and even strangers they will never meet, including the officials of the state who demand their obedience. For state leaders, that means creating 'a negotiated process relying on the skills of the theater to achieve spontaneous cooperation between human actors' (Hindson and Gray 1988:8). Elaborate ritual has been key in forging a semblance of oneness among disparate peoples and groups. As in the theatre, rituals have been used to arouse passions, to create affective ties between audience and spectators. Even the elaborate capital cities that every state has laid out and the costly public buildings they have erected are integral parts of the theatrical production. Analysing Burke, Hindson and Gray (1988:31) write:

> The physical arena within which political drama was enacted, was another feature of great importance to Burke's dramatic metaphor. The arena should be imposing and majestic. It should overwhelm the imagination of the populace, and awe them into acquiescence. The arena should be the architectural summit of human achievement, vast, impressive, and sublime.

---

6   Runciman (1997) contrasts this sort of model with a more pluralist model in the context of theatrical metaphors. He notes Hobbes's notion that all freedoms lie with the author of the drama, who is the sovereign (237). He contrasts that view with the one of Ernest Barker, the early twentieth-century British political theorist. 'Initially, Barker is happy to describe all the state as a stage, just as he is to describe all the persons within it as actors treading across its boards. The literal image of the state, however, is rather too passive to convey that sense of agency on which Barker's idea of the state depends. So he extends his analogy to take in those agents—the dramatist and producer— with whom responsibility for the staging of any drama rests...' (251).

E.P. Thompson, who certainly would not disparage the role of material forces in maintaining states' power and cohesion, noted that such forces go only so far in explaining why people obey. 'A great part of politics and law is always theater; once a social system has become "set," it does not need to be endorsed daily by exhibitions of power...what matters more is a continuing theatrical style' (Thompson 1974:389). Theatre moulds 'the images of power and authority, the popular mentalities of subordination' (Thompson 1974:387). And those images have remained important far past Geertz's and Thompson's nineteenth-century cases (for example, see Esherick and Wasserstrom 1990). 'Thrones may be out of fashion, and pageantry too', writes Geertz, 'but political authority still requires a cultural frame in which to define itself and advance its claims, and so does opposition to it' (Geertz 1983:142–3). The ability of any state to remain intact rests on its ability to produce that cultural frame, linking itself to the sacred through a set of rituals, and to transform itself so as to fit into a cultural frame that has resonance among key elements of the population.

Informal behaviour in the public sphere

Whether one leans towards an impresario or collective model for the theatrical metaphor, the state's position is central. Its success comes in creating some harmonious whole out of disparate parts. Another dimension having a deep impact on the state's ability to remain intact lies outside its direct control. Yet, this factor too is key in the fashioning of shared meaning in society, in the forging of a social unity that naturalises and sustains states. This dimension involves informal interactions in public space.

The concept of public space or the public sphere has been much discussed during the last generation, in good part due to the influence of Habermas (Habermas 1991; Calhoun, ed. 1996; Edgell, Walklate and Williams, eds 1995). His concern is with the debate on public issues by private people (as opposed to policy makers or others whose vocation make them part of political society or the state). Any number of practical discourses may proceed simultaneously on varied issues.

Habermas and those who followed him have been largely preoccupied with the quantity and quality of public debate and its effect on democratic politics. Nonetheless, some important presuppositions have gone into their thinking that raise questions related to our concern, the ability of states to remain intact. For one, the public sphere is understood to be an egalitarian space, that is, one in which 'arguments and not statuses determine decisions' (Calhoun, ed. 1996:1). Beyond that, the public sphere implies, not only the quality and quantity of rational conversations on public issues, but also an unwritten set of rules about how give-and-take should take place. Benhabib (1992:105) calls these conditions *universal moral respect* and *egalitarian reciprocity*. She goes on to say that: 'Democratic debate is like a ball game where there is no umpire to definitively interpret the rules of the game and their application' (106–7). Somehow, without the state or other authoritative umpires, rules for conversation among strangers do develop, at least in some societies.

The kinds of rules of the game to which Benhabib refers have to do with social interaction geared towards civic engagement. She is certainly right that these sorts of rules are preconditions for conversations that can influence political decisions and that such influence is essential in a democracy. But it is not only democratic debate that is like a ball game without an umpire. All societies, democratic and non-democratic alike, have broad dimensions of public life—life outside the walls of one's home—where social interaction is frequent and largely ungoverned by state law. And these, too, require rules without the benefit of an umpire, in part to insure social tranquillity but also to create a sense of unity or solidarity among those in society.

In the section on law above, I referred to these sorts of rules as a form of non-state law consisting of what various groups of people in society think is just and use as their guide to proper behaviour. The arena outside one's private or family domain can be threatening and frightening, and state laws have been able to provide only a modicum of security there. No matter how effective or pervasive the state apparatus, it cannot alone provide the kind of security that Hobbes imagined. Indeed, the perceived *effectiveness of the state rests on how well other sorts of implicit law or rules guide proper behaviour* and limit to some manageable level the deviance with which the state must deal.

Thinkers through the years have made reference to these non-state rules. Burke, for example, characterised them as the 'human "links", which, although having no legal status, act to constrain and restrict, as well as to give motion to the organised activity of a society' (Hindson and Gray 1988:8). Contemporary writers, too, continue to dwell on the issue of the rules of social engagement. Putnam (1993) relates the amount of civic engagement, including such mundane things as membership in choral societies and football clubs, to the effectiveness of governance in different regions of Italy. And he worries about the decline of 'social capital'—'networks, norms, and social trust that facilitate coordination and cooperation'—in the United States (Putnam 1995a:4). He argues that 'networks of civic engagement foster sturdy norms of generalized reciprocity and encourage the emergence of social trust' (1995a:4). In a similar vein, Laitin (1986:175) stresses the importance of societies developing what he calls shared 'points of concern'. These are a critical foundation for forging common understandings about what the public agenda should be and agreement on the proper ways to disagree.

How and why do strong social networks form in public space? Which societies manage to hammer out shared points of concern that determine what is up for discussion and what not, and which societies fail to do that? How do forms of engagement with others whom one encounters only fleetingly become established? All societies have multiple sites of juris-genesis, law creation, but which ones have some dovetailing of the understanding of what is proper and appropriate public behaviour? Unfortunately, scholars do not yet have answers to these questions, so essential for understanding the cohesion of states.

What one can say at this point is that the public space in modern times has been marked by three related characteristics, all of which have complicated the ability of societies to create and maintain a semblance of social solidarity. First, *the rules for engagement in the public space have been constantly renegotiated.* Urbanisation, migration, tourism, mass media, and women's liberation, among other powerful processes, all have repeatedly introduced new groups and individuals into the public space as well as different ideas of proper modes of interaction. In short, the public space has continued to expand dramatically. That never-ending process has put tremendous pressure on social stability and solidarity. In some cases, the new faces in the public space have assimilated into existing conventions; at other times, they have successfully induced changes in the existing ways of doing things to accommodate them; and, in still other instances, they have precipitated fierce struggles over who should rightfully participate in the public sphere and whose conventions will prevail. These conventions may include everything from how to behave when two people are walking directly towards each other on the sidewalk (who gives way?) to how much emotion to display in a conversation.

Second, *the claim for egalitarianism has energised the entry of new groups into the public space.* Habermas emphasises the importance of bourgeois society in the creation of the public sphere (1991:23) and the notion, mentioned earlier, that in egalitarian space arguments and not statuses determine decisions. Once introduced, the idea of equal claims on the right to participate in and shape the conventions of the public space is insidious. It did not end with the demands of the bourgeois stratum, by any means. Whatever a group's social basis for participation in the public sphere, whether class, gender, ethnicity, or some other, it has used the claim of equality to challenge others' feelings of entitlement to dominate public space. And that has been a very powerful demand indeed.

Third, *egalitarian assertions have precipitated counter-claims,* leading to contentious struggles about who properly belongs in the public space. In some of the most intense struggles, such as the fight over slavery in the United States of America or the Taliban's campaign against women in Afghanistan or the mutual claims for exclusion among ethnic groups in the former Yugoslavia, the state actually did disintegrate in the process. In all cases of claims and counter-claims, severe pressure was put on the unity of society. Why some societies could reconstitute their public space and develop practices that could continue or re-establish social unity is a question that scholars cannot yet answer. But it is one that holds great import for states and their ability to remain intact.

Conclusion

International factors, such as the globalisation of capital and the actions of United Nations agencies, have both buffeted and sustained the state. But any thoroughgoing explanation of why so many states have avoided collapse and stayed intact must deal with issues beyond these systemic, environmental factors. We must look to the direct relations between states and those they aim to govern. Organisational theorists point us towards social exchange, where individuals trade loyalty for selective access to public goods. Underlying this notion is an understanding that the state's efficient allocation of goods in that exchange will enhance its chances for survival. While that is a very helpful notion, it still leaves us wondering how so many grossly inefficient states continue to withstand disintegrative forces. How do states sustain loyalty and compliance even when their delivery systems falter?

Our answer starts with the dictum that 'the heart has its reasons which the mind does not suspect' (Shils 1975:135). The argument here has implied a realm of feelings and implicit understandings that go beyond rational calculation. Relying exclusively on provision of services or material goods to its population, whether directly through a complex bureaucracy or indirectly through an umbrella for patron–client ties, is a flimsy foundation for states. Their staying ability will ultimately rest on how well they tie into people's hearts.

Where states have tapped into the creation of shared meaning in society, they have become naturalised and the thought of their dissolution or disappearance has become unimaginable. That shared sense that the state is as natural as the rivers and the mountains has gone far in combating the effects of disintegrative forces, including the states' own inefficiency. This chapter has identified three areas in which changes in society and the nature of ensuing state–society relations can bolster or batter the cohesion of the state. The three are the generation of law in society, the sharing of public rituals between state and society, and the ongoing renegotiation of the rules of informal behaviour in the public sphere.

What I cannot say at this point is under what conditions changes in these areas will work to keep the state intact. What I can suggest is how they can work to sustain the state. First, the three areas of state–society engagement can both alert state officials to important changes in society— to *who is participating*, to *what practices are emerging*, and to *what import or meaning the changes hold*—and induce the state to adapt to the reconstitution of society. Second, changes in *participants*, *practices*, and *meaning* can lead, at times, to more social solidarity or unity, enhancing the unquestioned presence of the state. More than that, states can provide symbols, forums, and institutions that can increase the chances that social changes will dovetail to create social solidarity. Third, these sorts of changes, when they do dovetail, can increase social stability. Informal practices in the public sphere and other forms of non-state law can lead to greater public civility and tranquillity, further enhancing the state. Finally, these practices can seriously lighten the burden on the state. A state like one envisioned by Hobbes, responsible for all social security, would simply be stretched too thin. Where non-state practices provide security in their own right, the state is in a position to marshal and deploy its scarce resources more successfully.

Can one expect changes in informal practices and in the groups clamouring to be heard in the public space to help states remain intact or hurt them? From Habermas (1991) on, a dark pessimism has pervaded discussions of changes in the public sphere and the future of (democratic) states. In the United States, in particular, expressions of the deterioration of the public sphere have been commonplace (for example, Oldenburg 1989; Putnam 1995b). One encounters foreboding book titles, like *The Fall of Public Man* (Sennett 1977), or references to the 'American trauma' (Marty 1997).

My own inclination is to be more cautious about proclaiming an imminent apocalypse or even a slow deterioration of a public space that can produce social solidarity. It is tempting to view the public sphere as beleaguered, in part, because it is an area of ongoing renegotiation, contestation, and struggle. Present-day clashes take on an ominous cast and precipitate a nostalgia for some idyllic past, when the public sphere was really a civil space.

It is doubtful that such a heart-warming past did exist in the period from the Industrial Revolution on. But, more than that, those characteristics of contestation and struggle also give the public space countless possibilities for rebirth and new vigour. Claims and counter-claims surrounding the public sphere signal and spur parts of the state to change themselves and to renegotiate their coalitions with segments of society. Encounters in the public space also goad some in the state to nudge diverse social changes in common directions, building complementarities rather than fostering divisions. Out of these processes may come reinvigorated states. Focusing on these sorts of state–society relations in the future should give us an indication of when that happens, and when not.

3 In Weakness and Strength— State, Societies and Order in Papua New Guinea

SINCLAIR DINNEN

Papua New Guinea's burgeoning problems of order have contributed to the apocalyptic tone of many recent commentaries. An implicit—sometimes explicit—invocation of disintegration pervades such accounts.[1] While the disintegration thesis comes in various guises, there is broad agreement that the limited capacity of the Papua New Guinea state is a major contributor to current problems. For many, the most alarming aspect of this weakness of state is its inability to contain rising levels of lawlessness, criminal violence and social disorder. As Migdal reminds us, a defining feature of the modern state is its aim 'to impose a uniform and ultimate conformity on social life within far-reaching...boundaries' (Migdal 1997:209). It is the extremely limited success of the Papua New Guinea state in maintaining compliance to its authority and laws that is viewed by many observers as its most fundamental sign of weakness.

There is no denying that Papua New Guinea is experiencing major problems of order and that these have, in turn, caused extensive suffering, high levels of personal insecurity and impeded economic growth. These problems are manifested in endemic gang violence, euphemistically referred to as *raskolism*, social banditry in certain rural areas, the resurgence of so-called 'tribal fighting' in parts of the Highlands and, of course, the

---

1   The conservative Australian critic B.A. Santamaria was one of the most consistent and vocal proponents of the disintegration thesis in respect of Papua New Guinea. For an illustration of his views and a spirited riposte, see Griffin (1988). A more recent and sophisticated version addressing the Pacific Island states is the 'doomsday' scenario propounded in some of the work published by the National Centre for Development Studies (NCDS) at the Australian National University, for example, Cole, ed. (1993). Critiques of this latter perspective can be found in Pirie (1995), Hayes (1995) and Fry (1997).

bloody and inconclusive secessionist war on the island of Bougainville. Corruption is another notable concern and has fuelled growing popular disenchantment with the formal political process. Likewise, the diminishing capacity of the state's principal instrumentalities of law and order cannot be denied. Amongst other things, the weakness of state controls provides the rationale for the massive capacity building exercise presently being undertaken in the law and order sector and funded by Australian aid (see below).

There are, nevertheless, definite limits to an exclusive focus on disintegration. The processes underlying current problems of order are altogether less certain and predictable than implied in depictions of monolithic collapse. Much disorder in Papua New Guinea occurs in enclaves and is episodic in character. The performance of state institutions in this area has also been extremely uneven and an assessment of state responses requires the disaggregation of what is clearly not a unitary actor. Some institutions, such as the Ombudsman Commission and, for much of the post-Independence period, the superior courts, appear to have worked extremely well.

Underlying much of today's disintegrative talk is the unfavourable contrast drawn between the weak post-colonial state in Papua New Guinea and its allegedly stronger colonial predecessor. The 'collapse of law and order' in recent years has been associated with the failings of the former, while the era of colonial peace is often attributed to the strengths of the latter. Such a contrast oversimplifies a complex transformation in state–society relations that has taken place in the historical period concerned and is seriously misleading on a number of grounds. In the first place, it ignores the profound changes that have occurred in Papua New Guinea's social, economic and political environment in recent decades and that provide the context for current problems of order. Second, it seriously overstates the strengths of the colonial state and its role in securing colonial peace. Third, it provides an overly reductive portrayal of the post-colonial state, neglecting its combination of weaknesses and strengths, as well as the crucial way in which the state is itself constituted through interaction with the societies in which it operates.

Forecasts of Papua New Guinea's imminent disintegration have, of course, been heard for many years. While the organisation of both state and society may have weakened in significant ways, there have also been more positive building processes at work. The notion of disintegration fails to capture the fullness of these developments. Ample evidence testifies to the resilience of older social forms that have by no means crumbled under the impact of recent change and that, on the contrary, have had a transformative impact on many institutions of more recent origin. Current problems of order, it is suggested, may be more usefully viewed in terms of the emergence of a different kind of order, rather than as symptoms of total collapse.

This chapter examines the role of the Papua New Guinea state in the control of crime and social disorder. Analytic focus is placed upon the changing character of state–society relations in recent Papua New Guinea history and the manner in which these changes have influenced the current law and order environment. It is argued that an understanding of today's problems of order and, hence, the formulation of possible solutions, is advanced by viewing them in terms of the mutually transformative interactions that have occurred between state and society in the transition from colonial to post-colonial periods. At the broadest of levels, these changes have involved a progressive blurring between state and society in post-colonial Papua New Guinea that has, amongst other things, contributed to a growing reliance on violence as a political strategy on the part of both state and societal actors.

The chapter begins with an historical section, providing an abbreviated account of social ordering in stateless Melanesian societies, the impact of colonial intrusion, and the major institutional changes accompanying decolonisation. This historical background informs the subsequent discussion of contemporary problems of order and the particular responses of the post-colonial state. The concluding discussion draws these various strands together and provides a broad assessment of the weaknesses and strengths of the post-colonial state in Papua New Guinea.

Order in Papua New Guinea—An Historical Perspective

Stateless societies

While pre-contact Melanesian polities displayed a remarkable diversity of styles and substances, some broad generalisations are possible. Societies were typically small, parochial and isolated. Political units comprised the largest groups within which organised warfare would not normally occur. In the lowlands and coastal areas, these groups rarely exceeded several hundred people, although they rose to over a thousand in parts of Sepik and in the more populous Highlands (Chowning 1977). Political units seldom coincided with cultural–linguistic units, which were often much larger. Differences in size related principally to factors of ecology and the variable and often harsh terrain, as well as to the need for efficient divisions of labour in subsistence horticultural and other tasks. Patterns of residence ranged from dispersed homesteads to elaborate nucleated villages. Wide differentiation existed in kinship systems, patterns of land ownership, and in the stability of residential groups.

Social relations within these small scale societies were essentially kinship relations. The rights and obligations of each individual were relatively well defined and flowed from membership of the extended family. Patterns of inheritance for land, special knowledge and personal property could be patrilineal or, as in some coastal societies, matrilineal.

Reciprocal obligations between kin formed the basis of Melanesian morality. Reciprocity was commonly manifested in the ritualised exchange of food and gifts. Exchange practices sometimes evolved into elaborate trading partnerships with other groups over considerable distances. As well as constituting a significant means of social control, gift exchange was a vehicle for trade and a way of establishing and sustaining alliances with other groups.

Although links developed between groups as a result of trading or defensive alliances, or kinship ties through marriage, most communities remained insular. This insularity was reinforced by high levels of suspicion, inter-group warfare, and fear of sorcery. Reconstructions of pre-contact history suggest that, subject to local variations, warfare was endemic in many areas (Berndt 1962).

Melanesian societies were 'stateless' in the sense that they lacked any centralised political or administrative organisation equivalent to a 'government' that could weld together those sharing a common language and culture (Larmour 1992). Relations between individuals in such societies were highly personal, with members dependent upon one another's actions. Contrary to idealised representations of egalitarian and organically cohesive traditional communities, social divisions did exist, not least in terms of gender and leadership. As May and Tupouniua point out 'intense factionalism' was a common feature of Melanesian societies (1980:423).

Political units were usually led by a man, or several men. Men were politically dominant, even in matrilineal societies. While both ascribed and achieved leadership were found in such societies, achieved leadership—subject to the usual variations—appears to have been more usual. An aspiring leader engaged in perpetual competition with others to build his reputation and cultivate a personal following through the skilful manipulation of resources and social relations. Social power was ultimately generated through the personal power of big men. The authority of the successful Melanesian big-man rarely extended beyond his own small group and was contingent upon him fulfilling the expectations of followers, as well as outmanœuvring leadership rivals. The perpetual struggle between leadership contenders contributed, in turn, to the inherent political instability of such societies.

Each society evolved its own particular means of settling disputes, varying according to the status of the parties concerned and the relations between them (Epstein 1972:632). Taylor has categorised the means of social control in stateless societies as the threat of retaliation or 'payback', the threat to withdraw reciprocity, sanctions of approval and disapproval, and threats of sorcery and supernatural sanctions (1982:81–90). While there was a role for compulsion in securing conformity, inducement was equally significant in many such societies. This was achieved primarily through the manipulation of wealth in exchange relationships that were constantly validated through material transactions (Pospisil 1979:133).

The effectiveness of these strategies of control ultimately depended on the smallness and relative stability of these communities, the closeness of social relations linking members, and their shared system of beliefs and values. These social forms did not, of course, simply disappear with the advent of colonial rule and, subject to continuous adaptation, remain the most significant basis of indigenous social organisation and individual identity. Papua New Guinea's continuing social diversity is reflected today in the existence of over 800 recorded languages among a population of approximately 4.5 million. It is the sheer scale of this diversity that vests state–society relations in Papua New Guinea with their particular multi-faceted character.

Colonial impact

Although colonial intervention did not officially occur until the late nineteenth century, an assortment of missionaries, traders, gold prospectors and foreign adventurers had begun visiting coastal and island areas from the 1830s. The Dutch, who had asserted a claim to the western half of New Guinea in mid-century (Dutch New Guinea), did not establish an administrative presence until 1898 (Turner 1990:3). At the behest of commercial interests, the German imperial government annexed the northeastern portion of New Guinea in 1884 (German New Guinea). In the same year, the British declared a protectorate over the southeastern portion of the island (British New Guinea). Constitutional uncertainty about the status of the protectorate led to British New Guinea being annexed as a full colony in 1888, prior to its subsequent transfer to Australia—and renaming as Papua—in 1906.

The spread of colonial influence was an extremely slow and uneven process in both Papua and New Guinea and had varied impacts on different local populations, ranging from substantial to very little. The initial response to foreign incursion by indigenous communities also varied enormously. While some groups mounted overt resistance, thereby incurring punitive responses, others cooperated for a variety of strategic reasons. Fear of superior government firepower and the indiscriminate violence of punitive raids may have motivated some groups. For others, cooperation with Europeans—government or otherwise—was viewed pragmatically, as a means of forging powerful new alliances in the fight against traditional enemies (Kituai 1988:165), or as an opportunity for developing trade links, pursuing alternative strategies of prestige building, or acquiring new forms of wealth and knowledge.

In German New Guinea, colonial influence was extended by establishing government stations from which armed police patrols led by district officials set out to pacify indigenous peoples. Local men were appointed as *luluais* to represent the government at village level and some were made *tultuls* or interpreters. The district officer sought to pacify his district, stop inter-group fighting and, thereby, make it safe and profitable for European settlement. Australia formally took over the administration of New Guinea as a mandated territory of the League of Nations in 1921. Gold mining provided a significant proportion of the administration's revenue and lay behind the subsequent opening up to Europeans of the fertile and populous Highlands of New Guinea in the 1930s. In practice, both territories were jointly administered from 1942.[2]

In Papua, the expansion of British–Australian colonial influence proceeded at a leisurely pace. Apart from the gold prospectors scattered around the islands in the southeast and parts of the mainland, there were relatively few settlers and virtually no plantations. By 1940, the area of land under lease in Papua was actually less than it had been in 1911. The area under crops in 1918 (24 000 hectares) stayed about the same for the next 30 years, while the size of the European population in 1939 had not increased significantly since 1913 (Griffin, Nelson and Firth 1979:24). For many indigenes in both territories, the colonial order was personified by missionaries and traders rather than by government officials. The administration in Papua was almost entirely dependent on a modest Australian subsidy which severely restricted its operations. As in New Guinea, government control was to be gradually extended through a system of patrolling, radiating outwards from newly established government stations. These patrols were led by European patrol officers (*kiaps*) with an armed native constabulary.

The administration in Papua saw its principal goal as the protection of the indigenous peoples from corrupting Western influences and their gradual induction into the pale of 'civilisation'. This 'civilising mission' was to be accomplished through a benign and paternalistic system of 'native administration'. A system of village constables was established. These officials, like the *luluais* in New Guinea, were appointed to represent the administration at the village level. By 1940, approximately two-thirds of the inhabitants of the two territories were governed by patrol (Griffin, Nelson and Firth 1979:61). This included most of the Highlands by the late 1940s (Standish 1984:26). In practice, government by patrol often meant little more than a couple of visits a year for villages close to administrative centres, a single visit every one or two years for more distant villages, and even rarer visits in less accessible areas. The *kiap*, assisted by government appointed village officials, would inspect the village, collect taxes, complete the census book and hear minor criminal cases.

Retrospective accounts of the colonial period (almost entirely written by foreigners) emphasise the importance of district level administration and, in particular, the pivotal role of the *kiap* in suppressing inter-group warfare and extending government authority. Whether appreciative or

---

2   Joint administration occurred under the Australian military administration in 1942 in those areas not under Japanese control. In 1949, the United Nations formally agreed to a joint administration.

critical of what has been described as Australia's 'benevolent type of police rule',[3] it has often been assumed that colonial peace was something imposed from above upon bellicose indigenous communities. Such an assumption overstates the purchase of what were, in effect, extremely tenuous colonial controls. The colonial state was in most respects extremely weak, with the meagre resources available to it being insufficient to contain resistance on any significant scale. As noted in the Enga context:

> Numerous early patrol reports testify to the fact that by himself, with his small contingent of police, the kiap was unable to stop fights, even if he wanted to (Gordon 1983:210).

The incremental spread of a weak colonial presence provided little immediate threat to most Melanesian social institutions and ensured that their adaptation to change occurred largely on their own terms. As we have noted, it was missions rather than the colonial state that provided the catalyst for change in the daily lives of villagers in many parts of what is now Papua New Guinea. Until very late in its life, the colonial state evinced only a desultory interest in 'development', placing more value on 'stability' and the creation of a semblance of order.

Colonial peace was achieved as much by the inducements and opportunities it provided local populations, as by the compulsion of colonial force. According to one early observer of pacification in the Papua New Guinea Highlands, the desire for goods was the most significant constraint upon indigenous hostility to colonial intrusion (Reed 1943). Coercion did, of course, play a significant role in colonial pacification but was by no means the sole, or principal, factor. As Strathern has remarked in the Highlands context, colonial authority was accepted 'out of a combination of fear and self-interest' (1993:42). The emphasis upon colonisation as an imposed process has also neglected agency on the part of Melanesian actors and institutions and the crucial role these played in the mediation of colonial power. *Pax Australiana*—lasting less than 30 years in most parts of the Highlands—could never have been sustained without the acquiescence of local groups.

Insofar as the *kiap* system was successful, this was largely because it did not seek to displace local structures or overtly interfere in local politics. In practice, elements of the colonial system could sometimes be captured by local actors and turned to their own interests. The arrival of the *kiap* courts, to take one example, did not destroy existing mechanisms of dispute resolution. Rather, they provided additional forums that could be incorporated into local political strategies. Local litigants could graft these courts onto existing unofficial (officially illegal) mechanisms and engage in imaginative strategies of 'forum shopping'. Decisions of unofficial 'courts'—where most local conflicts were decided—could now be

---

3 Lord Hailey, a member of the Permanent Mandates Commission of the League of Nations (in Mair 1948:xvi).

confirmed or contested in the new forums provided by the colonial state. In this way interactions between indigenous and colonial systems of law often served to reinforce, rather than undermine, each other:

> Unofficial courts served to make kiap's 'law' 'strong' because of the nature of cooperation which existed between kiaps and unofficial 'magistrates' (Gordon 1983:211).[4]

These instances of mutually-reinforcing interactions between colonial and indigenous laws provide an illustration of what Migdal, in this volume, refers to as the 'naturalisation' of the state, whereby an otherwise weak state—in this case, the colonial state—is able to resist powerful disintegrative forces as a result of 'gaining legitimacy from the changes society imposed upon' it.

Reconstructions of colonial history focusing upon the experiences of the colonised, as opposed to the colonisers, also confirms the critical role of Melanesians working as junior officials in the shaping of colonial order (Schieffelin and Crittenden, eds 1991). The cumulative effect of recent studies of colonial policing, for example, is to portray 'colonialism' as the work of individual Papua New Guinea policemen, placed in large population centres throughout the Highlands and elsewhere, imposing their will by playing local politics and forming tactical marriage alliances (Kituai 1988, 1993; Gammage 1996). Melanesian policemen were 'aggressive and enthusiastic agents of change' (Kituai 1988:157).

Decolonisation and the 'Opening Up' of the State

The rather modest objectives of the colonial state prior to the modernising period preceding independence were never really in danger of provoking the level of resistance and conflict that has greeted more ambitious plans in later years. The acceleration in the pace of socio-economic and institutional change generated new opportunities, as well as new tensions and social divisions. With the inevitable weakening of colonial legitimacy, the spread of the cash economy, urbanisation, Western education, population growth and changing popular expectations, it is unlikely that the colonial peace would have lasted much longer than it did.

From the early 1960s, colonial authorities engaged in a belated process of institutional reform aimed at laying the institutional foundations of the modern state. The 1960 Derham Report provided the blueprint for the institutional transformation of law enforcement and judicial administration that was to be bequeathed—albeit in incomplete form—to Papua New Guinea at independence. The report advocated the gradual dismantling of

---

4   Fitzpatrick (1984:115) has used the concept of 'integral plurality' to describe this process whereby 'state law is integrally constituted in relation to a plurality of social forms'.

the decentralised and undifferentiated system of district administration. Instead, it was to be replaced by a unitary and centralised system of judicial administration based upon a clear division of labour between the police, judiciary and prison service (Derham 1960). While the modernising vision was relatively clear, at least in the minds of its Australian architects, the implementation of the reforms and their reception at local levels were less straightforward.

In 1961, the police force was separated from the Department of Native Affairs and in 1966 it was removed altogether from the direct control of the Public Service Commission in order to ensure its 'neutrality' (Gordon and Meggitt 1985:83). The system of courts, which had remained virtually unchanged from early colonial times, also underwent significant change from the mid-1960s, with a shift away from the relatively informal *kiap* courts to more formal court procedures (Oram 1973:13). Local and district courts were established in 1963 and connected through appeal to the superior courts. The local court was intended to replace the *kiap* courts. These, in turn, would eventually be replaced by the district courts staffed by a professional magistracy. Most of the native regulations enforced by the *kiaps* were repealed in 1968 and replaced by summary offences codified in modern criminal statutes. Belated provision was made for the training of indigenous magistrates with the opening of the Administrative College in 1966.

These institutional changes were to have an important influence on social control at local levels. This can be best understood in terms of their impact on those factors that had contributed to the relative success of the colonial *kiap*. In practice, the juridical powers of the *kiap* could be regularly supplemented by powers issuing from his various agency functions (Gordon 1983:220). These included options for rewarding, as well as for punishing, individuals and groups. The *kiap*, thus, had a wide choice of sanctions with which to influence behaviour, as well as considerable discretion in exercising this choice. These sanctions, moreover, could be applied immediately, with minimal formality or delay.

By contrast, the discretion of the professional magistrate, who displaced the *kiap* as official adjudicator of local level conflict, was restricted by the detailed provisions of substantive, evidential and procedural rules. Professional, as opposed to *kiap*, justice took longer and entailed a cumbersome, formalistic process guaranteed to bewilder the uninitiated. As well as weakening the standing of the *kiap* by depriving him of one of his most potent roles, these changes contributed to growing dissatisfaction on the part of local litigants. Official concern with due process, a narrow focus on individual culpability, and the emphasis on punishment rather than restitution, offended local perceptions of how disputes should be resolved. Compared to *kiap* justice, professional justice was viewed by many Melanesians as 'soft', partial and profoundly unjust (Strathern 1972, 1976). The authority of the police was also undermined by this separation of powers, with the formerly powerful and prestigious agents of pacification now subject to regular and humiliating 'defeats' in court, often on technical grounds.

The rapid process of localisation initiated during this period also had a significant impact upon the purchase of state controls. This was not only because of the institutional consequences of replacing experienced officers with less experienced personnel. It also related to the significant diminution in social distance between state officials and their societal clients flowing from the localisation process. While, as we have seen, individual Melanesian policemen operating at the most junior levels of the colonial hierarchy engaged directly with local power structures, expatriate *kiaps*, magistrates and other officials exercised considerable autonomy in their dealings with indigenes precisely because of their foreignness. Their apparent disinterest in competing with Melanesians through engaging in local politics and their immunity to the pressures of 'wantokism',[5] contributed to their appearance as 'independent' and 'impartial'. The basis of these local perceptions was fundamentally altered once Melanesians began filling these positions. Irrespective of their individual abilities and performance, indigenous officials were immediately vulnerable to accusations of 'wantokism' and to concerns that they would become rivals in local political competition. These problems associated with diminishing autonomy of state officials were exacerbated by the role fragmentation resulting from institutional reforms which, as mentioned, also reduced the power and prestige of *kiaps* and police.

These changes did not, of course, occur overnight but entailed a prolonged and uneven period of transition. Their cumulative effect, however, was to weaken both the capacity and legitimacy of state controls, drawing attention to the weakness of state rather than bolstering the myth of state strength. This process, in turn, has progressively deepened during the post-colonial period for a variety of reasons discussed below.

Indigenous participation in wider political processes also began in the early 1960s. A United Nations Visiting Mission in 1962 had been highly critical of the lack of political development in the territory and advocated a number of measures to increase indigenous participation. Among these was the establishment of a House of Assembly elected by all adults and the development of higher education to train Papua New Guineans for senior positions in the bureaucracy (Turner 1990:14). Despite the protestations of many residents, indigenous and foreign, the pace of political change began to quicken from the mid-1960s against a background of rapid decolonisation in other parts of the world.

---

5 The term 'wantok' in Papua New Guinea Pidgin literally means one who speaks the same language (that is, one talk) but is popularly used to describe relations of obligation binding relatives, members of the same clan or tribal group, as well as much looser forms of association. In the context of modern institutions, 'wantokism' is generally used to describe nepotism.

The first Papua New Guineans to be elected in a general election took the majority of seats in 1964 in a House of Assembly that was effectively dominated by official European members (Griffin, Nelson and Firth 1979:133–4). Their election, nevertheless, marked the beginning of the opening up of the state to local participation at the highest levels. It also signified the emergence of indigenous politicians as a new and significant category of power broker linking local power structures to more encompassing arenas of state. These individuals would proceed to play an important role in the decolonisation process and, more significantly, in the shaping of the post-colonial order.

Independence, Development and Problems of Order

While viewed with great trepidation by many,[6] the granting of independence in 1975 was a time of optimism for other Papua New Guineans. Popular aspirations, fuelled by nationalistic rhetoric, were directed at the anticipated development opportunities that political independence would provide indigenous citizens. For Papua New Guinea's first generation of state leaders, the most pressing tasks were to secure the material conditions for national development, on the one hand, and dealing with law and order problems, on the other. On the first matter, PNG's major source of revenue at independence was an annual grant from Australia which accounted for 40 per cent of public expenditure (Turner 1990:36). Following the Eight Point Plan for national development (King, Lee and Warakai 1985), the Constitution set economic self-reliance as one of the national goals. In the long term, this meant gradually reducing reliance upon Australian budgetary support by developing alternative sources of revenue. As well as expanding established agricultural exports, such as coffee, cocoa and copra, this meant exploiting the country's vast wealth in natural resources.

On the second matter, decolonisation coincided with the emergence of a number of areas of social conflict that challenged, in varying degrees, the authority of the new state. Impending independence fuelled micronationalist tensions in some of the more developed regions, notably Bougainville, the Gazelle Peninsula, and parts of Papua. On Bougainville island, the discovery of sizeable copper reserves and plans for a massive open-cast mine, which took little account of the wishes and aspirations of local land owners, set in motion a complex conflict that was to re-ignite in the late 1980s as the Bougainville war. The fragility of national unity was most vividly demonstrated when Bougainville leaders proclaimed a

---

6   Many Highlanders, with a significantly shorter experience of colonial rule, considered independence premature and were concerned that their better prepared lowlands compatriots would have an unfair advantage in the development stakes.

unilateral declaration of independence—a mere fortnight before PNG's national independence in September 1975. Lack of international recognition and some adept political manœuvring by the coalition government led by Michael Somare resulted in the—albeit temporary—defusing of the crisis in 1976. In Papua, the spectre of secession was raised by leaders apprehensive about the social impact of large scale migration from other parts of the country, particularly the Highlands (Oram 1976:144).

The revival of 'tribal fighting' in parts of the Highlands in the early 1970s provided another challenge to the writ of centralised authority. For many observers, the reappearance of this form of conflict—effectively suppressed during the colonial era—demonstrated the folly of replacing the old colonial system with a remote, centralised system of criminal justice. In particular, the centralisation of institutional controls was seen as resulting in a withdrawal of state from the most local levels.[7] The resurgence in 'tribal fighting' represented a reversion to older 'self-help' strategies, largely in response to the absence of state or the 'weakness' of its solutions. As Feil commented in the Western Highlands context:

> ...the perceived ineffectiveness of a weak indigenous administration [has] offered few alternatives to western highlanders, aside from violence, for settling grievances, disputes, and for pressing claims (Feil 1987:276).

While the 1977 Inter-Group Fighting Act—which criminalised participation in such conflicts—appears to have resulted in a temporary lull, subsequent outbreaks led to progressively more coercive policing responses. In 1979, for example, the national government declared a state of emergency in all five Highlands provinces. Tribal fighting has continued sporadically in different parts of the Highlands. The introduction of modern weaponry has led to substantial increases in fatalities, destruction and protracted cycles of retributive violence. Growing pressures on land in the densely populated Highlands have also been implicated in contemporary fights as, in recent years, have disputes over electoral outcomes (Dinnen 1996; Standish 1996).

Conflict in urban areas was manifested in the growth in street crime— *raskolism*—from the mid-1960s. Juvenile gangs appeared against a background of urban growth following the removal of colonial restrictions over indigenous social movement. The abolition of these restrictions opened up the towns—formerly the preserve of the European élite—to migration from rural areas. The removal of the prohibition on the indigenous purchase of alcohol in 1962 was another factor in early gang formation, providing the 'spark which ignited the flame' (Harris 1988:8).

---

7   The Paney Committee Report on Tribal Fighting stated that it had 'heard many complaints of a lack of judicial and police presence at village level and considers this lack as one of the prime causes of increased lawlessness in the Highlands. Government influence in these fields is stopping at Sub-District level while at the village level an administrative vacuum is developing' (PNG 1973:7).

The first gangs were primarily mechanisms for coping with the dislocative effects of socio-economic change and, in particular, those facing young male migrants in the unfamiliar urban environment. Criminal activities were initially confined to petty theft, mainly of food, beer and cash (Parry 1972). *Raskolism* has since spread to many other parts of PNG and criminal activities have become increasingly more sophisticated and violent, particularly in the main towns. As with tribal fighting, the widespread availability of illegal firearms has contributed significantly to growing violence on the part of *raskols*. According to one observer, by the late-1980s *raskol* gangs had become:

> ...efficient criminal organisations which operate with little fear of appre-
> hension...They have strong links with other criminal groups in the country
> for the distribution and sale of stolen goods; they are heavily involved in
> the drug trade; and they have close links with some politicians and
> businessmen who use them for political purposes and to 'pay-back'
> enemies (Harris 1988:1).

Demographic factors and new forms of socio-economic marginali-sation provide an important part of the explanation of the rise of *raskolism*. Between 1966 and 1977, the capital, Port Moresby, experien-ced a dramatic 12.2 per cent annual growth rate (King 1992:22) and doubled in size during the first decade of independence (Dorney 1990:299). Whereas most early growth was the result of migration, later growth reflects a natural increase in fertility among urban residents. Despite persistent calls to repatriate 'troublemakers', many of today's urban youth have only tenuous links with rural villages. In practice, a growing proportion of the urban population have become 'permanent urban dwellers' (Morauta 1980).

Of the current national population, approximately 43 per cent are under the age of fifteen (Dalglish and Connolly 1992). According to the 1990 national census figures, approximately 50 per cent of the population of the national capital district (Port Moresby and its environs) are under twenty years of age, and approximately 62 per cent are aged under 25 years (NSO 1993). While over 50 000 school leavers join the labour market each year, the formal economy can only absorb about 10 000, leaving over 40 000 to seek alternative avenues in the informal economy. Many leave or are 'pushed out' of school because parents cannot afford the fees or because of difficulties encountered with the urban-oriented education system. This orientation contributes to the marginalisation of village youth, while simultaneously drawing them to the towns. Crime, in this situation, constitutes a relatively accessible strategy for acquiring resources, particularly in the fully monetised urban milieu where employ-ment and subsistence options are limited. The weakness of state controls, in turn, adds to the attractions of this strategy.

In contrast to media stereotypes of *raskols* existing apart from 'respec-table society', members of criminal groups are often extremely well integrated into their immediate social environment. This integration is not only owing to reasons of self-interest, with criminals dependent on their residential communities for safe haven in times of conflict with state authorities. It is also because bonds of kinship and association outweigh externally imposed criminal labels. More significant, for our purposes, is the powerful sense of grievance shared by *raskol* and non-*raskol* residents in many village and settlement communities. This is expressed in a broad rhetoric of social disadvantage directed, in particular, at the breakdown of government services, deepening socio-economic inequalities and burgeoning levels of government corruption. Criminals use this rhetoric to legitimate activities that, in practice, tend to victimise the socially disadvantaged more than the socially privileged. They have, nevertheless, become adept at connecting with these broader currents of popular discontent and using them to their advantage.

Growing levels of popular disenchantment with political leadership and the integrity of government processes, in turn, stem from the failure of successive post-independence governments to provide development opportunities and improve the quality of life for ordinary citizens. This failure has been increasingly attributed by many to the corrupt dealings of individual public office holders. The recent constitutional crisis and instability catalysed by the Chan government's decision to hire foreign mercenaries to resolve the Bougainville conflict—the so-called Sandline affair[8]—provides the most vivid demonstration of this growing concern with corruption at the highest levels of state.

General impressions and available indicators confirm a progressive decline in the quality and delivery of government services during the later part of post-independence period. In many rural areas, existing services have ceased or been effectively paralysed owing to shortage of resources and personnel, and, in some cases, have been withdrawn in the face of local problems of order. The creation of new public infrastructure has been minimal and uneven, while the maintenance of existing facilities has been seriously neglected. Economic growth has been poor and outpaced by population growth. A recent UNDP Human Development Report placed PNG at the bottom of the Pacific region for life expectancy, adult literacy and the status of women (UNDP 1994). While a small urban-based élite enjoys the material and other benefits of a sophisticated international lifestyle, the urban poor and rural majority continue to eke out a living in informal and subsistence economies.

Corruption in PNG has been described by a former Governor of the Bank of Papua New Guinea as 'systemic and systematic' (*The Press* [Christchurch], 3 July 1995). While difficult to define and quantify, there is widespread agreement, including among national leaders themselves, that corruption and other forms of financial abuse have become pervasive in recent years. Popular perceptions of corruption relate to the way in

---

8   For an account of the Sandline Affair, see Dinnen, May and Regan (1997).

which political leaders ostensibly abuse their positions to accumulate personal wealth, rather than to more technical definitions covering procedural malpractice. The privileged access to public funds granted to politicians, in combination with the weakness of legal and administrative controls, has facilitated abuses at this level.

The volatile character of electoral politics and processes of government formation in post-colonial PNG provide other opportunities for corrupt practices. Each of the 109 members of the national parliament is eligible for substantial discretionary grants for the development of their constituencies. Such funds have been commonly used to buy votes and consolidate local power bases through the strategic dispersal of a variety of development projects. In practice, they have also been used to build up the private wealth of individual politicians and their associates. Public funds are also allegedly used to buy the loyalties of independent members in the process of putting together governing coalitions following general elections. The diversion of state revenues necessary to fund these strategies also serves to subvert bureaucratic delivery services, with departmental appropriations disappearing into these discretionary mechanisms or into extravagant ministerial schemes.

State Responses

The institutional weakness of state controls has had an important influence on the escalation of crime and disorder in the post-independence period. This relates in part to the relative ease with which criminals have been able to evade detection and apprehension. It also relates to the counter-productive outcome of the militarised policing which has become a standard response to localised outbreaks of disorder. At the same time, the increasing demands placed upon PNG's under-resourced law enforcement sector would provide a major challenge to the best-resourced and most technically sophisticated law and order agencies.

Dorney has described the police force handed over to PNG on the eve of independence as 'the most crippled of any government agency' and whose responsibility in 1975 'covered only ten per cent of the land area and forty per cent of the population' (Dorney 1990:296). The size of the force has not kept apace with subsequent growth in population and crime. In 1975, when crime rates were relatively low, the national population was slightly more than two million with a police force of 4100—a police–population ratio of 1:476. By 1996, with crime a major concern, the population had doubled to over four million, while the number of police personnel remained at approximately 5000 uniformed staff and 300 civilian support staff (Nenta 1996). The police–population ratio now stands at 1:800.

The coverage provided by police today is still distinctly uneven, with many rural areas having little, if any, police presence. Shortage of financial resources remains a major constraint. It is not unusual, for example, for police vehicles to be temporarily immobilised owing to a lack of funds for fuel or maintenance. Related—if less visible—difficulties have been experienced with other law and order agencies (Clifford, Morauta and Stuart 1984).

The limitations of state policing, in combination with high levels of insecurity, have contributed to the massive growth in private security companies in PNG over the past two decades. A recent conservative estimate claims that there are approximately 200 registered and unregistered security companies, employing about 10 000 staff or, put another way, over twice the number of uniformed state police (*The Independent*, 18 April 1997). This largely unregulated industry is concentrated in the urban centres and offers a range of protective services. Individual companies vary widely in size, organisation, services offered and degrees of professionalism. Clients are likewise diverse, including virtually every office complex, businesses (large and small), banks, schools, colleges, hospitals, hotels, clubs, restaurants, supermarkets, shops, some open-air markets, and most institutional and high covenant residences. Concerns are regularly aired about 'cowboy' elements in the industry and the often thin line dividing lawful security operators and criminal elements.[9]

As mentioned earlier, the shortcomings of criminal justice in general, and policing in particular, provide the rationale for the substantial proportion of Australian aid directed at capacity building in PNG's law and order sector (Engel 1994). Similar reasoning lies behind the practice of periodically supplementing criminal justice processes with extraordinary measures such as states of emergency,[10] curfews[11] and special policing operations. These measures have sought to restore order in designated areas through a combination of restrictions on movement, police raids and orchestrated displays of militaristic strength. Such displays belie the actual capacity of PNG's security forces to control disorder on any significant scale. In practice, the police are sometimes joined by members of the defence force and prison service on such occasions. Police mobile squads have also been deployed on Bougainville during the current crisis. As well as exacerbating the shortage of police in other parts of PNG, these joint ventures on Bougainville have also contributed to the militarisation of

---

9 Such concerns were accentuated by the murder of four youths at Dogura beach outside Port Moresby, allegedly by security employees carrying out a 'payback' on behalf of their employer (*Post-Courier*, 31 November 1996).

10 A state of emergency was declared in the national capital district in 1985 in response to *raskol* violence.

11 Prior to 1987, a curfew could only be imposed under the auspices of a state of emergency declared by the head of state under section 228 of the Constitution. The Curfew Act 1987 allows for curfews to be declared independently of states of emergency, by empowering the head of state to proclaim a curfew over designated areas, between particular hours, for limited durations.

mainland policing, particularly in parts of the Highlands (Standish 1994: 78–80).

Special policing operations and raids against settlements and villages reflect the failure of routine processes of criminal justice to apprehend suspects or detect stolen goods. These raids, targeted on the basis of secondary evidence, often end up as indiscriminate 'fishing expeditions'. Evidence of any 'possible' crime is seized. Property that cannot be accounted for with receipts may be confiscated. These strategies are punitive in intention and execution and in many respects resemble the punitive expeditions of early colonial pacification. Allegations of serious human rights abuses and destruction of property often follow.[12] Where the services of a lawyer or local law student can be procured, a civil action for damages against the state may also be initiated. As Filer wryly observes:

> The 'strong arm of the law', which once forced people to make peace with each other, now merely provokes a further round of claims against the state itself (1997a:171).

Such actions contribute to high levels of mutual distrust between police and local communities in many, particularly rural, areas. This naturally undermines the cooperation necessary for effective investigative police work. In its submission to a National Crime Summit in 1991, the Papua New Guinea Chamber of Mines and Petroleum stated that:

> One of the major problems that has developed over recent years is the communities' distrust of the police, particularly in rural areas. Much of this is due to a lack of discipline and efficiency in parts of the police force to the extent that the community has become more frightened of the police than they are of the criminals (PNGCMP 1991:6).

Militaristic policing generates a destructive, reinforcing cycle in police–community relations, whereby lack of local cooperation is cited by police as justification for punitive methods which, in turn, results in further local antagonism towards police and so on. In extreme cases, the police may be viewed as little more than a hostile army of occupation. As with colonial strategies of pacification, the punitive strategies of the post-colonial state are also susceptible to capture by local groups to further their own parochial interests, as when one group informs on another (Dinnen 1997:250). Where the police are caught in such a situation, the ideal of neutral policing is further subverted. In urban areas, militaristic policing contributes to an escalating cycle of retributive violence between police and criminal groups, fuelled by an abundant supply of sophisticated firearms.

Militaristic state responses can also inadvertently strengthen criminal organisation and commitment. In practice, curfews and special policing

---

12 An illustration of a recently reported police raid is documented in Dinnen (1997).

operations often serve to displace criminals from high crime areas to areas unaffected by these restrictions. As such, they have the unintended effect of contributing to the dispersal of criminal networks. Harris has remarked that Port Moresby gangs became more professional as a result of the restrictions imposed under the 1985 state of emergency (Harris 1988:34). Violent encounters with police have become an integral part of *raskol* induction in urban centres. Imprisonment has similarly been incorporated into the constitution of *raskol* identity, providing another means for building criminal status.

The incidence of state violence in PNG is highest in those environments where societal tolerance of violence is high. What is perhaps most disturbing here is the manner in which state and societal violence have become increasingly entangled in a reinforcing spiral in recent years. Growing levels of violence, in turn, fuel its legitimacy as an acceptable political strategy among both state and non-state constituencies. In the 'frontier' environment of the rural Highlands, it is often difficult to tell the two apart and, indeed, there are numerous illustrations of 'state' officials using their coercive power in pursuit of essentially 'private' ends, as when a policeman uses a police raid to punish an adversary in a marital dispute (Standish 1994:74). This blurring process is most apparent in those rural areas where the presence of the state is weakest. Reay has observed how some village court magistrates in the Western Highlands were 'contemporary fight leaders who see nothing anomalous in urging their groups to battle while being paid to implement the law' (1987:74). For many villagers in these areas, state police are incorporated into 'traditional' ideational frameworks that have long governed inter-group relations. As such, the police are to be alternatively resisted as enemies and co-opted as allies as local circumstances prescribe. Speaking in the context of contemporary Enga province, Bonnell remarks that:

> It could be said that police in many areas...are often viewed as an enemy clan. Community groups may fight the police as an enemy clan or they might try to co-opt police assistance as an ally for grievances against another enemy clan (1994:83).

Discussion

The weakness of the post-colonial state clearly constitutes a crucial dimension of PNG's current problems of order. Mann's notion of infrastructural power—'the capacity of the state actually to penetrate civil society, and to implement logistically political decisions throughout the realm' (1986:113)—provides a useful way of conceptualising state power, and its limitations, in this respect. Lack of infrastructural power in PNG is evident in the uneven presence of state and the poor, and deteriorating, quality of basic government services. It is most apparent in the limited purchase of state controls and, in particular, their manifest failure to counter growing levels of violence and social disorder. This has contributed to the revival of older Melanesian strategies for dealing with conflict. Tribal fighting and 'pay-back'[13] provide obvious examples. These strategies, themselves, rely on violence, thereby posing a direct challenge to the state's ostensible monopoly over force.

Where the state does react to societal violence, it often does so in militarised ways. Such responses, as we have seen, have had distinctly counter-productive outcomes. They have aggravated marginalisation and fuelled vicious cycles of retributive violence on the part of targeted groups. They have also played a critical role in the evolution of *raskolism*. Militarised responses reinforce public distrust and fear of the police, which undermines willingness to cooperate with police inquiries, leading to mounting frustration on the part of the police. The substantial sums of public funds spent on such responses also represents monies denied basic government services, the creation and maintenance of infrastructure, and more productive development activities. This, in turn, contributes to further marginalisation.

Reliance on militarised solutions can, at one level, be viewed as a way of compensating for state weaknesses by relying upon its ostensibly strongest aspect. Proposing coercive solutions is generally an easier option than the more onerous task of designing and implementing strategies that address underlying problems. The post-colonial state, as we have seen, does not have the capacity for this latter, and more complex, task. The tendency for militaristic solutions may also be related to the time constraints under which national administrations operate. Coercion offers the prospect of more immediate results than those likely to flow from lengthy bureaucratic processes.

Given its weakness in institutional terms and manifest failure to provide basic services and infrastructure, perhaps the only way the post-colonial state can assert itself in practice is through the use or threat of force. Not being capable of mobilising popular support through the positive inducement of government provision (unlike colonial regulation), it has to resort to coercion towards the same end. The broader educative message issuing from such actions is, of course, that might is right. The nexus between state violence and wider societal violence has, thus, become a mutually reinforcing one, each reflecting and sustaining the other. In this respect, the distinction between legality and illegality (upon which statist law and order debate is premised) fails to capture what is going on in both state and non-state coercive action in contemporary PNG. In practice, the question of a monopoly of violence neither characterises the post-colonial state nor legitimates its actions.

---

13 'Payback' is one of the mechanisms of social control in stateless societies discussed by Taylor. It is a self-help remedy carried out against the offender (or close relative of the offender) by the victim, or victim assisted by kin, or kin alone where the victim is dead or incapacitated (1982:82).

The lack of internal legitimacy of the PNG state relates to its recent origins in a relatively short period of distinctly uneven colonial rule, the scale of social diversity within its territorial boundaries, as well as the absence of a unifying independence struggle. There remains a lack of organic unity or shared values between state and societies and, in particular, an absence of widespread commitment to the introduced system of government. Such commitment as does exist, has been severely tested in recent years as a result of deteriorating government services and perceptions of endemic corruption. Even though it may be unusually important in materialist terms, the PNG state has by no means secured its predominance within the national society, remaining merely one of a number of collective entities competing for popular allegiances. It has no automatic legitimacy at local levels. Social power continues to be widely dispersed among a multiplicity of parochial organisations consisting of loose, often symbolic, associations of kinship and lineage. This is a classic case of what Migdal refers to as 'dispersed domination', whereby:

> ...neither the state nor any other social force has established an overarching hegemony; domination by any one social force takes place within an arena or even across a limited number of arenas but does not encompass the society as a whole. Social life is then marked by struggles or standoffs among social forces over questions ranging from personal and collective identity and the salience of symbols to property rights and the right to use force. People's identities and moral codes remain remarkably diverse in such a society (1994:27).

Dispersed domination is to be contrasted with an ideal of 'integrated domination' which is 'inclusive' and 'society-wide', with the state playing the central role in the creation and maintenance of social control (Migdal 1994:27). Evidence from PNG shows how, in many respects, the actions of the post-colonial state—and, sometimes, its failure to act—have contributed to the further dispersal of domination. An illustration lies in the evolving political culture, comprising a blending of older Melanesian modalities of leadership and personal power within the institutional framework of the modern state. Electoral candidates attempt to win or maintain political power by concentrating their vote-buying strategies on tiny proportions of their formal constituencies, with whom they are often linked by kinship. If successful, the benefits of political power will be directed at these key support bases, inevitably at the expense of other parts of a member's constituency. These highly personalised relations between contemporary politicians and their strategic voters serve to sustain and deepen political fragmentation and, thereby, the dispersal of domination within the wider society.

While the PNG state is undoubtedly weak in the manner outlined above, an exclusive focus upon the fragility of state power detracts from its central role in materialist terms. A major paradox of the post-colonial state in PNG lies precisely in its weakness in institutionalist terms and simultaneous strength in materialist terms. It is, in this sense, both weak and strong. Lack of alternative sources of comparable wealth have contributed directly to the centrality of the state as the single most important controller of resources in modern PNG. The relative wealth of the state and rhetoric of political leaders has inflated material expectations at local levels. More particularly, it provides the context for the progressive primacy of politics in post-colonial PNG, where access to state power is a means to material wealth, as well as political power. The growing turbulence of election competition is indicative of how the struggle for government has assumed a 'pathological dimension' in recent years (Clapham 1985:40).

Arguably, it has been the external legitimacy granted the PNG state by the international community, through PNG's progressive integration into the global economy, that has enabled its survival in the face of diminishing internal legitimacy. Papua New Guinea is heavily dependent upon the international economy in terms of imported manufactured goods, markets for raw materials, and foreign investment and personnel. It is also a recipient of substantial overseas aid, mainly from Australia. As mentioned earlier, Papua New Guinea is now subject to a structural adjustment program agreed with the International Monetary Fund and World Bank. These international linkages have helped sustain the weak state in PNG, as elsewhere in the post-colonial world (Clapham 1996).

State–society relations in Papua New Guinea have undergone a significant transformation in the transition from colonial to post-colonial statehood. As we noted earlier, these relations at the lower end of the colonial hierarchy were often the outcome of active processes of interaction and negotiation. These provided Melanesians with a significant role in the shaping of colonial order at the most local levels. In other respects, however, the colonial state operated at a considerable social distance from Melanesian societies. The fact that the administration was almost exclusively run by foreigners reduced its susceptibility to permeation from indigenous society at all but the most junior levels (that is, the native constabulary). At the most senior levels it was, in fact, staffed from outside the territory altogether. This capacity to remain remote and disengaged from local politics has contributed to the myth of the strong colonial state. Decolonisation entailed the gradual opening up of state institutions to indigenous participation at all levels. This process of localisation accelerated dramatically in the period after independence. Politicians and state officials in the post-colonial period have become part of the indigenous political process and are readily identifiable with local-level social organisations and politics.

Contrary to the closed character of many parts of the colonial state in relation to indigenous social forces, the post-colonial PNG state has become a more uniformly porous entity, like many of its counterparts in post-colonial Africa (Chazan 1994:267). The increasingly personalist exercise of power evident across the spectrum of state institutions in the post-colonial period represents a continuation of the strategies of indige-nous engagement evident at the most local levels during the colonial administration. These strategies have been inserted into the commanding heights of the post-colonial state. As a result, the boundaries between state and society have progressively blurred, and the state has itself become less coherent. This process inverts Habermas's contention that the 'lifeworld' is increasingly colonised by the 'system' in late industrial society (Habermas 1987). In non-industrial PNG, it is the state (as 'system') that appears to have been increasingly colonised by the Melanesian 'life-world'. The resulting lack of delineation has been facilitated by the unde-veloped character of civil society in PNG, which might otherwise serve as an intermediary between state and local-level social organisations.

As the boundaries between state and society have blurred, the com-promised character of the post-colonial state has become more and more apparent. We have also seen how state agencies, notably the police, have themselves become implicated in those very areas of disorder they ostensibly seek to control. The actions of political leaders and the com-modification of the electoral process have also become important catalysts for conflict. The fervent struggle for political power is increasingly con-ducted not through policy or doctrinal differences but through 'contexts of violence and cash payments' (Strathern 1993:56). This form of politics has been inimical to public-regarding leadership, nurturing inequitable practices of gifting that benefit the few while neglecting the majority. In the process it has devalued bureaucratic processes, undermined state legitimacy and contributed to the further dispersal of domination. What we hear endlessly debated under the ubiquitous 'law and order' banner is less about the collapse of order and more about the emergence of a distinctive and vigorously contested new post-colonial order.

4 State, Society and Governance: Reflections on a Philippines–Papua New Guinea Comparison

RON MAY

For some time students of comparative politics, as well as aid donors and international agencies such as the World Bank, have been concerned with the poor performance of many states in Africa, Asia, the Pacific, Latin America, and more recently Eastern Europe and Central Asia. This has been reflected in the proliferation of such terms as 'weak states', 'collapsed states', and (going back some years) 'broken-backed states'. Since the appearance of Joel Migdal's *Strong Societies and Weak States* (1988) the ideas of weak states and strong (and weak) societies have been employed frequently in analyses of Southeast Asian and island Pacific polities, where state–society relations have long been a focus of scholarly and policy-oriented attention.

This chapter attempts to relate the concepts of weak state, strong–weak society, and state capability (which might be roughly equated with 'governance') in two countries of the region, both democratic, one with a weak state and strong society (the Philippines) and one with a weak state and weak society (Papua New Guinea). Essentially, it asks how far similarities and differences in the configuration of states and societies can explain similarities and differences in state capabilities. It finds— employing Migdal's (1988:32–3) indicators of social control—that in both countries *compliance* is weak and *participation* is in some sense strong, but, paradoxically, that *legitimation* appears to be higher in Papua New Guinea than in the Philippines. This finding is related to questions of who occupies the institutions of the state and how representative the interests of those occupants are; it is suggested that the apparently higher level of legitimation in Papua New Guinea might be explained in terms of its greater 'representativeness', given the absence of major class or ethnic

60

cleavages and the frequent turnover of state office holders. While at any point in time a substantial section of the population may be indifferent to the state, seeing it as largely irrelevant to their lives, over time virtually all of the population feel they have a stake in the state, as an institution which delivers public goods and services. This appears to be consistent with the trend of recent constitutional reforms and proposals in the two countries, which have tended to be state-limiting in the Philippines and state-strengthening in Papua New Guinea.

Comparing the Philippines and Papua New Guinea

At first glance, the Philippines and Papua New Guinea are not obviously comparable. The Philippines, with a well-educated and internationally mobile population of around 70 million, has experienced over four centuries of colonial rule, a relatively long period of integration into the world economy, and half a century of independence, and now sees itself as an 'Asian Tiger' cub. Papua New Guinea, on the other hand, once referred to as 'the last unknown' (and more recently described somewhat cryptically by its national airline as 'like no place you've never been') had a comparatively brief contact with the outside world before achieving independence in 1975, and its roughly four million people, who speak some 800 different languages, are still predominantly subsistence farmers, with comparatively low levels of formal education and technical skills.

Notwithstanding these differences, in political terms the two countries share a number of more or less common features.

- Both enjoyed a relatively smooth and amicable transition to independence, without, therefore, creating the sorts of 'heroic' leaders, parties or armed forces that have emerged in countries which had to fight for their independence.[1]

- Although the Philippines inherited, from the US colonial regime, a presidential-style system while Papua New Guinea chose (largely from a reading of Westminster-style African models) a parliamentary system, unusually for the Asia–Pacific area both countries—with the comparatively brief exception of the Philippines under President Marcos (from martial law in 1972 till his downfall in 1986)—have maintained robustly democratic systems.[2]

---

1   The Philippines fought its revolution, and produced its heroes, in the nineteenth century struggle for independence from Spain, but with no great practical relevance for politics in the second half of the twentieth century (which is not to say that the country's revolutionary heroes are not still revered).

2   The latest available Freedom House index rates Papua New Guinea (on a scale of 1 [most free] to 7 [least free]) 2 for political rights and 4 for civil liberties, and the Philippines 2, 3.

With the same (but qualified) exception for the Philippines under Marcos, both countries:

- have competitive political party systems, though parties have tended to be fluid, for the most part not sharply ideologically differentiated, and often rooted in the politics of personality or region (Wurfel 1988:93–106; Landé 1965, 1996; Villanueva 1996; May 1984),

- have held regular and (albeit with some manipulation)[3] genuinely contested elections,

- have experienced regular and constitutionally-mandated changes of leadership,

- have maintained quite strong traditions of judicial independence and—at least in rhetoric—popular support for the rule of law, and

- have enjoyed a free and active press.

- While both countries—particularly the Philippines, but to a minor extent also Papua New Guinea—have seen the military exercise political influence, both have substantially upheld a tradition of Huntingtonian military professionalism and neither has succumbed to a military coup[4] (though some people interpreted the 1986 'People Power Revolution' in the Philippines as a military coup to restore democracy—incorrectly in my view).

- Both have embraced political decentralisation, with limited success (though Papua New Guinea is currently in the process of reversing this—ostensibly in the name of further decentralisation) (Tapales 1993; May and Regan with Ley 1997).

- Both countries have maintained relatively open, capitalist economies, in which government has played an important developmental role (Golay 1961; Doronila 1992; de Dios and Fabella 1996; Connell 1997; May 1997).

- Both countries have experienced armed regional separatist rebellions (the Philippines in the Muslim south and to a lesser extent in the northern Cordilleras; Papua New Guinea on Bougainville), which they have attempted to deal with by a mixture of military and political means (Che Man 1990; May 1990; Wesley-Smith, ed. 1992; May 1996).

If this list of similarities does not impress, then one might consider the comparison of the Philippines and Papua New Guinea against, say, that of

---

3 On the Philippines see Carbonell-Catilo, de Leon and Nicolas (1985) and Santiago (1991).

4 See, for example, chapters by Selochan and May in May and Selochan, eds (1998).

the Philippines with any of its Association of Southeast Asian Nations neighbours and that of Papua New Guinea with such other South Pacific Forum member states as Fiji, Samoa or Tonga.

With so many apparent similarities in what might be termed 'political performance indicators', it would seem reasonable to expect to find some parallels in political institutions and/or 'political culture'. To the extent that these can be measured, to what extent is this so?

The State[5]

The state in the Philippines

There seems to be general consensus that the Philippines state, in terms of its capacity 'to *penetrate* society, *regulate* social relationships, *extract* resources, and *appropriate* or use resources in determined ways' (Migdal 1988:4), is relatively weak.[6] Its weakness may be traced to the country's colonial history. The 'state' in the Spanish colonial period was a loose structure, essentially Manila-centred and substantially reliant on the clergy and private enterprise to sustain the colonial enterprise beyond Manila. Apart from the Muslim sultanates in Mindanao and Sulu, and the few bastions of Muslim influence in the Visayas and Luzon which were quickly overthrown, pre-colonial society was politically fragmented into largely autonomous *barangays* (hamlets). Spanish colonialism effectively created a sense of Filipino identity, promoting the growth of prominent local families, in part through intermarriage and the integration of immigrant Chinese. By the end of the Spanish period there was a well-developed, locally-based, *ilustrado* (élite) class; during the American colonial period this class consolidated its position through political leadership in the democratic system promoted by the Americans (the Philippine literature commonly uses the term 'élite democracy') and

---

5   The 'state' is used here—as in Migdal (1988:xiii fn. 2, 19–20) and in other contributions to this volume—in an essentially institutional, Weberian sense. This broadly corresponds with the usage employed by Stepan (1978:xii), where the state is seen as 'the continuous administrative, legal, bureaucratic and coercive systems that attempt not only to structure relations *between* civil society and public authority in a polity but also to structure many crucial relationships *within* civil society as well'. For further discussion see Migdal (1994:11–18, 1988, 1997), Stepan (1978:chapter 1), Goulbourne, ed. (1979), Evans, Rueschemeyer and Skocpol, eds (1985), Hall (1986), Mann (1986), Bratton (1989), Navari (1991), and Evans (1995).

6   See, for example, Villacorta (1994), Rivera (1996) and Kerkvliet (this volume). For a more detailed discussion of state and society in the Philippines see Wurfel (1988:chapter 3), Hutchcroft (1991), Timberman (1991), Hawes (1992), Gutierrez, Torrente and Garcia (1992), McCoy (1994), Rivera (1994). Also see Machado (1972) and Carroll (1994).

economic dominance based on land ownership and the translation of this into equity in a burgeoning industrial sector.

In the post-independence period, social tensions, particularly between import-substitution manufacturing interests and those supporting an export-oriented development strategy, not only hampered coherent policy making but created the political instability which facilitated the election of Ferdinand Marcos in 1965. However, the increasingly authoritarian regime of President Marcos did little to improve the capability of the state to achieve its leader's objectives (except perhaps the objective of enriching the Marcos family); indeed, it might be argued that Marcos became entrapped in a kleptocracy of cronies in much the same way as previous governments had been constrained by self-seeking élite competition. The People Power Revolution of 1986 only partly changed this, the Aquino regime being heavily dependent on winning the support of local élites just as Marcos had been (indeed in some places the local élite simply switched allegiance from Marcos to Aquino). Only under President Ramos (1992–98) does there appear to have been some strengthening of the state (see Miranda 1993).

What is interesting about the Philippines, however, is that even under Marcos, the *institutions* of the state remained largely intact: apart from the early years of martial law, elections were held (albeit being heavily manipulated), parliament met (though it was dominated by Marcos loyalists and much policy making was done by presidential decree), and the judiciary maintained a measure of independence. Moreover, political parties operated (albeit under various constraints), and an active press and radio were tolerated. Thus, when the challenge to Marcos came in 1986 (significantly, as the result of an election), the opposition had leadership, organisation, and the means of mobilising popular support; in the event, it was also able to call on a degree of Huntingtonian military professionalism.[7] (The contrast with what happened in Burma two years later is striking.)

The state in Papua New Guinea[8]

Pre-colonial Papua New Guinea was also intensely fragmented into small-scale political entities, with little overarching organisation or hierarchical leadership. (Traditional society in Papua New Guinea has commonly been referred to as 'stateless' and 'acephalous'.) The state was very much a colonial creation and for much of Papua New Guinea's population the experience of colonial administration was brief (in some parts, less than two decades). Although the colonial administration has been des-

---

7 See, for example, Mackenzie (1987), May (1989).
8 For a more detailed discussion of state–society relations in Papua New Guinea see Dinnen (this volume) and Standish (1994).

cribed as highly centralised,[9] district officers frequently exercised considerable autonomy. After independence in 1975, separatist movements on Bougainville and elsewhere resulted in the establishment of a system of provincial government, decentralising political power and in the process inevitably creating tensions between provincial politicians and national Members of Parliament (MPs).

A legacy of the latter years of the colonial experience has been the widespread view of the 'state' as a provider of goods and services. With limited mobilisation of resources outside the government sector, access to those goods and services is best achieved by occupying the institutions of the state. Politics is thus seen as a major form of *bisnis*, with elections eagerly contested (despite a high cost of contesting, frequently upwards of 40 candidates compete, in a first-past-the-post poll, in 89 single-member open constituencies of around 25 000 to 50 000 voters),[10] and around 50 to 55 per cent of members losing their seats at each election. Since 1972, all governments have been coalitions, and in every parliament since 1977 government has changed in mid term as a result of shifts within coalitions. The consequent concentration on factional dealing and pork barrelling has contributed significantly to the inability of the Papua New Guinea state to commit itself to policies with a longer-term perspective, and to the growth of corruption and nepotism. The state's ability to deliver services and to maintain its presence, especially in more remote rural areas, is limited by the capacity of its bureaucracy, availability of resources, and difficulties of terrain. The outbreak of armed rebellion, beginning in 1988, in Papua New Guinea's relatively prosperous North Solomons (Bougainville) Province, primarily over unsatisfied demands by land owners for a larger share of revenue from the huge gold and copper mine at Panguna, tested the coercive powers of the state; after almost a decade, the conflict has not been resolved.

Society in the Philippines and Papua New Guinea

If the 'state' is sometimes an ambiguous and contested concept, 'society' is analytically even more difficult. 'Society' is used here, loosely, to refer to what Woods (1992:77) has described as 'patterns of political participation outside of formal state structures and one-party systems'.[11] In this sense, there is an overlap between 'society' and what I refer to below as 'regime'.

---

9 See, for example, the report to the Constitutional Planning Committee, on central–provincial government relations (Tordoff and Watts 1974:2/2).

10 In a parliament of 109 seats there are also twenty provincial seats, of around 25 000 to 400 000 voters.

11 For a more detailed discussion, see, for example, Bratton (1989), Stephen White (1994), Diamond (1994), Hutchful (1995–96).

The 'strength' of society in the Philippines lies in two, largely opposing, directions: the existence of essentially locally-based patrons, *caciques*, dynasties or warlords (all four terms, and others, recur in the Philippines literature) on the one hand, and on the other, the existence of a vibrant 'civil society' which includes a mind-boggling array of non-governmental organisations (NGOs), a strong labour movement, a powerful church (especially the Roman Catholic Church) network, a highly politicised academic community, and a strong Left incorporating worker, peasant, church and other sectoral groups and a Communist Party. The former, with some rotation of players, have over time substantially penetrated and appropriated the resources of the state; the latter ('civil society') has been less successful in capturing government, but has asserted itself in other ways, including 'everyday politics' (Kerkvliet 1990) and armed insurgency, and in these ways exercised a restraining influence on an élite-dominated state (most dramatically in the overthrow of Marcos in 1986).

In Papua New Guinea, on the other hand, 'society' is arguably weak: traditional social groups are small and often in conflict; the labour movement (in a country where formal sector employment is relatively small and dominated by government) is at a low level of development. NGOs are embryonic (and having been partly co-opted by government following the June 1997 elections seem less likely to act as a restraint on the state). Christian churches play an important role socially but are not particularly active politically and are divided by denomination. And political parties lack a mass base. Yet the high rate of turnover of Members of Parliament, and the necessity for national MPs to deliver to their local constituencies, suggest that civil society exercises some influence over the state.

In terms of Migdal's matrix (1988:35, Table 1.1), Papua New Guinea would seem to be a clear case of weak state, weak society; but it is doubtful whether it can be described, as Migdal labels this cell, as 'anarchical'. Indeed, in terms of the classic criteria—regularity of elections, number of changes of government, and the constitutionality of those changes—it has been a remarkably stable polity.

State, Society and Governance

Having provided these thumbnail sketches of one country with a weak state and strong society and one with a weak state and weak society, where do we go from here? Can we explain similarities and differences in state capabilities in terms of these characteristics?

An obvious approach would be to examine government performance in several comparable policy areas as a measure of state capability. This might reveal, for example, that both states, for more or less similar reasons (to do with the difficulties of placing long-term development strategies above short-term gains) have been poor managers of their economies; that both, for more or less similar reasons (to do with the limited reach of the state) have had difficulties maintaining law and order, and so on. I would expect, however, that on any measure the Philippines would have a better record on policy formulation and a somewhat better record on policy compliance. But I suspect that the more detailed the examination, the more difficult it would become to measure capability, to reconcile the indicators of compliance, participation and legitimation, and to disentangle state from society.

This suspicion appears to have been borne out in several chapters in this volume, which have concluded from studies of particular countries that the 'strength' or 'weakness' of the state can vary both from one policy area to another and one region to another, and, within a single policy area or region, over time (see, for example, Kerkvliet, in this volume). If this is the case (and there is little doubt that it is), do the concepts of state and societal strength or weakness retain any analytical usefulness?

Some of us, at least, would feel that, despite the inherent problems of definition, the ideas elaborated by Migdal in 1988 have provided sufficient analytical insights that we should be wary of throwing out the conceptual baby with the proverbial bath water. But some development of the initial analytical framework is clearly needed. Two conservationist strategies might be considered.

One would involve the compilation of an index of overall 'state strength' (and perhaps an index of 'societal strength'), along the lines of the Freedom House Index of Democracy or the Wall Street Journal/ Heritage Foundation Index of Economic Freedom, which would make it possible to locate states (and societies) along a scale of strength–weakness according to the characteristics identified by Migdal (1988) or some other basket of indicators.[12] While such an index might find a ready market, my impression is that, like the Freedom House Index and the Index of Economic Freedom, in the process of aggregation it would conceal as much as it revealed.

A second strategy would be to pursue the difficult task of clarifying the relationship between state and society (a task which Migdal and others have already addressed in Migdal, Kohli and Shue, eds 1994, and Migdal 1997).

Thus, to return to the Philippines–Papua New Guinea comparison: it has been argued that the Philippine state has been dominated by a landed capitalist élite (Villacorta 1994) which has largely (though not exclusively) used the state to promote its own social and economic interests; as against this, the contrasting societal forces of a strong democratic ethos, arguably grounded in the Philippines pre-hispanic culture but certainly nurtured under American colonial rule, and locally-based power structures which penetrate but do not coincide with the Philippine state, have for the

---

12 Migdal (1988:279–86) seems to have had this possibility in mind in including an appendix on (quantitatively) 'Assessing Social Control'.

most part exercised fairly effective restraint over autocratic tendencies in the Philippine state. In consequence, with reference to Migdal's indicators of state strength, policy making is vigorously debated and legislative programs (somewhat less vigorously)[13] enacted but implementation and *compliance* is frequently weak—especially (in areas such as land reform, forestry, and environmental management) when the interests of local power brokers do not coincide with nationally legislated policies. The inability of successive Philippine governments, notwithstanding pressures from the International Monetary Fund, to enact much needed tax reforms is a striking case in point.

On the other hand—and apparently contrary to Migdal's (1988:32) notion of '[i]ncreasing levels of social control'—*participation*, on almost any measure, is quite high, with a wide range of civil society organisations active in formal and informal politics, and public demonstrations and strikes (*welga*) over policy issues reasonably frequent and largely tolerated by government. Nevertheless, although elections are well contested and voter turnout is comparatively high, political patronage remains important in the continuing dominance of prominent families—for example, see Soriano (1987) on the first post-Marcos election—and there is widespread popular cynicism about politics, especially as directed towards 'traditional politicians' (*trapos*). Correspondingly, popular perceptions of the state's legitimacy (*legitimation*) in the Philippines appear to be mixed. The common claim that 'Filipinos respect a strong leader' suggests a high degree of state legitimation, but evidence for this is weak. President Marcos held on to power, from 1972 to 1986, only through the declaration of martial law and systematic state repression in the face of growing opposition. Successive governments have faced armed insurgencies from the Communist New People's Army and the Muslim Moro National Liberation Front and Moro Islamic Liberation Front (and for a while also the Cordillera People's Liberation Army); and after the 1986 change of government President Aquino faced a series of attempted coups by rebel factions of the armed forces. Moreover, the recent strong public reaction to moves to amend the constitution to enable President Ramos to seek a second presidential term (see below) suggests that even a successful and generally popular president, who appears to have significantly raised perceptions of state legitimacy in the Philippines, exercises a limited mandate.[14]

In Papua New Guinea, the state has been more broadly representative, and in the absence of the sort of major class or ethnic cleavages which have characterised many other societies, and with a relatively high turn-

---

13 Dickson-Waiko (1994:134) records that during 1987–91 just over five per cent of 104 bills and resolutions introduced into Congress (some, admittedly, addressing the same subject) were enacted into laws.

14 A more systematic analysis of legitimacy would need to distinguish, at least, between performance-based and moral or 'democratic' concepts of legitimacy.

over of members of parliament, it is arguable that no substantial social group (except women as a gender group) feels itself to be systematically excluded from the possibility of sharing in state power. State and society are thus more broadly integrated. *Participation* is, in this sense, comparatively high, and is reflected in the large number of candidates contesting elections, the high voter turnout, the demands made on members of parliament by their constituents, and ultimately, the relatively high turnover of members.

A notable feature of state–society relations in Papua New Guinea, on the other hand, is the very low level of development of formal civil–society organisations (apart from churches) between the local community and the state.[15] The integration of state and society and the high rate of participation in politics, however, makes for the 'pork barrelling' style of politics noted above. With all national governments in Papua New Guinea's political history being coalitions—with generally weak, poorly disciplined, and not ideologically sharply differentiated parties—candidates have increasingly stood as independents (in order to maximise their bargaining position, should they be elected, in the process of government formation) and elected MPs engage in an ongoing process of bargaining to maximise the benefits from office to themselves and their line (as noted above, every Papua New Guinea parliament since independence has changed government in mid term as a result of shifts within coalitions).

As I have argued elsewhere (May 1997), employing Ekeh's (1975) notion of 'primordial' and 'civic' realms, this is not an environment favourable to sound policy making and *compliance*. Problems of compliance are further exacerbated by the limited capabilities of many administrators, which inhibits government service delivery,[16] and the frequency of political interference in administration at the local level. In such a context there is a good deal of cynicism about politics and politicians, and perceptions of state *legitimacy* tend to be low among those who are not currently recipients of state benefits. But while, at any time, most people have little regard for the state, there has not been (apart from Bougainville) the sort of direct opposition posed to the state that the Philippines has faced with the Moro National Liberation Front and the New People's Army, since those who at present have poor access to the state and its benefits might, at the next election, be the winners. Thus, paradoxically, with a weak state and a weak society Papua New Guinea

---

15 This observation was made during the Workshop on Weak and Strong States in Melanesia and Southeast Asia (12–14 August 1997), by Michael Ong of the Australian Parliamentary Research Service. It is not obvious whether the low level of civil society development reflects a low level of ('modern') political development generally, the satisfactory working of electoral representation, or simply a high level of political indifference at the national level.

16 Compare the comments of Kabutaulaka and Dauvergne (1997) concerning the administrative incapacity of the state in the Solomon Islands.

has enjoyed a generally higher level of state legitimation and political stability than the Philippines.

This Philippines–Papua New Guinea comparison suggests two propositions of more general application. First, consistent with the approach of defining the state in institutional terms and seeing it, in neo-Weberian terms, as mediating conflicting claims and establishing social values, it is necessary to distinguish the state from those who, at any time, occupy or control the institutions of the 'state'. In a research project on Regime Change and Regime Maintenance in Asia and the Pacific, we have attempted to accommodate this by distinguishing between the *state* (defined in institutional terms), *government* (those who occupy the legislative and executive offices of the state at any time), and *regime* (as in popular usage—for example, 'the Marcos regime'—those who at any time occupy the institutions of the state or exercise significant continuous political influence over it).[17] In practice, governments may change relatively frequently (in democratic systems principally as the result of regular elections) without any change in the state; regime change, on the other hand, occurs less readily and usually involves a dramatic event, such as a military coup, revolution, or foreign invasion. Changes of regime, unlike changes of government, generally imply changes in state structures. In the Philippines, the declaration of martial law marked a regime change (the ascendance of President Marcos, backed by the military, a political machine—the *Kilusang Bagong Lipunan* (KBL), New Society Movement—and a 'crony' business élite) and a change in the state (the suspension of the constitution). The 'People Power Revolution' of 1986, and subsequent passage of a new constitution, brought another change of regime (and state). The Philippine state under the authoritarian rule of Marcos was very different, in its relations with society, from the essentially democratic Philippine state under Aquino or Ramos. In contrast, there have been several changes of *government* in Papua New Guinea, but without a fundamental change of regime the role of the state in society has been essentially unchanged (though there have undoubtedly been differences in governing style).

Second, having established who occupies the institutions of the state, it is necessary to ask how representative that group is. There is little doubt, for example, that the Philippine state under Marcos placed considerable weight on the interests of the Marcos family and its supporters ('the Marcos regime'). While many would argue that the Philippine state under Aquino and Ramos was still dominated by the interests of a landed capitalist oligarchy, few would dispute that under Aquino and Ramos the Philippine state was representative of a much broader range of interests (though many Muslims would argue that no Philippine state has really represented their interests).

---

17 Also see Calvert, ed. (1987:248), Fishman (1990:428) and Lawson (1991).

In much of the writing about the state—even when the diversity of society is recognised—there is a tendency to assume that 'nation building', the creation of a sense of *national* identity (and thus identification with the nation-state) among socially diverse populations, can be achieved, as a by-product of 'modernisation' or through specific policies of national ideology.[18] The evidence to support such a view, particularly in the Asia–Pacific region, however, is weak. Most states are systemically biased in their representativeness, whether in privileging the interests of dominant ethnic, religious, class or cultural majorities (as in Fiji's 'paramountcy of Fijian interests', or Malaysia's 'New Economic Policy') or in making concessions to minority groups (as in the creation of an Autonomous Region of Muslim Mindanao and the recognition of indigenous 'ancestral domain' in the Philippines). In many states, moreover, there are significant groups who regard themselves as permanently denied the possibility of exercising political power at the national level (the Muslims in the Philippines, and perhaps workers, peasants and indigenous cultural communities provide examples). Sometimes such groups simply disengage from the state (compare May, ed. 1982); where they are sufficiently large and can be organised politically there is always the possibility of insurrection against the state.

This has implications for the assessment of state strength or weakness: different elements of society may judge indicators of state strength differently. The mining industry in the Philippines, for example, may see delays in the passage of mining regulations as evidence of state weakness where an indigenous minority may see the state's concern over ancestral domain (a major cause of this delay) as evidence of state strength. Similarly, a government's performance on decentralisation may be judged to be strong or weak depending on whether one takes the perspective of a national planner or a provincial governor. Performance on land reform may be judged differently by a land owner and a peasant. Performance on export-oriented industrialisation may be judged differently by workers and the owners of capital. And, ultimately, a state may be judged 'strong' if it successfully counters an insurgency, regardless of the moral justification for such action.[19] It is for this reason that democratic theory emphasises such factors as turnover and tolerance of minorities.[20]

---

18 Migdal (this volume), for example, speaks of the 'naturalisation' of the state, as a 'shared sense that the state is as natural as the rivers and the mountains'. Similarly see Migdal (1988:16). It is not clear, however, how much 'coherence' states must have in order to survive; sometimes, indeed, they survive through the political disinterest of their citizens, or through the superior coercive force of the national government. Like families, states may be dysfunctional, yet survive.

19 Kerkvliet (this volume) recognises this in proposing that 'perspective' be added to Migdal's (1988) indicators of state strength. But while compliance, participation and legitimation are, at least in principle, quantifiable, perspective is inevitably subjective. Kerkvliet (fn.22), moreover, sets aside

Reforming the State

In this context (perceptions of whose interests the state represents), it might be instructive to briefly consider and compare recent debates in the Philippines and Papua New Guinea concerning constitutional reforms.

Following the fall of President Marcos in 1986, a Constitutional Commission was created to draft a new constitution. The new constitution was ratified in 1987. One outcome of the Marcos experience was a new provision to limit terms of public office. Under the 1935 constitution presidential office was limited to two terms. It is generally believed that it was the ineligibility of Marcos to stand for a third term in 1974 that precipitated his declaration of martial law and suspension of the constitution in 1972. A new constitution, pushed through in 1973, removed this constraint. Under the 1987 constitution a president was granted only one term (of six years). Senators are allowed two consecutive terms of six years and members of the House of Representatives three terms of three years. In 1997, with President Ramos's term of office due to end in 1998, Ramos supporters campaigned to 'change the charter' to allow the president to recontest in 1998 (and to extend the allowable term of other offices). Despite Ramos's considerable popularity, the move provoked heated opposition from across a broad political spectrum, with accusations that Ramos intended to reimpose martial law. The president's popularity plummeted, and the move was defeated. (Earlier proposals during the Ramos presidency for a shift from a bicameral, presidential system to a unicameral, parliamentary system, ostensibly in the interests of greater efficiency and democracidity, were similarly opposed as covert moves to prolong Ramos's term in office.)[21] A second aspect of the 1987 constitution concerned the role of political parties. Prior to martial law the Philippines had had a broadly two-party system, though the two major parties were not sharply differentiated ideologically, were élite-dominated, and membership was fluid. (Marcos himself had stood in the presidential election of 1965 as a Nacionalista Party candidate after being denied nomination by his chosen Liberal Party.) Under martial law, parties were initially banned and then allowed to re-establish under restrictive conditions; Marcos's KBL dominated politics from its establishment in 1978 till

consideration of Muslim separatism in the Philippines on the grounds that it 'challenged the legitimacy of the very idea of the Philippine nation', unlike the two political legitimacy crises he considers, 'which accepted the nation but challenged the legitimacy of those governing it'.

20 It is notable that the Philippines, which is generally regarded as a weak state, felt able to make constitutional provision in 1987 for autonomous regions in Muslim Mindanao and the Cordilleras, while Indonesia, generally regarded as a strong state, has refused to consider substantive autonomy to East Timor, Irian Jaya or Aceh, on the grounds that such action could precipitate a fragmentation of the Republic.

21 For a summary of, and commentary upon, this debate see Bolongaita (1995).

1986, when it virtually collapsed. In the wake of 1986, some commentators confidently predicted the re-emergence of a competitive two-party system (see, for example, Landé 1987:31–2). Amongst Filipinos, however, there was a good deal of hostility towards 'traditional politics' and the party system. This was reflected in the 1987 constitution (Art. VI S.5(1), (2)) which provided that a fifth of the membership of the House of Representatives should be elected through a party-list system of registered national, regional and sectoral parties or organisations. As a transitional measure (for three consecutive terms after ratification of the constitution), however, half of the seats allocated to party-list representatives were to be filled 'by selection or election from the labor, peasant, urban poor, indigenous cultural communities, women, youth, and such other sectors as may be provided by law, except the religious sector'. In a detailed study of the party-list system as it operated during the eighth congress (1987–92), Corral described the objectives of the party-list system in the following terms:

> The party-list provision was proposed to open up the political system to a pluralistic society through a multiparty system...The party-list system...in effect, equalizes political power such that the traditional two-party system in Philippine politics is dismantled...The party-list system, with its transitory provision of sectoral representation, institutionalizes people power and broadens participatory democracy (1993:6–7).

Corral's study suggests that the provisions may not have yielded the results hoped for by their proponents—even apart from the fact that during the first two post-1987 congresses all seats were allocated to sectoral representatives, with some members representing more than one sector—but the system has been retained and the first election under the full party-list system is planned to take place in 1998. (Further evidence of hostility towards 'traditional politics' was the inclusion in the 1987 constitution's 'Declaration of Principles and State Policies' of a statement (S.26): 'The state shall guarantee equal access to opportunities for public service, and prohibit political dynasties as may be defined by law'; to date no such legislation has been enacted.) A third element of the post-1986 reform in the Philippines was a major effort at political decentralisation through a new Local Government Code (1991). Although progress in some areas has been slow (and notwithstanding a belated concern that decentralisation might deliver political power into the hands of local warlords and political oligarchs), decentralisation has gathered pace over recent years. A significant aspect of this decentralisation has been the formal involvement of NGOs.

In all three areas the predominant rationale for reform has been to prevent the re-emergence of a dominating central state. When in 1992 Singapore's President Lee Kuan Yew advised Filipinos that what they needed was discipline rather than democracy, he was quickly reminded, by President Ramos, of the Philippine's 'ill-fated flirtation with authoritarianism' (see *Far Eastern Economic Review* 10 December 1992:29).

In contrast, much recent debate in Papua New Guinea has been concerned with ways of strengthening the state. At independence Papua New Guinea adopted an essentially Westminster constitution, which included provision for removing the prime minister or other ministers by a parliamentary vote of no confidence. In 1991, following repeated votes of no confidence in successive prime ministers, the constitution was amended to give an incoming government a grace period of eighteen months (previously only six months) before facing a vote of no confidence, in the interests of political stability. In contrast to the opposition to charter change in the Philippines in 1997, there was no significant opposition to this amendment. In a second significant initiative, prior to the 1987 national elections in Papua New Guinea, concern over the growing number of candidates contesting elections (and the consequent decline in the percentage of the vote gained by winning candidates) prompted a move to raise the candidate deposit from K100 (then roughly $US90) to K1000. Although this proposal (which would have given Papua New Guinea, with average per capita GNP of $US1130 in 1993, one of the highest candidate deposits in the world) was dropped, on legal advice, it was successfully revived in 1992 and retained in 1997, when there were suggestions that it be increased to K2000. (Despite this, the number of candidates has continued to rise.) A third topic of discussion has been possible ways to strengthen the party system, with the aim of promoting accountability, discipline and stability; favoured measures have been legislation to discourage 'party hopping'[22] and public funding for political parties. There have also been proposals (which were to have been put into effect in 1997) to shift from a first-past-the-post electoral system to a preferential voting system. More recently, leading opposition figure, Sir Rabbie Namaliu, left the opposition to join the government in order, he said, 'to strengthen the government and provide good governance to the people' (*National* 16 December 1997). With respect to political decentralisation, the pre-independence Constitutional Planning Committee in Papua New Guinea recommended a system of decentralisation to provincial governments. Although initially dropped from the independence constitution, provincial governments were put into place in 1976–77

---

22 In June 1997, as votes were being counted in the national election, Papua New Guinea's Electoral Commissioner Reuben Kaiulo announced that he would prepare and publish a list of all newly elected members showing their political party affiliation according to their nomination form, so that any member changing party allegiance could be identified. Kaiulo proposed to distribute this list to the chief ombudsman, the police commissioner, churches, and the press (*Independent* 27 June 1997). Legislation to prevent 'political turn-coatism' has also been introduced into the Philippine Congress, but to date has not been enacted.

following separatist demands from Bougainville. Early opposition from members of the National Parliament and local government councillors, both of whom saw the new political tier as a threat to their local power bases, resulted in several attempts to shift power back to the centre. In 1995, the Organic Law on Provincial Government was replaced by a new Organic Law on Provincial Governments and Local-Level Governments, which abolished the elected provincial assemblies. Although the rationale for the provincial government reforms was stated in terms of greater decentralisation (increasing the powers of local-level governments) the general consensus has been that the new legislation represents a recentralisation of authority to the national government. Other evidence of centralist tendencies might include the increasing use of the army in law and order operations and the frequent expression, in political circles, of admiration for models of 'social control' drawn from Singapore, Indonesia and Malaysia. While such centralist tendencies might be partly explained as attempts by sitting politicians to consolidate their authority and perpetuate their terms in office, the fact is that there has been little public opposition to them and, indeed, a good deal of popular support.

The general hostility towards state-strengthening reforms in the Philippines and apparent widespread acceptance of the need for state-strengthening measures in Papua New Guinea is consistent with the suggestion above that, notwithstanding a relatively low level of *compliance*, the state in Papua New Guinea enjoys greater *legitimation* than that in the Philippines, and that this may be explained by the closer integration of state and society, or greater representativeness of the state, in Papua New Guinea.

Afterword

Migdal (1994:14–15) has argued for a 'new "anthropology of the state"'. In his earlier study, Migdal (1988:xvi) characterised the literature on the Third World, critically, as generally falling into two categories: one which 'often remain[ed] enmeshed in the intricacies of social life at the local level', with scant attention to the state; the other which focused 'on life among the most influential elements', which by implication tended to produce overly state-centred accounts. It is doubtful whether this criticism can be sustained for either Papua New Guinea or the Philippines. Studies of politics in Papua New Guinea—where state and local politics are deeply interpenetrated—have often been criticised for being too 'anthropological' and insufficiently engaged with grand theory. To a lesser extent the same 'criticism' might be levelled at those who write about Philippine politics, in which the state and local oligarchies are often difficult to disentangle. Insofar as they have focused on the complex interaction of state and society, however, the literatures on Philippine and Papua New

Guinea politics provide a fertile ground for comparative studies of 'the state'.

5 Migdal in Melanesia

PETER LARMOUR[1]

In Joel Migdal's original formulation (1988), state strength was defined as the ability of state élites to impose their preferences on the rest of society. It could be measured by popular compliance with legislation, popular participation in state run institutions, and the legitimacy accorded by the population to state élites (1988:32).

In 1994, Migdal tempered the sharp distinction between state and society, disaggregated both, and traced the 'recursive and mutually transforming nature of state society interactions' (1994:11). Subsequently, in chapter two of this volume, he goes on to ask why so few states have, in fact, fallen apart. He proposes three reasons: international support; successful exchanges with their citizens; and their ability to create and sustain meaning through law, public ritual, and public space.

Here I want to use Migdal's successive and cumulating frameworks to reflect on relationships between state and society in Melanesia, the chain of Pacific island states running from Irian Jaya, in the west, to Fiji, in the east. Before colonial rule, the societies in the region were governed by big men, elders, and chiefs. Centralised, bureaucratic states were introduced after Melanesia was divided up between different colonial powers in the second half of the nineteenth century. The recent introduction of the state makes it seem quite natural to draw a conceptual distinction between 'state' and 'society' in the South Pacific (Larmour 1992).

New Caledonia remains an Overseas Territory of France, and Irian Jaya has been absorbed into Indonesia. The other four parts of Melanesia that became independent as Fiji (in 1970), Papua New Guinea (1975),

1 I am grateful for comments by Sinclair Dinnen and Anthony Regan, and two reviewers, and also to Adrian Leftwich who kindly provided me space at the University of York to do a first draft. Responsibility, of course, is my own.

Solomon Islands (1978), and Vanuatu (1980) are the focus of this chapter. Migdal's work provides different lenses through which they can be compared. The chapter looks first at the arguments in *Strong Societies and Weak States* (1988), then at those in *State Power and Social Forces* (1994) and, finally, at the arguments in chapter two of this volume. The evidence from Melanesia raises theoretical questions about state and society, discussed in the conclusions.

Table 5.1 Population and GDP

	Population (000)	GDP/capita (US$)
Papua New Guinea	3862	999
Solomon Islands	355	529
Vanuatu	160	1020
Fiji	761	1991

Source: UNDP (1994).

Table 5.1 shows the four independent states claiming to control populations ranging from about 3.8 million (PNG) to 160 000 (Vanuatu), which is about the size of a metropolitan municipality, or one of the Greek city states that provided the West with its early ideas about democracy. Half of Fiji's population consists of indigenous people, and half are descendants of migrants and settlers during the colonial period, mainly from India. Indigenous people are the vast majority in the others.

Strength and Weakness

Papua New Guinea is now regularly described as having a 'weak' state (for example, by Wanek 1996). Dauvergne writes of Solomon Islands as 'weak' in this volume. Vanuatu is often similarly characterised, but Fiji tends not to be. In *Strong Societies and Weak States*, Migdal identified several indicators of state strength, relative to society: compliance, participation, and legitimacy. What evidence can we find for weakness, so defined, in Melanesia?

The most spectacular and well documented absence of compliance with policy and legislation in Melanesia may be in the forestry industry, described for Solomon Islands by Dauvergne in this volume. In PNG in the late 1980s, the Barnett Commission of Inquiry found that the government's 1974 statement of forestry policy 'was being followed in hardly any respect at all' (quoted in Asia–Pacific Action Group 1990:11). Monitoring of timber exports was 'seriously inadequate' (13). Tax on profits was being avoided by transfer pricing, and by mis-declaration of the species being exported. Ministers, officials and local leaders were accepting gifts from timber companies in exchange for licences.

The Barnett inquiry concluded that corruption in the forest industry in PNG was taking place within a wider framework of botched decentralisation, inadequate staffing, funding and transport, official inexperience and lack of political support for field officers (quoted in Asia–Pacific Action Group 1990:14). The Ombudsman Commission found very similar malpractices in the forestry industry in Solomon Islands (Larmour 1998; Dauvergne this volume). Other official inquiries have found corruption embedded in administrative weakness in other sectors. A Commission of Enquiry into an education project in Solomon Islands criticised officials for allowing themselves to be 'manipulated' by an Australian consultant and for failing to familiarise themselves with, and apply, regulations (Larmour 1988). In Vanuatu, the Ombudsman found

> ...many—indeed most—of our officials and office holders have very little idea of 2 things—firstly the realistic demands of the job they have been allocated, and secondly, the moral and ethical standards by which the public is entitled to be served (Larmour 1998).

Popular compliance with policy and legislation is particularly difficult to assess in pluralistic legal systems like those in each of the four countries. In each country a customary system of law coexists with an introduced one. There are problems of compliance in both systems: older people complain that young people no longer 'follow custom', while police prosecute some of those who break the introduced law. Sometimes the two apply to the same activity, relationship, or piece of land. Hence, compliance with 'custom' may mean breaking the law, and vice versa.

Overlap and contradiction seem to have been particularly intense in areas of sexual behaviour, family law, and land tenure.

> ...in most rural Papua New Guinean societies the legal offences of sodomy, bestiality, homosexual dealing and bigamy are not regarded as offences at all, while adultery is regarded as a serious offence. A recent survey of attitudes to legal offences found that rural Papua New Guineans regarded adultery as more serious than murder, although in terms of legal penalties murder is ranked first and adultery twelfth. The views of urban respondents, however, fitted the ranking of legal penalties more closely (Clifford, Morauta and Stuart 1984:I:11–12).

Writing about family law, Pulea describes how conflicts have arisen when '..."kerekere", the Fijian custom of borrowing, is interpreted as larceny, or when a writ of habeas corpus is issued over a customary adoption' (1986:2).

Traditional rights are now being reasserted over areas of land that were bought or taken during colonial rule, and since then owned under statutory law. In each country, descendants of traditional owners have occupied private plantations or government owned land, and are refusing to leave. By complying with 'custom', traditional claimants are breaking the law, and vice versa. The most extensive occupations took place in Vanuatu, just before independence, when the Vanua'aku Pati declared a 'Peoples

Provisional Government'. Plantation occupations led to violence on PNG's Gazelle peninsula in the 1960s and early 1970s. They have been quieter, and small scale, in Solomon Islands and Fiji.

Election data provide a partial indicator of popular participation, Migdal's second criterion of strength. Compared to the global average of 63 per cent, popular turnout in parliamentary elections has been relatively high in PNG and Vanuatu, low but growing in Solomon Islands, and lower and falling in Fiji (voting is voluntary in each country).[2] There is a particularly high level of participation by candidates in PNG: the number standing per seat rose from an average of 5.5 per electorate in 1964, to 15.2 in 1992 (Saffu 1996:8).[3] The high levels of participation by candidates, however, do not apply to women, who made up only one per cent. In Vanuatu, political parties act to limit the number of candidates in order to prevent their vote being split (Van Trease 1995:155).

Migdal's third criterion of strength was legitimacy. The recent introduction of states to Melanesia puts them in an uneasy relationship with tradition, or 'custom', as a source of legitimacy. Constitutional deference to traditional institutions increases the further east you travel. The preamble to PNG's constitution refers to the 'worthy customs and traditional wisdoms of our people', and the 'national goals and directive principles' include that development takes place 'primarily through the use of Papua New Guinean forms of social and political organisation' (Brunton and Colquhoun-Kerr 1985:1, 21). Village Courts had, since 1973, been settling disputes according to traditional principles, and the Constitution also made custom the basis of the underlying law (Goldring 1978:149–72). Solomon Islands regards incorporation of traditional leaders as a matter for provincial rather than national institutions, but a recent Decentralisation Bill was subsequently found to be unconstitutional for providing for unelected chiefs in local government (Nanau 1998). Vanuatu's constitution creates a National Council of Chiefs, with advisory powers. Fiji's Great Council of Chiefs exercised strong influence on governments after the 1987 coups, and the former coup leader, Sitiveni Rabuka, went on to create a political party claiming particular loyalty to chiefs. It became the largest party in parliament after 1992.

---

2   PNG turnout has steadily increased from 67 per cent in 1964 to 79 per cent in 1992. Vanuatu turnout rose from 75 per cent in 1983 to 81 per cent in 1995 and 91 per cent in 1995—higher than the 90 per cent recorded in the crucial election just before independence (Yosef 1995:161). Turnout in Solomon Islands is lower, but grew from 55 per cent in 1980 to 61 per cent in 1993. In Fiji, however, it fell from 64 per cent in 1992 to 56 per cent in 1994 (IDEA 1997:51–82). 1992 was the first parliamentary election after the coups.

3   It may lead to a lower level of legitimacy of results, as candidates in PNG's first past the post system win with small pluralities—in 1992, for example, nine candidates won with less than 10 per cent of the vote, the lowest gaining only 6.3 per cent (Reilly 1996:57–8).

Legitimacy may be an attribute of the state itself, or of the government which temporarily inhabits it. It is not a single undifferentiated attribute. The attitudes of the élite, or the army, may be more important than those of ordinary citizens, from whom the state, or government, may simply need acquiescence rather than legitimacy (Barker 1990:107–25). In 1987, elements of the army deposed the recently elected coalition government in Fiji, but in 1992 the coup leader was elected to parliament and became, and remains, Prime Minister. In 1997 in PNG, the army appealed to popular opinion against a government decision to engage foreign mercenaries to put down a secessionist rebellion (Dinnen, May and Regan 1997). Popular demonstrations outside parliament, marshalled, in some cases, by disaffected soldiers, eventually forced the Prime Minister to step aside, though the coup leaders were eventually brought to trial for mutiny.

PNG's dissident commander claimed he was acting against 'corruption' in government, exemplified by the mercenary contract. Throughout Melanesia, the legitimacy of elected governments is undermined by widespread perceptions of corruption, expressed by members of the élite, as well as gang members. Vanuatu's President announced on 1993 Constitution Day that 'corruption seems to be gaining ground in the highest ranks of our leadership', while in 1995 PNG's Governor General warned, '...innuendos, manipulations, undercover deals, greed and corruption are becoming deeply rooted in this society' (*Australian* 14 June 1995).

Paradoxically, however, the widespread talk about corruption may involve more than attitudes to the state. It also involves a wider rejection of economic inequality, suspicion of trading minorities, anger at failures to distribute wealth, and a Christian sense of moral decline (Larmour 1998).

In formalising his argument about state and society, Migdal argued that strength and weakness were relational. States were weak or strong in relation to forces in society, richly described as, '...chiefs, landlords, bosses, rich peasants, clan leaders, *za'im, effendis, aghas, caciques, kulaks* (for convenience, "strongmen") through their various social organizations' (Migdal 1988:33).

Land tenure played an important role in Migdal's argument: the ability to impose statutory law over customary tenure is one measure of the relative strength of states *vis-à-vis* the societies they nominally governed. Land issues have been particularly important for state–society relations in Melanesia.

Table 5.2 Customary Ownership of Land in Melanesia

	Customary land (as % of total)
Papua New Guinea	98
Solomon Islands	84
Vanuatu	99
Fiji	83

Source: Larmour (1990).

Table 5.2 shows that the majority of land in Melanesia is held under tenure recognised by the state, and to some extent protected, as 'customary', 'traditional' or 'native' ownership. The smaller but more valuable amounts of land that have been 'alienated', and held under statute, are under pressure from descendants of traditional owners wanting it back. Supporters of the 1987 coups in Fiji claimed that the new 'Indian-dominated' government posed a threat to indigenous Fijian land ownership. The local conflict that precipitated the Bougainville rebellion was over compensation payments due to traditional owners around the copper mine. In 1996, a World Bank structural adjustment program for PNG was stalled after riots and demonstrations against proposals that customary land be more easily available for development.

The weakness of the states in relation to customary land is in part a result of the strong legal protections for customary ownership installed by their colonial predecessors in Fiji, Solomon Islands and PNG. The colonial regime in Vanuatu was less protective, and traditional rights were even more strongly reasserted at independence.

Migdal's 1988 analysis drew attention to the character of society as well as the character of the state; it was the combination of the two that determines the difference between a diffused system of power, and 'anarchy'. In Melanesia, a notion of 'society' may be as much a recent introduction as the 'state'. It is not simply that Melanesia consisted of a number of pre-existing 'societies' brought under several states. Traditional political units—those within which people routinely accepted a responsibility to resolve disputes without fighting—were very much smaller than the colonial states that encompassed them, but as Filer argues, these smaller units were not particularly coherent themselves.

> ...Melanesian communities have always been on the verge of disintegration, even in pre-colonial times, and it has always taken special qualities of leadership, in each succeeding generation, to prevent them splitting apart at the seams. In pre-colonial times, such efforts were directed to the pursuit of warfare, the practice of initiation, and the organization of large-scale gift-exchange, but the rules of these games were no more permanent than the social groups whose continuity depended on the outcome (1990:86).

More fundamentally, Marilyn Strathern (1988) argues that the idea of an overarching 'society', populated by 'individuals', is inimical to Melanesian thinking, which (to simplify) conceptualises people more in terms of relationships than identities.

State-in-Society

Migdal's next formulation addressed the interactions between state and society, rather than the opposition between them. His introduction to *State Power and Social Forces* argued that:

We need to break down the undifferentiated concepts of state—and also of society—to understand how different elements in each pull in different directions, leading to unanticipated patterns of domination and transformation (Migdal 1994).

He proposed a picture of 'the state' as its officials, deployed at different levels (field, province, centre) and engaging in different settings with different groups.

Such a multi-levelled, personal, contested view of the state makes sense in several historical periods in Melanesia. Traditional forms of government by 'big men' depended on personal forcefulness. Boutilier describes how individual district officers imposed colonial rule in Solomon Islands by judiciously aligning themselves with local forces: his local informant told him 'the government is the district officer' (1982:35). In Vanuatu and Solomon Islands even the modern central government is small and personal in style.

At independence, there were deliberate attempts to intensify the interaction between state and society by decentralisation to provincial governments in PNG and Solomon Islands, and regions in Vanuatu. PNG created nineteen new provincial governments after independence. The aim was to bring government 'closer to the people' by creating new, more accessible arenas for interaction between state officials and social forces. The system that emerged was highly differentiated: the legislation allowed devolution to proceed at different rates for different provinces, and for each to adopt different constitutional arrangements. Some moved more quickly than others. Some adopted a presidential system, with a popular vote for their chief executive, and some a parliamentary executive system.

In each country, decentralisation was driven by the desire to pre-empt secession, as much as by a wish to reduce central interference. Central government in PNG reasserted itself, at first indirectly, through using its powers to suspend provincial governments on grounds of financial mismanagement (Regan 1997:49–53), and then by legislation, replacing elected provincial assemblies with delegates from local level governments, chaired by a national Member of Parliament, acting as 'Governor'. A similar process of devolution followed by reassertion of central parliamentary control, combined with greater rhetorical commitment to local rather than provincial government, has taken place in Solomon Islands (Nanau 1998). The issues are more complicated in Vanuatu, where decentralisation has become identified with the defence of Francophone linguistic minorities against an Anglophone central government. It followed a different course from PNG and Solomon Islands. Eleven local government councils were set up at independence, with a lower tier of 'area councils'. In 1994, the eleven councils were amalgamated into six better funded provinces, and the lower tier abandoned. There was no parallel in Fiji, though its provincial councils have been granted, and sought, greater autonomy since the coups.

Decentralisation formally increased the possibilities for interaction between state officials and local forces. It also enhanced opportunities for the development of patron–client relations and corruption.

The last of the four states to become independent, Vanuatu, did so in 1980. Since then the world has changed around them. Migdal's most recent thinking on the state, expressed in this volume, goes to issues of survival.

Survival

All four states have faced, but so far weathered, crises that threatened either their constitutional government, or territorial integrity. As we have seen, there have been military threats to constitutional government in PNG and Fiji, while Vanuatu has also faced down a mutiny by its para military police. What explains their survival? Migdal's chapter in this volume suggests three reasons: international support, successful interactions with their citizens, and their ability to create meaning for their citizens.

International support

States in Melanesia are to some extent creatures of an international system that pushed for the ending of colonial empires, and recognised their independence. The 'New Guinea' part of what became PNG was formally a UN Trust Territory. The UN Committee on Decolonisation oversaw the decolonisation of the other parts of Melanesia.

The Melanesian governments are jealous of their sovereignty, though PNG, Solomon Islands and Vanuatu depend to a degree on aid from other states, as shown in Table 5.3. All are active in regional international organisations: the South Pacific Commission, founded in 1947, the South Pacific Forum (1971), and the Melanesian Spearhead Group, which was founded by PNG, Solomon Islands and Vanuatu in 1985, and which Fiji recently joined (Henningham 1995). None of these imagines any future unification, like (say) the European Union. Vanuatu has relationships with the other Francophone countries, as well as (with the others) the Anglophone Commonwealth. They have differing capacities to field overseas missions, and sustain the military apparatus of sovereignty. They also have different interests at stake in their relationships with each other, and the international community. PNG is trying to manage its secessionist crisis. Fiji was excluded from the Commonwealth after its military coup, but was readmitted in 1997 after its parliament accepted changes to its constitution removing biases in favour of indigenous people. Fiji also has a stake in the international system as a supplier of troops for United Nation's peacekeeping missions. All are considering how to adjust to liberalising international trade, with Fiji's sugar industry particularly vulnerable.

Table 5.3 International Support and Recognition

	Aid as % of GDP	EEZ (million square kilometres)
Papua New Guinea	16	3.1
Solomon Islands	21	1.3
Vanuatu	31	0.7
Fiji	5	1.3

Sources: World Bank (1997), Asian Development Bank (1996:44), Economic Insights (1994a) (for PNG).

Their international sovereignty is, itself, a resource in which they can trade. It entitles them to declare and licence the exploitation of 200 mile Exclusive Economic Zones (see Table 5.3). Vanuatu runs a shipping register for vessels that never need visit, but welcome a relaxed regime. Its legislation dealing with offshore transactions allows it to attract foreign companies to register in Vanuatu to limit their tax exposure at home.

That international recognition, however, is coming at a rising domestic price. Since the end of the Cold War, larger states, international agencies and non-governmental organisations have become more willing to look behind claims to sovereignty and criticise the domestic policies of independent states. Thus, PNG's actions in Bougainville have been criticised by Amnesty International. Its land policies have been scrutinised by the World Bank. The claims of customary land owners against the PNG government's mining policy have been heard in a Melbourne court. Australia has criticised Solomon Islands' forestry policies.

It is not unusual for larger countries to interfere in smaller countries' internal affairs. Banks have often sought policy changes as a condition for approving loans. Aid and military assistance comes with strings. However, emerging international norms and the politics of the Cold War for many years protected the sovereignty of what Jackson (1990) rather sourly called 'quasi states'. This protection is now lifting, as aid donors, the World Bank, and the Asian Development Bank adopt policies promoting 'good governance' among their clients. 'Governance' includes 'public sector management, accountability, the legal framework for development, transparency and information' (World Bank 1994). The impact on Melanesia has been in donor and bank pressure to reduce the size of the public sector in the economy. So far, PNG has committed itself to reductions as part of a structural adjustment program negotiated with the World Bank, while Vanuatu and Solomon Islands are negotiating with the Asian Development Bank. Table 5.4 suggests such reductions may strain the relationship between state and society, by reducing the state's ability to provide jobs and subsidise social services.

Exchanges with citizens

Table 5.4 shows how the state spends half of the national income of Vanuatu and Solomon Islands, and provides between a third and a half of all non-agricultural jobs in each country. These are immediate and material reasons for people to support the existence, and continuation, of rule by the state. Nevertheless, the benefits are paid for by local taxes, and charges for services, as well as aid. If aid declines, and more people are drawn into the net of taxation, they may begin to question the terms of their exchange with the state.

Table 5.4 The State in the Economy

	Public expenditure as % of national income	State employees per 100 inhabitants	State employees as % of non-agricultural employment
Papua New Guinea	32	2	36
Solomon Islands	53	4	43
Vanuatu	50	3	32
Fiji	27	6	49

Sources: World Bank (1997), Asian Development Bank (1996:44).

The strongest claim that states have made for support has been the ability to deliver 'development'. The concept may be complex, and difficult to define, but according to Goddard 'presents itself simply and tangibly' to people in PNG: 'Particularly in rural areas, the Tok Pisin transliteration *developmen* connotes cash, infrastructure, and services such as schools and medical centres' (Goddard 1995:67).

Politics in PNG and Solomon Islands often consists of an exchange of votes for promises of development: 'Communities vote for the candidate who offers the greatest material reward and candidates normally offer the greatest reward to their own community' (Filer quoted in Saffu 1996:4).

Both PNG and Solomon Islands have created funds from which Members of Parliament (MPs) can draw directly to benefit their constituents, without going through the state apparatus of budgeting and accounting. PNG MPs each qualify for Kina 300 000 per annum in 'Electoral Development Funds' (EDF) (Reilly 1996:68). These have since risen to about Kina 500 000 per annum, and are known as 'Rural Action Programs' (Sinclair Dinnen, personal communication). A Solomon Islands discretionary fund introduced in 1992 was renamed 'Constituency Development Fund', and provided MPs with SI$200 000 per constituency by 1994 (Alasia 1997:12). Vanuatu's equivalent might be the generous provision for ministerially appointed political staffs.

Yet it is a system of exchange that is bound to disappoint, as candidates bid up promises, favour one part of the electorate before another, and fail to deliver in hard budgetary times. Standish found in Simbu that

EDF funds became 'something of a liability for MPs', as it was impossible to satisfy everyone, though one MP did well by funding the purchase of ambulances which bore his name (Standish 1996:298).

In PNG at least, the state seems increasingly unable to fulfil its side of the exchange with its population. A World Bank report on 'delivering public services' found a 'serious deterioration in the quality of many essential services', including, 'an alarming spread of familiar diseases amid sharp declines in health services and central supervisory activities' (1995a:2).

It was not for lack of money. Compared to similar developing countries, PNG's central government spent a relatively large share of the country's GDP, and spent relatively more per capita on services. The trouble was that 'most of this money is spent on administration and non essential functions', as national agencies, and their cumbersome procedures, squeezed out local authorities and initiatives (World Bank 1995a:3). There is anecdotal evidence of declines in services in Solomon Islands and Vanuatu, where high rates of population growth are also reducing per capita expenditures.

Manipulation of meaning

The anthropologist Jeffrey Clark asked his local collaborator what he thought of belonging to PNG:

> ...he immediately replied 'I hate PNG' with a vehemence that surprised me, and confessed to feelings of shame about Papua New Guinea. He qualified his answer with reference to the ways in which government inefficiency, corruption and wantokism (nepotism) in particular, hold back development (1997:75).

States are moral, or immoral, orders in several ways. In the Weberian ideal type, they have their own internal values of impersonality, and conformity to rules. As actors in the international system they also have to conform to its morality including (as we have seen) new concerns with 'good governance'. They may draw on, or express moral principles external to themselves. They may also campaign to transform the morality of individual citizens. Thus, Corrigan and Sayer describe English state formation as a kind of 'cultural revolution' (1985:4).

'Development', which we discussed above in material terms, has also become a kind of moral duty on governments imposed on them as a consequence of their membership of the international system.[4] The

---

4   In 1919 the Charter of the League of Nations entrusted the 'welfare and development' of non self governing peoples to countries like Australia, whose mandate to govern former German New Guinea required it to 'do her utmost to promote the material and moral welfare and the social progress of the inhabitants of the territory' (in Latouche 1987). The 1945 Charter of the United Nations states that: 'The United Nations will work to raise standards of

Melanesian states became independent in the 1970s, a high point of the international moral climate in favour of state-led development, and at the end of the long post-war boom which could fund it. They attracted very high levels of aid per capita, which was justified as contributing to 'development'. By the early 1990s, however, international disappointment was setting in. The World Bank surveyed the performance of its seven Pacific island member countries in the 1980s (including Solomon Islands, Vanuatu and Fiji, but not PNG), and identified what it called the 'Pacific Paradox': 'virtually no growth occurred in average real per capita income during this period despite a favourable natural and human resource endowment, high levels of aid, and reasonably prudent economic manage-ment' (World Bank 1993a:1).

The Melanesian states have other less material ways of providing meaning. States not only borrow authority from autonomous competing sources (Barker 1990). They make the additional claim of their unique ability to express them. Thus, the Fiji state does not simply draw on the autonomous authority of 'tradition' or 'indigenousness'. It makes a more ambitious claim to a unique ability to express these values (for example, 'only through the state can tradition be maintained', or 'only through the state can indigenousness be promoted'). The Fiji example also shows how divisive, and hence self defeating, such appeals may be. By appealing to indigenous and Christian traditions the state deeply alienated its Indo-Fijian population: 40 000 emigrated since the coups (Fiji 1996:37). Fiji's new constitution tries to appeal to all groups, not just indigenous Fijians.

States may displace, from above and below, identifications with race, ethnicity, family, clan and place. On the one hand they are totalising, representing people to themselves as members of a single community: Papua New Guineans, Solomon Islanders, ni-Vanuatu, or Fiji Islanders, claiming to override divisions of race, clan or region. On the other hand, they are individualising, addressing people as voters, taxpayers, or students. They can also create new, intermediate, units of identity, such as provinces.

States are also involved in the construction, and maintenance, of gender identities and differences. The state itself may be thought to have a gender. For some it may be a kind of traditional big man, expected to distribute wealth (Borrey, cited in Goddard 1995:70) For other men in Melanesia, the state is gendered dangerously female.[5]

---

living, for full employment and for conditions conducive to economic and social progress and development.' In the 1970s, supporters of a New Inter-national Economic Order proposed an expansive duty for the state. Article 7 of the Charter of Economic Rights and Obligations: 'Every government has a primary responsibility to promote the economic, social and cultural progress of its people.'

5 Clark (1993) shows how Huli men interpret the manifestations of 'the state' at the Mount Kare gold mine in terms of their own, Huli, conceptualisations of gender. To simplify, men and women led largely independent lives, and men

Colonial states aimed to transform their subjects by training, education, resettlement and planning. Colonial native regulations made detailed petty interventions into daily life (Wolfers 1975). The independent states have not given up nagging and chivvying their populations into behaving in respectable, modern ways. Foster (1992) looks at 'National Law Week', and campaigns against spitting in public places, as examples of the way the PNG state engages in moral education to produce modern citizens. National Law Week addressed people as individuated citizens, with human rights, rather than people defined by their membership of a particular clan or tribe. The campaigns against spitting addressed a moral general notion of manners, but took on a powerful symbol of indigenous identity: the betel nut that people chewed, and spat out. Foster shows these campaigns to be internally opposed: membership of a modern nation requires conformity with other models of nationalism, yet the claim to separate nationhood is based on distinct cultural identities.

Nationalism has been the standard way in which modern states have naturalised themselves through meaning. It is often presented as relatively weak in Melanesia, compared to more local loyalties, or to more heroic nationalist movements in other former colonies. Yet in the 1970s, Australia faced strong and violent pressure against its rule on the Gazelle peninsula, including the killing of a District Commissioner, while the Vanua'aku Pati in Vanuatu waged a classic nationalist campaign of mass mobilisation, provisional governments, and appeal to the UN. There are long-standing nationalist feelings on the Indo-Fijian side of Fiji politics, and a more robust indigenous nationalism since the coups. Whether or not these sentiments count as 'nationalism' may be simply a matter of definition.[6] However, Anthony Smith's theories of nationalism in Europe and elsewhere suggest similar processes have been at work in Melanesia. He argues that nationalism is not simply nostalgic, or backward looking. It amounts to 'communal regeneration in any and every sphere of human life' (1995:13). Smith distinguishes two routes to nationalism, aristocratic and vernacular, both taken in Europe and Melanesia. The first he calls 'bureaucratic mobilisation', wherein an élite ethnicity extends itself into the periphery, and downwards into lower social strata. In the second,

---

believed menstrual blood to be dangerously polluting. The men who went to work at the gold mine at Mount Kare suffered respiratory infections, typhoid and sexually transmitted diseases. They blamed the gold, which they interpreted as like menstrual blood, and for them their illness indicated a wider loss of control to the world outside: to people from the coast (nambis), and the PNG state itself.

6   For Anthony Smith, nationalism is 'an ideological movement for the attainment and maintenance of autonomy, unity and identity on behalf of a population deemed by some of its members to constitute a "nation"'. Which in turn is 'a named human population which shares myths and memories, a mass public culture, a designated homeland, economic units, and equal rights and duties for all members' (1995: 56).

vertical, process indigenous intellectuals return to their roots, rediscovering and reinterpreting local language, traditions and art. In Melanesia, bureaucratic mobilisation took place through British, French and Australian colonialism. Indigenous rediscovery of displaced 'kastom', land tenure systems, and vernacular languages was aided by institutions such as the University of the South Pacific's Institute of Pacific Studies, or the Institute of PNG Studies, or the Research School of Pacific and Asian Studies at the Australian National University.

Smith identifies two further stages of national regeneration: politicisation of the rediscovered culture, and purification of the community (1995:68). Politicisation took place in the various 'micro-nationalist' or 'new' social movements which brought together educated leaders and rural villagers, of which the Vanua'aku Pati was the most conspicuously successful. Such movements also proliferated around the first generation of university students in PNG. There were nasty overtones of purification in the aftermath of the 1987 coups in Fiji, directed as much against indigenous moderates, as against Indo-Fijians.

In chapter two of this volume, Migdal suggests three particular areas in which states create meanings that, in turn, naturalise themselves: law, ritual and public space. We have already noticed, in our discussion of compliance, a degree of legal pluralism in Melanesia, particularly in matters of family law, sexual behaviour, and land tenure. 'Custom' sometimes contradicts statute, but states have also moved to codify some aspects of traditional land tenure systems. The colonial state in Fiji recorded clan boundaries and membership. PNG and Solomon Islands introduced and abandoned a series of experiments in registering the ownership of customary land, but were widely suspected of wanting to register land in order to make it easier to alienate (Larmour, ed. 1991). Vanuatu attempted a more radical reconciliation of the two: its constitution asserts that custom will form the basis of land law, with a statutory system of leases floating on top of it. But none has managed to get it right: in each country, 'land' is tied up with personal and political identity, as well as material interests, and remains an issue that quickly generates popular distrust of government.

The colonial state in Fiji was the best of the four at conjuring up ritual and ceremony, including its reconstruction of Fijian chieftaincy. Arts Festivals displayed the products of nationalist regeneration at the time of independence, while international sporting competitions provide opportunities for young people, this time including women, to compete under national flags. Regular elections provide opportunities for drama. Foster (1996) sees the act of voting as a 'secular ritual', demonstrating membership of the wider horizontal community of the nation, and briefly constituting 'the state' for rural people who otherwise rarely come into contact with government officials. Concretely, voting 'singles people out' from a list, in alphabetical order, marks their fingers with ink (to show they have voted, and prevent them voting again) and invites them to make a private choice between candidates. Back outside the polling area they are reunited with kin (Foster 1996:158–65).

The past is reframed as 'custom' (or, in Vanuatu 'kastom'), but new Melanesian national rituals are being invented. Dinnen notices the new phenomenon of criminal gang surrenders in PNG:

> Surrendering groups often carry home made placards written in English or Tok Pisin asking forgiveness and requesting assistance for their chosen rehabilitation strategies...Groups from rural villages will often walk considerable distances to surrender in town, where they can attract maximum publicity and have more chance of connecting with government and private sector resources (1997:256–7).

The state in Vanuatu has been particularly keen to turn 'kastom' to public purposes. On a hill above the capital, Port Vila, a newly constructed parliament looks across an open space to the traditionally constructed meeting house of the National Council of Chiefs. On another side is the massive Cultural Centre, and a new building being constructed (with foreign aid) for the National Council of Women. The open space has become an arena for national ceremonies, such as traditional pig killing aimed at reconciliation after rioting and a state of emergency was declared in the capital.

> The ceremony is the chiefs' way of showing that they accept that the damage is done, now it is 'face cleaning' time towards putting the wrong right. The government has promised to compensate the victims (*Trading Post* 28 January 1998).

Yet this engaging example also shows the limits of ritual, and public space. The shopkeepers whose stores were damaged refused to attend, and there were grumblings around town that the police, in enlisting the help of chiefs, had compromised the authority of the state.

The possibility for the Melanesian states naturalising themselves through what Migdal called norms and networks of civic engagement, and the creation of 'public space', may be limited by low levels of urbanisation in PNG, Solomon Islands and Vanuatu (Connell and Lea 1993). However, their towns are growing fast. In PNG high levels of violent crime keep people suspicious of strangers, and locked up in their houses at night, reducing the possibilities of civic engagement.

Conclusions

Migdal's arguments clearly travel well. They illuminate the differences between the four countries, as well as suggest issues in common, and link the study of Melanesia to broader studies of politics, society and culture in developing countries. The study of Melanesia also brings into question the underlying problematic of 'state' and 'society' which Migdal has been uncovering.

Pre-colonial Melanesian societies are often called 'stateless'. Clastres points to the ethnocentricity of the assumption that they were 'missing something—the state—that is essential to them' (1974:189). More positively, they demonstrate the conditions under which people can govern themselves without centralised authority. These conditions—small scale, common values, intense personal relationships—turn out to be quite stringent (Taylor 1982). What does the state amount to for Melanesians? Foster argues that:

...Tangans, perhaps like most citizens of Papua New Guinea, do not imagine the state as a reified entity or transcendent abstraction—something that exists independently of the flesh and blood public servants who operate (or not) in its name (1996:145).

That may be true, but it may be true everywhere. The importance of the idea of a state (impartial, abstract, rather chilly) in the constitution of an actual state goes wider than Melanesia. Dyson has argued that societies where this idea is weak, or attenuated, are to that extent 'stateless' (1980). The idea is part of the institution. He was thinking of liberal societies like Britain or the United States, rather than Melanesia, and he was comparing them to continental European societies with their stronger state traditions. Such traditions have carried over into modern ideas of the East Asian 'developmental state', mobilising national power to catch up with the liberal West. Current complaints about state weakness in Melanesia often compare the states with their colonial predecessors, or with images of East Asian states, or with the development tasks they face. Such strong state traditions appeal to some members of the Melanesian élite, and to officials in aid agencies who channel resources to 'institutional strengthening' projects in Melanesia. It may be that any actual state these days is 'weak' in relation to such an ideal. The East Asian states are looking less worthy of emulation since the financial crisis that began in mid 1997. That is not necessarily, or wholly, a bad thing. Civil libertarians might value the absence of an overbearing state, and welcome the fact that Melanesian states now have self-limiting constitutional protections of human rights that limit their despotic power.

6 Indonesia's 'Strong' State

HAROLD CROUCH

In the middle of 1997 Indonesia exhibited many of the characteristics of a strong state. In contrast to the two decades of political instability and upheaval that preceded the establishment of the New Order in the mid-1960s, Soeharto's military-based regime had been in power for more than 30 years and faced no major organised challenge from society.[1] Certainly the regime was forced to deal with occasional outbreaks of urban rioting while small-scale separatist rebellions persisted in several outlying provinces but the political dominance of the state was never in question. Meanwhile, the strong state brought about a transformation of the Indonesian economy. The opening of the economy to foreign capital resulted in rapid industrialisation and by the mid-1990s Indonesia's economic achievements were being widely praised. It was expected that Indonesia would soon be graduating into the ranks of the newly industrialising countries.[2]

Yet the 'economic miracle' turned into an economic disaster during the second half of 1997. The Asian financial crisis, which began with the collapse of the Thai baht in July 1997, quickly spread to other countries in

---

1   In this discussion I do not make a sharp distinction between 'state' and 'regime'. I am regarding the New Order as a distinct type of state in Indonesia compared to Guided Democracy, Liberal Democracy and the Dutch colonial state. But since the establishment of the New Order in 1966, there has been no change in regime. As Lawson points out, 'In nonwestern states it is often much more difficult to distinguish among state, regime, and government, and in some cases there may be no discernible distinction' (Lawson 1993a:187).

2   One World Bank research report had already described Indonesia as a newly industrialising economy and placed it among the eight 'high performing Asian economies (HPAEs)' (World Bank 1993b).

the region—Malaysia, the Philippines, South Korea and Indonesia—which all experienced devastating depreciations of their currencies. But, by early 1998, it was the apparently strong state of Indonesia that was suffering most. As the value of the rupiah against the US dollar fell by 80 per cent in little over six months and several million workers lost their jobs as their employers went bankrupt, the government appeared incapable of carrying through the reforms needed to win back international and domestic business confidence. It was only after the International Monetary Fund (IMF) intervened several times that the government introduced substantial measures, but by then many Indonesians no longer looked to the government for a solution but perceived the government as being part of the problem.

Nevertheless, the state continued to dominate society. By coincidence the economic crisis reached a peak five weeks before a scheduled session of the People's Consultative Assembly in March 1998. Despite growing public dissatisfaction with the government's performance and open calls for President Soeharto to resign, the five-yearly session of the assembly unanimously re-elected the president—as it had on six previous occasions. As usual, the questions of the presidency and vice-presidency were settled behind closed doors while organisations representing important parts of society were excluded. In a sense, therefore, Indonesia was still a strong state, but the 1997–98 financial crisis showed that its capacity to implement policies at a critical time was extraordinarily weak.[3] This chapter argues that the weaknesses of Indonesia's strong state in dealing with vital policy issues were not due to the state's inability to cope with strong pressures from society but arose from its own character.

Using Joel Migdal's theorising about strong and weak states as a starting point, this chapter will discuss four main issues:

- Why was the New Order state stronger than earlier forms of the state in Indonesia? To what extent does Migdal's model in *Strong Societies and Weak States* (1988) fit the Indonesian case?

- In his introduction to *State Power and Social Forces*, Migdal (1994) argues that we need to disaggregate the state. In what ways was the New Order state strong and in what ways weak?

- Although the New Order state was very strong in some respects, it also exhibited many characteristics of a weak state. Does the explanation lie more in the strength of society or in the characteristics of the state itself?

- Is a strong society necessarily incompatible with a strong state? Could a stronger society enhance the capacity of the state?

---

3   This book went to press days after Soeharto was forced from office on 21 May 1998 in the wake of a devastating riot in Jakarta. It is too early to assess the nature of the new government headed by President Habibie.

The Historical Phases of the Indonesian State

There was, of course, no 'Indonesian' state when the Dutch first established a trading post in Batavia at the beginning of the seventeenth century. Instead, political authority in the territory which later became Indonesia was divided among numerous indigenous states ranging from the Mataram sultanate based in central Java to small sultanates in the eastern part of the archipelago. The most powerful, the Mataram sultanate, was sufficiently well organised to mount a serious military challenge to the Dutch but was eventually subjugated. The Dutch gradually extended their control throughout the archipelago by imposing treaties on various sultans, rajas and local chieftains but it was not until the early twentieth century that the borders of the Netherlands East Indies were finally established.

Although Dutch exploitation of the Indies economy intensified during the nineteenth and twentieth centuries, the Dutch state preferred to preserve traditional indigenous ruling élites. As its economic interests deepened, the regions brought under direct Dutch administration expanded. Nevertheless, a small part of Java and a large part of the Outer Islands were governed indirectly as 'native states' (numbering 282 at the time of the Japanese invasion in 1942) under the nominal authority of traditional rulers who had been more or less forced to acknowledge Dutch authority (Cribb 1992:501). Although the colonial government could intervene in the affairs of these states and had the right to appoint rulers, in practice it maintained traditional ruling élites as its local agents. Even in regions directly ruled by the Dutch, local administration was headed by indigenous aristocrats under the supervision of Dutch officials. Dutch officials made up only ten per cent of state personnel in the 1920s.

Dutch rule in the Netherlands East Indies, therefore, fits in part the pattern of British colonial rule in Sierra Leone described by Migdal in *Strong Societies and Weak States*. Writing of Sierra Leone, Migdal explained that: 'Such rule minimized costs by relying on the chiefs as legislators, judges, and administrators, while it attempted to ensure against concerted rebellion through policies that fragmented indigenous social control' (1988:122). While the sheer territorial extent of the Indies meant that the Dutch often faced local resistance, the archipelago's ethnic diversity and the consequent absence of an Indonesia-wide identity before the twentieth century virtually ruled out the possibility of coordinated multi-ethnic rebellion. Dutch rule in Indonesia had probably progressed further towards administrative unification than had British rule in Sierra Leone and its penetration of society was deeper, especially on Java, but it was still true, as Migdal wrote of Sierra Leone, that 'the goals of stability and security could be better achieved through policies that created and perpetuated a fragmented, weblike society with numerous poles of power, even though such a society posed formidable constraints on mobilization of human and material resources' (1988:127).

In one sense, of course, the Dutch colonial regime constituted a strong state. The state was certainly strong enough to prevent the emergence of an indigenous political challenge to its rule. Although nationalist organisations had mobilised some popular support in the second and third decades of the twentieth century, most radical nationalist leaders were imprisoned during the 1930s and it was not seen as absurd for a Dutch governor-general to anticipate that the first 300 years of Dutch rule would be followed by another 300 years (Benda 1972:237–8). It was only after the Indies was occupied by the Japanese during World War II and the Netherlands itself devastated by German occupation that the foundations of Dutch rule were shaken. As strong as the Dutch colonial state had appeared to be before 1941, its inability to mobilise the indigenous population in its defence and its collapse in a matter of weeks as the Japanese occupied its territory, exposed the hollowness of its claims to strength.

Despite the territorial unevenness of the Dutch administration, Dutch sovereignty laid the basis for the emergence of a multi-ethnic 'imagined community' of educated Indonesians during the twentieth century. Anderson describes how a small number of young Indonesians obtained Dutch education in their home areas and gravitated to the centres of higher education in Java where they met fellow-students from other parts of the archipelago and acquired a sense of being Indonesian (Anderson 1983: chapter 7). It was these young people who joined nationalist organisations which supported the Proclamation of Independence following the defeat of Japan in 1945.

The Indonesian National Revolution lasted for four years during which the newly proclaimed Indonesian state competed with the returning Dutch colonial state (see Kahin 1952). The Indonesian state exercised little effective power not only because much of its claimed territory remained under Dutch control but also because of its own internal divisions. The nationalist forces included nationalist, Muslim, communist and socialist organisations which were often at loggerheads with each other. The Indonesian National Army consisted of poorly trained and ill-equipped local guerrilla units whose loyalty was usually given to their immediate commander and not to the central military leadership (see Sundhaussen 1982:chapter 2). During the revolution it was not uncommon for troops to depose centrally-endorsed commanders and replace them with officers of their own choice. Military officers were also divided in their political allegiance and on one occasion dissident troops even detained the Prime Minister. Fighting between various nationalist forces was common. Communist-aligned troops rebelled at one stage and Muslim troops at another time. Moreover, the central government exercised no effective authority in the regions outside Java. Nevertheless, the Indonesian forces were able to prevent the Dutch from re-establishing control and made the costs of continuing their campaign prohibitive. Under American pressure, the Dutch eventually agreed to negotiate the transfer of sovereignty to an independent Indonesia at the end of 1949.

The new Indonesian state's control over the territories it inherited from the colonial regime was tenuous. Never fully integrated into the colonial state and ethnically distinct, many regions in the Outer Islands were reluctant to accept rule from Jakarta. In some regions local élites had sided with the Dutch, while in others participants in the struggle for independence complained that they had not fought and made sacrifices in order to be dominated by a government based in Java. In region after region local rebellions broke out, often led by former nationalists who were disappointed with the fruits of independence. Regionalism was often mixed with religious identity. Orthodox Islam was more deeply entrenched in many regions of the Outer Islands than in Java where the traditional aristocracy had followed a syncretic blend of Islamic and indigenous religious beliefs. Some regional rebellions were identified with Islam indicating the frustrations of strongly Muslim populations with national governments in which adherents of what Geertz called 'the religion of Java' were prominent.[4] Even in West Java, adjacent to the national capital, a Muslim rebellion continued into the 1960s. By the middle of the 1950s, dissatisfaction in the Outer Islands had reached boiling point and coordinated rebellions led by military officers took place in several parts of Sumatra and Sulawesi. The outcome was the collapse of parliamentary democracy and the introduction of martial law in 1957.

Governments during the era of parliamentary democracy from 1950 to 1957 were weak in many ways (see Feith 1962). The agreement with the Dutch had provided for the establishment of a parliament to which both nationalists and representatives from Dutch-controlled regions were appointed. Reflecting the ethnic and regional diversity of the new nation, the members of the parliament represented a wide range of parties, most of which were linked to ethnic and religious communities. When the first national election was held in 1955, no single party obtained even one quarter of the seats in parliament. Three of the largest four parties had their strongest followings in Java. The National Party and the Communist Party (PKI) won support in that part of the Javanese community which did not identify with political Islam, while the Nahdatul Ulama had its base among rural Muslims, especially in East and Central Java. The fourth large party, the Masyumi, tended to be supported by urban Muslims and had a strong base in West Java but drew most of its support from the Outer Islands. Smaller parties represented the Christian community (with separate parties for Catholics and Protestants), small Muslim groups and various regions.

As a result, it proved impossible to form strong governments. In the seven years between 1950 and 1957, no less than seven coalition govern-

---

4   On the Muslim rebellions see van Dijk (1981). On the 'religion of Java', see Geertz (1960).

ments rose and fell, the longest holding office for about two years and the shortest for only six months. Such governments were preoccupied with maintaining their majorities in parliament. Policies were neglected for what Indonesians call 'cow-trading' as parties bargained for the best deal in coalition governments. Migdal's description of post-independence politics in Sierra Leone applied equally well to Indonesia. 'Politics', he wrote, 'has been neither the expression of state autonomy nor the dominance of a single class, but it has been a display of disparate acts of "accommodation and persuasion". Appointments and manipulation, not social control and mobilization, remain the outer limits of state capabilities' (1988:137).

The failure of the central government to deal effectively with regional rebellions paved the way for the introduction of martial law in 1957 and the establishment of President Sukarno's 'Guided Democracy' in 1959 (see Lev 1966). Expressing popular disaffection with parliamentary democracy, Sukarno had called on the nation to 'bury the political parties' and establish a new system of 'democracy with leadership'. The president's proposals were supported by the military leadership which gradually regained control of the rebellious regions and became Sukarno's main partner in the government. The Guided Democracy regime, however, was riven by sharp internal divisions and proved incapable of providing effective administration. Sukarno needed civilian support to balance the growing power of the military and turned increasingly to the PKI which was the only major party that had not participated in the coalition governments of the discredited parliamentary era. The military and the communists were natural rivals and politics became increasingly polarised between them. In an effort to mobilise popular support, Sukarno launched military campaigns first to wrest West New Guinea from Dutch control and then to oppose what he saw as the British-sponsored project to form Malaysia. Meanwhile, the economy declined precipitously as foreign investors withdrew, exports fell and infrastructure deteriorated.

In this context the rivalry sharpened between the military and the PKI, each supported by their allies. Migdal's 'necessary condition' for the emergence of a strong state is the occurrence of a calamity involving massive social dislocation such as wars and mass migrations (1988: chapter 8).[5] In Indonesia, the involvement of PKI leaders in the assassination of the top military leaders provided the opportunity for the remaining military leadership to eliminate their main political rival. During the last three months of 1965 and the early months of 1966, some half-a-million supporters of the PKI were massacred throughout Indonesia. The killings were carried out largely by members of Muslim youth organisations with military encouragement. Another million or so PKI supporters were imprisoned (see Crouch 1978:chapter 5). The army-supported massacre

---

5   Migdal gives the examples of revolution and war in countries such as China and Taiwan, the two Koreas, and Israel. He also mentions mass migrations affecting Taiwan and Israel.

upset the balance of power on which President Sukarno's authority rested and enabled the military, headed by General Soeharto, to remove him from office in a series of manœuvres which culminated in Soeharto's effective election as president in 1967 and formal election in 1968.

Migdal also lists four 'sufficient conditions' which can permit the emergence of strong states. First, they need a favourable 'world historical moment'. In Indonesia's case, the military's annihilation of the PKI occurred at a time when the American engagement in Vietnam was intensifying so it naturally won the approval of the US government and its allies who quickly formed a consortium to provide economic aid. Second, it helps if the state is faced by a military threat—whether external or internal. In 1965 it was easy for the military and allies to portray the nation as threatened not only by the domestic communists but also by China which they claimed had given full support to the PKI. Migdal's fourth condition is the availability of skilled top leaders of the calibre of Ben-Gurion, Castro, Ho Chi-minh, Kim Il-sung and Mao Tse-tung (to mention those singled out by Migdal). Whatever else might be said about Soeharto, it could hardly be denied that he possessed extraordinary political skills, perhaps shown most clearly in the way that he edged Sukarno from power in a gradual process that stretched out over two and a half years. Migdal's third sufficient condition—a bureaucracy consisting of people with administrative skills and independence from existing social groupings—was less evident in Indonesia. However, under the New Order the military partly performed this function.

There can be no doubt that Soeharto's military-based New Order regime has been much stronger than previous versions of the Indonesian state.[6] The parliamentary coalition governments of the 1950s were so divided internally that they could not even maintain themselves in office for long, let alone deal with the regional challenges that threatened the unity of the new country. The successor system of Guided Democracy was also riven by internal rivalries which were so intense that they eventually brought about not only the overthrow of the government but a massacre that eliminated a crucial component of the regime. The emergence of the military as the dominant force in Indonesian politics under President Soeharto's New Order created a regime which was able to neutralise all opposition and reverse fundamental policies of the so-called Old Order. But, as Migdal pointed out: 'Many states have become formidable presences even in the far reaches of their societies, especially in North Africa, South America, and Asia...At the same time, state leaders in many societies have found it exceedingly difficult to bring about intended social changes.' What was the capacity of the New Order regime 'to achieve the kind of changes in society that their leaders have sought through state planning, policies, and actions' (1988:39, 4)?

---

6 According to Anderson, 'the New Order is best understood as the resurrection of the state and its triumph vis-à-vis society and nation' (1990:109).

The Strengths and Weaknesses of the New Order State

Migdal has argued that it is necessary to 'disaggregate' the state because it can behave in different ways and have different capacities in different sectors (1994). In Indonesia the New Order state was strong enough to repress organised political opposition but it could not ignore entirely societal pressures, especially those emanating from the Islamic community. In the case of economic policy, the state was not subjected to strong pressures from economic groups in society but its reliance on patronage to maintain internal cohesion was a major obstacle to reform, as was shown most decisively in the Soeharto government's reaction to the Asian financial crisis in 1997–98.

Politics

In contrast to the shifting coalitions of the era of parliamentary democracy and the short-lived Guided Democracy regime, Soeharto's New Order has maintained itself in power for three decades while facing no organised challenge from society. Soeharto's power is based on the military which is trained and organised primarily as an internal security force. The military justifies its political role by reference to its ideology of *dwi fungsi* (dual function) which claims the right for the military to participate as an autonomous force in national affairs. The military's political role is backed by its 'territorial' organisation which stations some two-thirds of the army's personnel in units spread throughout the entire country in provincial centres, small towns and even townships (see Lowry 1996:91–4). Military officers, both active and retired, have been appointed as cabinet ministers, senior bureaucrats, regional governors, district heads and ambassadors.

Following the elimination of the military's main rival, the PKI, in the massacre of 1965, Soeharto ensured the emasculation of the remaining political parties. The parties were forced to amalgamate in two new parties whose leaders were elected with the assistance of military intelligence officers who in effect supervised party congresses. National elections were held regularly under circumstances that guaranteed overwhelming victories for the military-sponsored *Golkar* party. Candidates in elections were vetted by military intelligence, criticism was permitted of neither the government nor its leaders in election campaigns, and the local bureaucracy, police and military were mobilised behind *Golkar* while the other two parties always pledged themselves to support the re-election of President Soeharto. Finally a substantial minority of seats in legislatures at the national, provincial and local levels was reserved for military representatives.

The government's control extended beyond the parties into civil society. Single corporate organisations were established for labour, peasants, business, youth, journalists and various professions. Critical newspapers or magazines were banned and the others either intimidated or owned by individuals or organisations aligned with the government. All political activity was monitored by the military's security apparatus which from time to time detained dissidents among students, journalists, trade unionists, Muslim leaders and, occasionally, disaffected military officers.

The state, therefore, was strong in the sense that it faced no significant organised political challenge from society. But the regime was also weak in that it was divided between factions, especially military factions, competing for favours from the president. Soeharto's power was partly derived from his ability to keep rival factions in balance so that he never depended excessively on any single group. It was particularly important for Soeharto to ensure that the military was never so completely united that it might pose a challenge to his own authority. Occasionally military factionalism ran out of hand as in 1974, when rivalry between senior officers contributed to the rioting that accompanied the visit to Jakarta of the Japanese Prime Minister. In the late 1980s, Soeharto's appointment of one military officer as vice president led to a breach with another group which continued to control the military and increasingly adopted an independent political position until Soeharto sacked the Minister for Defence and Security in 1993 and then purged his followers during the following years. During the 1980s and 1990s, Soeharto brought civilians into an increasingly complex political balance. By weakening the internal coherence of his regime, Soeharto was able to protect his own personal power.

The competing military and civilian factions within the regime were held together by Soeharto's judicious distribution of patronage opportunities. While the best opportunities were initially reserved for the military élite and their Chinese partners, the expanding economy provided ever-widening opportunities which extended to civilian supporters of the regime in the bureaucracy and the political parties both at the centre and in the regions. In contrast to the pre-New Order era when regional rebellions were commonplace, the Soeharto regime faced no serious challenges from the regions, partly because regional élites were effectively co-opted into the patronage network. Rapid economic growth, stimulated by the rise in oil prices during the 1970s, enabled the government to devote more resources to the official military budget and reduce the military's dependence on what were called 'unconventional' funds with the result that direct military involvement in business declined, but the patrimonial pyramid of patronage continued to hold the system together (see Crouch 1979). By the 1980s and 1990s, the main beneficiaries were no longer military officers but the civilian relatives and cronies of government officials.

The New Order state was, therefore, strong in that it was able to prevent the emergence of significant organised challenges from society. But it was weak in that it was riven by factionalism between competing élite interests which were bound together through the distribution of patronage. The state's power, therefore, rested on a fragile foundation in that its core leadership was dependent on its ability to buy the support of key elements within the regime. As long as the economy continued to grow and provide expanding patronage opportunities, President Soeharto could consolidate political support. But his regime was vulnerable to prolonged economic downturn. While it was not possible for organised opposition to overthrow the state, public disaffection in the form of demonstrations or rioting could precipitate shifts in power within the state.

Society

Although the New Order regime was strong in that it could prevent the emergence of organised opposition, it by no means exercised full control over society. Indonesia is a country of great ethnic and religious diversity. The Javanese (from Central and East Java) are the largest ethnic group making up about 45 per cent of the population, followed by the Sundanese (from West Java) with fourteen per cent. About one-third of the population belongs to a diverse range of ethnic groups from the Outer Islands and three per cent are of Chinese descent. About 87 per cent are classified as Muslim and ten per cent as Christian (both Catholic and Protestant). Although Muslims constitute a large majority, many Javanese identify more closely with traditional Javanese beliefs and practices than with orthodox Islam. In the Outer Islands, on the other hand, Islam is usually practised more strictly.

   One of the biggest challenges facing the Indonesian state is that of maintaining harmony between ethnic and religious communities. Although armed regional movements during the New Order period were confined to provinces with special histories—Irian Jaya, East Timor and Aceh—the memory of the regional rebellions of the 1950s remained strong. Those rebellions won most support in regions where regional interests, ethnic identity and religious affiliation reinforced each other. Religious conflict was always near the surface in the 1950s, when the main cleavage was between political parties which explicitly identified with Islam and those, especially in Java, which supported the concept of the *Pancasila* (Sukarno's five principles of the state). The first principle, 'Belief in One God', avoided the use of explicitly Islamic language and was understood to imply that the state would not be identified exclusively with Islam. The potential for religious conflict was demonstrated in 1965 when Muslim youth organisations were in the forefront of the massacres that eliminated the PKI whose followers were drawn mainly from that part of the Javanese community that had distanced itself from orthodox Islam. Muslim involvement in anti-Chinese rioting has also been common.

   The armed forces are among the strongest supporters of the concept of *Pancasila*. The officer corps is still disproportionately Javanese in composition, many among them being non-orthodox in religious disposition, while a significant number are Christian (see MacFarling 1996:chapter 8).

Even officers who are orthodox in their personal religious practices conform to the military's stance against political Islam. The military ethos has also downplayed ethnic differences and it has been common for non-Javanese officers to hold important command positions. For the military, the acronym SARA—standing for 'ethnic, religious, racial and class conflict'—encapsulates the main threats to national security.

The military had come to power after 1965 in the wake of anti-communist massacres which were sponsored by the military but largely perpetrated by Muslim youth organisations. While the military welcomed Muslim support at that time, they also recognised the challenge that political Islam might pose in the future. The non-orthodox military leaders in Soeharto's circle soon regarded political Islam as the main domestic political threat and pursued a strategy designed to contain Muslim activism. After forcing existing Muslim parties to amalgamate, they permitted the new party to contest elections but ensured that it was led by ultra-moderates who were often financially dependent on the government. The government also established an official council of pro-government Muslim scholars to advise on Islamic issues. The subjugation of political Islam proceeded further in the early 1980s, when the government legislated to compel all organisations to adopt the *Pancasila* as their 'sole fundamental principle'. Muslim organisations protested on the grounds that their sole fundamental principle was derived from the Koran but in the end virtually all backed down—although often with silent reservations. At the same time the military adopted severely repressive measures against Muslims who openly challenged the regime.

Despite the government's success in largely neutralising political Islam at the organisational level, a substantial part of society remained deeply committed to Islamic principles and susceptible to being mobilised by radical leaders. In 1974, for example, the government was forced to withdraw a proposed secular marriage law in the face of widespread Muslim opposition. In the late 1970s and early 1980s, small-scale terrorist attacks by Muslim extremists took place. Muslim frustration was regularly expressed over apparently peripheral, but in fact profoundly symbolic, issues like the timing of school holidays, the dress of Muslim girls at school, or government recognition of traditional Javanese beliefs. In 1984, following a clash at Jakarta's port, Tanjung Priok, when troops, firing on a hostile crowd, killed a large number of Muslim protesters, terrorist attacks were launched against Chinese-owned banks and shopping centres in Jakarta and an attempt was made to blow up part of the ancient Buddhist monument at Borobudur in Central Java. Many Muslim radicals were detained and some received long prison sentences.

In the late 1980s, however, President Soeharto changed his approach to political Islam. The government gave concessions to Islamic education and Islamic courts, an Islamic bank was opened and Soeharto and his family performed the *haj* in Mecca. In 1990, he supported the establishment of a new national Islamic organisation, ICMI (Indonesian

Muslim Intellectuals' Association) headed by his protégé, Dr B.J. Habibie (Hefner 1993). The new association attracted a wide range of Muslim activists, including some former radicals, who believed that the government had abandoned its previous suspicion of political Islam. Leading members of ICMI were appointed to high positions in the bureaucracy and several joined the cabinet in 1993.

Contrasting, but not necessarily contradictory, explanations have been proposed for Soeharto's new Islamic policy (Liddle 1996). Many observers noted a growing religious commitment in Indonesian society since the 1970s. This was often seen as part of a world-wide Islamic revival but it also had domestic roots. Orthodox Muslims, who had previously been under-represented in the upper-middle class, benefited from economic growth and the consequent spread of tertiary educational opportunities which allowed graduates from relatively humble backgrounds to enter the bureaucracy, the professions and business. These Muslims, although orthodox in their religious practices, usually adapted easily to urban middle-class lifestyles and could in no sense be regarded as 'fanatical' or 'extremist' but at the same time they often resented the Javanese aristocratic aura that pervaded the presidential palace and supported moves to give greater prominence to Islamic symbols. The adoption of 'pro-Islamic' policies by the government could therefore be seen as a response to powerful pressures emanating from a changing society.

The government's *rapprochement* with political Islam, however, was not simply a response to pressure from society but also the outcome of factional manœuvring within the regime. By the late 1980s a serious rift had developed between the president and the military leadership, headed by General Benny Moerdani, a Javanese Catholic. Although a protégé of Soeharto's, Moerdani had been alienated by a number of issues including the president's vice-presidential choice in 1988, his promotion of the interests of Dr Habibie, the favourable treatment given to his children in business and his Islamic policy. Moerdani did not launch a direct challenge to Soeharto's authority and Soeharto continued to enjoy the support of many military officers but it seems that Soeharto calculated that moves to win over Muslim support would strengthen his position in the event of a future showdown with the Christian Moerdani. In the end, Soeharto sacked Moerdani in 1993 and appointed officers from Islamic family backgrounds to head the armed forces.

Although the New Order government's strategy to contain and neutralise political Islam had been largely successful, Islamic political sentiment continued to be a factor with which the regime had to reckon. The Islamic revival of the 1970s and 1980s reinforced political Islam as the strongest potential opposition to the military. The state was clearly strong enough to block the rise of an organised Muslim opposition movement challenging the current regime but it was not able to prevent periodic outbursts of Muslim protest, often in the form of rioting directed against the Chinese minority. The government's promotion of a relatively moderate form of

Islam in recent years served both the president's interest in countering a potential challenge from the military leadership and the state's interest in dampening spontaneous Muslim protest from society. The continuing significance of Islam therefore constituted an important societal limitation on the power of an otherwise dominant Indonesian state.

Economy

When the New Order government came to power in 1966 it inherited an economy on the verge of collapse. After the new government issued a statement describing the economic state of the nation, two economists wrote that 'a picture of economic breakdown has been revealed to the Indonesian people and to the world which can have few parallels in a great nation in modern times except in the immediate aftermath of war or revolution' (Panglaykim and Arndt 1966:1). Inflation was running at an annual rate of 600 per cent, foreign exchange reserves were exhausted, food was in short supply, roads, railways and harbours were in disrepair, and per capita income was only US$40. Three decades later after a quarter century of average annual growth of around seven per cent, Indonesia's per capita income exceeded $1000 and it had graduated from the ranks of countries classified by the World Bank as low-income to the lower-middle-income category. Industry's contribution to gross domestic product had risen from nineteen per cent in 1970 to 39 per cent in 1993 while agriculture's contribution declined from 45 per cent to nineteen per cent. In the same period manufactured exports rose from one per cent of total exports to 53 per cent (World Bank 1982, 1995b).

The transformation of the Indonesian economy under the New Order was often attributed to Indonesia's strong state. Free of pressures from society, the military-dominated government had appointed a team of Western-trained academic economists to manage macro-economic policy. They opened the country to foreign investment, liberalised foreign trade and introduced market-oriented programs of deregulation. The reversal of economic strategy was welcomed by the West and Japan which supplied vast amounts of foreign aid. Fortuitously, the price of Indonesia's main export commodity, oil, skyrocketed during the 1970s, providing finance for a heavy-industry program. While the technocrats guided macro-economic policy, the military ensured the maintenance of political stability and freedom from trade union activity.

The technocrats, however, did not exercise full control over the economy. As described above, President Soeharto's political strategy in the early New Order period required the distribution of patronage to influential members of the military establishment who in turn ensured the loyalty of the military and financed Soeharto's political projects. In the early years of the New Order, the national oil corporation, the rice trading agency, the state tin mining corporation and various other state enterprises were headed by generals whose duty was to divert funds to the military and whose activities were exempt from technocratic control. As the economy expanded, influential military leaders were also able to provide lucrative benefits to private enterprises with which they, or their colleagues, were associated. During the 1980s, military officers became less prominent in business but other associates of leading members of the regime quickly took their place, especially the children of high officials, most notably the children of President Soeharto himself.

The technocrats were victims of their own success. The military leaders had turned to them to stabilise the chaotic economic conditions of 1966 and to lay the macro-economic foundations for future growth. But their success in creating conditions attractive to foreign aid donors and foreign private capital in fact reduced their influence. In the early 1970s, however, the mismanagement of several big military-run enterprises—particularly the bankruptcy of the oil corporation and the failure of the rice trading body to maintain food prices—brought on new crises which forced the government to turn again to the technocrats. But the revival of their influence was short-lived due to the extraordinary rise in the price of oil during the rest of the 1970s. Financed by oil money, the government embarked on a program of heavy industrialisation advocated by economic nationalists who resented the influence of the Western-oriented technocrats. Heavy industrialisation also provided enormous opportunities for patronage distribution as foreign corporations paid huge commissions to participate in mega-projects in such fields as steel, petrochemicals, electricity, telecommunications and so on. But the boom did not last. The collapse in the price of oil in the mid-1980s confronted Indonesia with a new economic crisis forcing the president to turn again to the technocrats who introduced a far-reaching program of liberalisation and deregulation aimed at dismantling what was euphemistically termed the 'high-cost economy'. In fact many 'patronage' projects survived—especially those connected to the president's entourage—but the technocrats' policies brought about rapid growth of manufactured exports (MacIntyre 1992; Bresnan 1993:chapter 10).

The authority of the liberal technocrats has been balanced since the 1980s by the growing influence of economic nationalists, often dubbed 'technologists', led by the Minister of Research and Technology, Dr Habibie. A German-trained aeronautical engineer, Habibie persuaded the president to isolate 'strategic' industries from the technocrats' reach. In contrast to the technocrats who emphasised export-oriented labour-intensive industrialisation, Habibie's technologists called for a technological leap into 'hitech' activities. At enormous cost Habibie established heavily-protected aircraft-construction, ship-building and other capital-intensive industries (see Shiraishi 1996).

The influence of the technocrats was also limited when their policies conflicted with the interests of palace-connected business groups. In 1993, five of the top ten indigenous tax-payers were either children or close relatives of the president while most top Chinese taxpayers had business ties with the president's family. The president's son, Bambang, headed a huge conglomerate with interests ranging from petrochemicals and satellite communications to a citrus fruit monopoly; another son, Hutomo, was awarded, among many other perquisites, a clove monopoly and the national car project; Soeharto's daughter, Siti Hardiyanti, dominated toll-road construction. The president's Chinese cronies, including Liem Sioe Liong, Bob Hasan and Prayogo Pangestu, also controlled enormous business empires based on special access to government favours.[7]

The Indonesian economy was riddled with what Indonesian critics called 'collusion, corruption and nepotism' when the Asian financial crisis struck in mid-1997. After the exchange rate for the rupiah against the US dollar had fallen from Rp2450 at the beginning of July to Rp3800 in October, the government was forced to turn to the IMF for assistance. Although the government agreed to abandon or postpone some high-cost infrastructural projects, it refused to withdraw support for the aircraft and national car projects, headed by Dr Habibie and the president's son respectively. As part of the IMF-imposed reforms, sixteen bankrupt banks were liquidated but one, owned by the president's son, Bambang, re-opened shortly afterwards under a new name. Later, several big infrastructure projects associated with presidential children and cronies were quietly exempted from the cut-backs. It was only when the rupiah had dropped to Rp10 000 in January 1998 that Soeharto agreed in another deal with the IMF to withdraw state support for family and crony-linked projects, including the aircraft and national-car projects, and to abandon various giant infrastructure projects awarded to family and other politically influential business groups. At the same time, major monopolies controlled by family and crony enterprises were withdrawn on IMF insistence.

Economic policy making during the New Order had been the product of a three-way struggle between liberal technocrats, economic nationalists and beneficiaries of the patronage pyramid with the nationalists often aligned with the patronage network. Soeharto usually heeded the advice of his technocrats whenever the economy's condition became critical but favoured the economic nationalists and technologists when funds have been available. At all times, however, Soeharto has been alert to the needs of the patronage network on which his own political power ultimately depends. It was only after the 1997 financial crisis had virtually bankrupted Indonesia that Soeharto finally agreed to measures demanded by the IMF and long advocated by his technocrats.

The Indonesian government's reluctance to take effective measures to deal with the 1997–98 economic crisis was not due to any weakness *vis-à-vis* society. It was not strong forces in society which obstructed the implementation of necessary reforms. On the contrary, the government's

---

7 On the Soeharto family, see Schwarz (1994:chapter 6); on Chinese business see Schwarz (1994:chapter 5) and Robison (1986:chapter 9).

weakness in dealing with the economic crisis must be attributed to the influence of strong elements within the strong state itself.[8]

The Weaknesses of a Strong State

The New Order state had many of the characteristics of a strong state. The regime successfully co-opted, neutralised or repressed all potential political threats for more than 30 years. It reversed the economic strategy of the previous regime and embarked on its own strategy which, by 1997, had transformed a poor, backward, and stagnant agrarian economy to one which was growing rapidly and industrialising. And faced with an ethnically diverse society with a history of regional revolts and religious tensions, it succeeded in holding the nation together while countering the threat posed by political Islam.

But the New Order state also exhibited some of the characteristics which Migdal associates with weak states, including the 'Politics of Survival'. Migdal points to the danger for a leader if he relies too heavily on single institutions, such as the army, which might eventually turn against him. In Egypt, for example, Nasser created his own political party to balance the power of the military. Migdal notes how leaders resort to the 'big shuffle' by regularly reshuffling leadership positions to prevent the emergence of alternative leaders although this is 'a mechanism of deliberately weakening arms of the state and allied organisations in order to assure the tenure of the top state leadership'. They also make non-merit appointments 'based on personal loyalty, cooptation, ethnic bargaining, and other nonmerit criteria [which] have limited the ability of states to make the binding rules of the society'; and they have practised 'dirty tricks' including 'illegal methods or quick changes of the law to remove key state figures, preempting the emergence of competing power centers, and weakening or destroying groups in agencies already powerful enough to threaten the rulers' prerogatives'. Dirty tricks sometimes involve illegal imprisonment, torture and death squads. Resort to these practices means 'attacks on the state's explicit or implicit rules of the game, its legal code and established modus operandi, by the leaders of the state themselves' (Migdal 1988:217, 222–4).

Much of this will be familiar to observers of Indonesian politics. Like Nasser, Soeharto came to power with the support of the military but eventually strengthened or created institutions which helped to balance the military's power—such as the bureaucracy, the government party *Golkar*,

---

8   In a study limited to financial policy in Indonesia, MacIntyre (1993:161) comes to a similar conclusion: 'Patrimonial imperatives and sheer bureaucratic incapacity have been the principal stumbling blocks. In short, the obstacles to decisive state action have not been the countervailing actions of societal groups but have been in the nature of the state itself.'

and more recently ICMI. Initially dependent on the military, Soeharto displayed exceptional skills in maintaining balance between rival military factions so that he was never wholly beholden to anyone. In particular, he consolidated his power by distributing patronage which was used to reward loyal friends and buy over potentially hostile enemies. 'Big shuffles' and surprise appointments were always a feature of his rule both within the military and in his cabinet while many such appointments could hardly have been primarily based on merit criteria (although he selected outstandingly talented technocratic economic policy makers). Soeharto's closest political advisors—often with military intelligence backgrounds—were no doubt appointed primarily because of their personal loyalty but they were also consummate practitioners of 'dirty tricks'. Many regime opponents were detained, some for many years, while others were ensnared in the patronage network.

Migdal asks 'Why have so many of these states failed to get their populations to do as state leaders legislate and decree...?' (1988:xiv). His answer is that states are confronted by strong societies in which local strongmen can frustrate the implementation of policies proposed by state leaders. He argues that 'The strong bargaining position and the capture of tentacles of the state by urban and rural caciques, or any other such strongmen, have made the outlook for widespread political mobilization by state leaders in these societies even more remote' (1988:269). Thus, 'Reshaping society...is way beyond the capabilities of many third-world states' (1987:430). In the Indonesian case, however, the weaknesses of the state are not primarily a consequence of its confrontation with a strong society. When social groups have attempted to prevent the implementation of state policies, it has usually been the social groups rather than the state that have given way.[9] The origins of the weaknesses of the Indonesian state have to be sought in the nature of the state itself, not in the strengths of society.

In a more recent study, Migdal reminds us that states are not homogeneous entities. He urges us 'to break down the undifferentiated concept of the state—and also of society—to understand how different elements in each pull in different directions, leading to unanticipated patterns of domination and transformation' (1994:8). He argues that: 'Different responses from within the state mean that we cannot simply assume that as a whole it acts in a rational and coherent fashion, or strategically follows a defined set of interests' (1994:9). As we have seen, Indonesian political history provides examples of regimes in which different elements pull in different directions. Like sultans in the patrimonial states of pre-colonial Java who retained power by maintaining a balance between competing

---

9   At one point Migdal refers to the capacity of local strongmen to obstruct 'the social justice state leaders would like' (1987:401). In Indonesia the problem has often been the inability of local strongmen to obstruct policies that caused social injustice.

aristocratic families, both Sukarno and Soeharto presided over regimes in which the component parts were rivals rather than partners and were held together by the careful balancing of positions and perquisites (Anderson 1990:chapter 1). Under the New Order the president maintained a balance between competing military factions, technocratic economists, techno-logical nationalists, Muslims and various state-linked business interests.

In conceptualising the Indonesian state and distinguishing it from society, a purely formal–legal approach is inadequate. It is not sufficient to regard the holders of political and bureaucratic offices as repre-sentatives of the state while classifying non-office holders as part of society. Certainly the ministers, senior bureaucrats and military and police officers must be regarded as key leaders of the state but the failure to include key 'private' individuals, groups or organisations outside the formal–legal state can lead to confusion when analysing state weaknesses. From one perspective the state appears to be weak when dealing with business people who, like Migdal's local strongmen, are able to ignore the state's rules and regulations whenever their interests are involved. But these business people are not members of a developed bourgeoisie resisting the impositions of the state. On the contrary, they are dependent clients (including sons and daughters) of those who hold formal positions in state institutions. Their interests are identical with those of their patrons with whom they share their profits.

The 'weak' characteristics of Indonesia's apparently 'strong' state are derived from its own nature. The various components of Soeharto's New Order state, like Sukarno's Guided Democracy before it, were not held together so much by a common goal of 'reshaping society'—although they each had their own visions of the future—but more by the patrimonial distribution of patronage. This is not to claim, of course, that all members of the Indonesian élite were motivated purely by the pursuit of material gains. It is to argue, however, that Soeharto's skilful management of the patronage network laid the foundations for his regime and was a major part of the explanation of its longevity.

This patronage pyramid also constituted a huge obstacle to reform, as was demonstrated when the Asian financial crisis hit in mid-1997. For several months the government seemed paralysed as the rupiah continued its sharp fall. The IMF-backed efforts of the Indonesian technocrats to implement reforms necessary to re-establish international confidence in the rupiah were resisted by the president whose priority was the main-tenance of the patronage network on which his regime was based. It was only when the value of an already severely weakened rupiah dropped by more than half in one week in January 1998 and threatened to continue its downward spiral that Soeharto reluctantly agreed to the IMF's conditions which promised to eliminate most of the special favours awarded to family and cronies. Economic reform was in effect imposed by external pressures.

Strengthening a Weak Society

If one takes the view, following Migdal, that the main obstacle to reform is the combination of a strong society and a weak state, the remedy is obviously to strengthen the state and weaken the society. But if the main obstacle lies within the state itself, further strengthening of the existing state would only exacerbate the problem. On the other hand, the weakening of the state and the strengthening of society might simply return Indonesia to the circumstances envisaged by Migdal and actually experienced by Indonesia before 1965.

The solution seems to lie in strengthening reform-minded elements in the state at the expense of anti-reform elements. But why should the opponents of reform give way to its advocates? In recent attempts by political scientists to explain political change, there is a tendency to stress the importance of visionary leadership and élite-level negotiations (O'Donnell and Schmitter 1986; Di Palma 1990). While leadership and negotiations are indeed important, we should not neglect pressures emanating from changing societies.

As discussed above, some of the most influential societal forces in Indonesia have been linked to Islam but political Islam has appeared in many guises. At one level, political Islam has expressed itself in disruptive ways. During 1996–97, for example, several riots took place in small towns in Java and elsewhere in which Chinese shops, Buddhist temples and Christian churches were destroyed by youths claiming to act in the name of Islam. On the other hand, Muslim organisations seem to have the greatest potential for mobilising popular opinion on political issues. While such issues sometimes focus on specifically Islamic concerns like gambling or perceived 'insults to Islam', Muslim organisations have also been in the forefront in calling for limitations on the power of the armed forces and criticising the corrupt links between government officials and big business. A strengthened moderate version of political Islam could, therefore, give societal support to reform-minded elements within the regime.

The growth of the middle class, as a result of Indonesia's rapid economic growth, is another societal factor which could add to the pressure for reform (see Tanter and Young, eds 1990). It has often been argued that members of the various strata subsumed under the broad middle-class category tend to want government that is more accessible, efficient, transparent and honest. Members of the middle class want higher standards of government administration not because their own ethical standards are necessarily higher than those of the rest of the population but because, as citizens having regular contact with government agencies, they stand to gain most from better administration. Further, members of the middle class are relatively well educated and urban with better access to the mass media and political gossip which means that they are usually more aware of corruption and other abuses perpetrated by government officials. And relatively well-off members of the middle class who feel directly disadvantaged by maladministration are more likely than less well-off classes to have the self-confidence to protest. The Indonesian middle class is still relatively small but it has grown significantly in recent years. Although middle-class expansion is likely to slow as a result of economic conditions following the 1997 crisis, in the long run it can be expected that middle-class pressure in favour of reform will provide reform-minded government leaders with stronger bases of support in society.

A major societal limitation on pressure for reform, however, lies in the nature of Indonesia's business class (see Robison 1986:Part III). Domestic big business continues to be dominated by Indonesian–Chinese business-people. In contrast to a rising bourgeoisie in ethnically homogeneous societies which is often able to mobilise political support from the rest of society, Indonesia's Chinese are effectively disqualified by their ethnicity from playing a leadership role in politics. As members of a small and unpopular minority, Chinese businesspeople have often felt insecure and have therefore turned to the indigenous political élite for protection. All major Chinese business groups have links with individuals in the military, bureaucratic and political élite, as described above. Chinese business-people therefore prefer to deal in an individual and informal way with government officials rather than attempt to apply collective pressure. The other component of the Indonesian business élite consists of the indige-nous partners of the Chinese. All but a few of the indigenous business élite have attained their business positions through their political connections rather than as independent entrepreneurs. Although there were some signs during the 1980s of some business groups attempting to influence government policy, the structure of domestic business makes it unlikely that it will become a major force for reform (see MacIntyre 1990). Instead, closely integrated with the state, it is likely to remain a major obstacle.

Conclusion

Soeharto's New Order state was undoubtedly much stronger than previous forms of the Indonesian state. The Soeharto regime established itself in an orgy of violence and continued to rely on coercion to prevent the emergence of political challenges. But it also brought about an economic transformation which benefited many sections of Indonesian society. After thirty years in power, the regime seemed impregnable and was often identified as a strong state.[10]

Despite its apparent strength, Soeharto's regime exhibited many of the characteristics identified by Migdal as those of a weak state. Although

---

10 Although Soeharto was forced to resign on 21 May 1998 following massive rioting in Jakarta, he was succeeded not by leaders of the organised opposition to his regime but by his vice president, Dr Habibie.

clearly dominating society, its power was not entirely without limits. In some respects its strength was limited by entrenched elements in society, especially those associated with Islam. But while the government was sometimes forced to take such social pressures into account, its grip on power was never seriously challenged by them. The most important weaknesses of the Indonesian state were not a result of the state being weak *vis-à-vis* society but were derived largely from its own internal structure. Riven by factional rivalries and bound together by patronage distribution, the government's capacity to deal with economic crisis was limited by Soeharto's need to maintain his patronage network intact. The state's weakness in this respect was demonstrated dramatically by its inability to take appropriate measures to deal with the Asian financial crisis in 1997. It was only when the economy faced virtual bankruptcy at the beginning of 1998 that it finally adopted measures in effect imposed on it by the IMF. But these measures were not enough to save Soeharto. Whether his state will survive remains to be seen.

7 Confucius in Singapore: Culture, Politics, and the PAP State

STEPHANIE LAWSON

Among the important factors in comparative and international political studies that are now linked to the strength, weakness or capacity of the state is 'culture'. While this concept has often been invoked as an explanatory variable, at least implicitly, in many kinds of political studies for at least the last 100 years, it has achieved much more prominence in the post-Cold War era. For example, it has become the principal theme, if not the overriding theme, in the current 'Asian values' debate. Assisted by some semi-scholarly prognostications about looming 'civilisational clashes', the culture concept is now the favoured trope employed by many contemporary state élites, especially in the Southeast Asian sub-region, in justifying certain political arrangements. Top-level political leaders such as Goh Chok Tong of Singapore and Dr Mahathir of Malaysia have found that it has multi-purpose political uses, ranging from culturally oriented conceptions of regionalism to culturally justified forms of political and social control within the state. And in the economic sphere, a generic brand of neo-Confucianism has been promoted by any number of political leaders, bureaucrats, business people, academics, journalists and others as the prime explanatory factor in East Asian economic success stories.[1]

The discussion of culture and politics in this chapter is relevant to all the spheres of debate and activity outlined above. More specifically, however, the chapter is concerned with a number of important issues in democratic theory and practice, especially as these relate to contemporary discussions about the role of culture in national state–society relations as

---

1   At the time of writing, however, a number of East Asian economies were experiencing currency and stock market crises. It is certainly doubtful whether 'cultural factors' will be deployed to explain this.

well as in international relations. The empirical focus is on some of the cultural dimensions of state authority in Singapore, paying particular attention to the role of Confucianism.[2] The discussion, however, is not a contribution to culturalist approaches to the analysis of states, state authority and state–society relations in the usual sense. Rather, my aim is to focus critically on the ideological uses of the culture concept itself as it is expressed in neo-Confucian terms and, by so doing, show that the utility of the concept as a major explanatory category in political studies cannot be taken at face value.

The discussion that follows sets out a broad critique of culturalist assumptions by elucidating some significant problems with the application of culture in political analysis. I begin with the 'return' of culture in the post-Cold War era and a preliminary critique of its analytic value, especially in relation to states like Singapore and the People's Action Party (PAP) government's project of constructing an 'Asian' model of democracy in which society is clearly subordinated to the state. I then consider some key issues in democratic theory and practice, including certain institutional factors. These include the role of political opposition in a democratic political system. Since political opposition in Singapore is permitted very little scope by the PAP government, and because Confucian ideas that deal with harmony and cohesion have often been used to justify this, a section on the role of political opposition in classic Confucian thought is included. This is interesting because although contemporary politicised versions of neo-Confucianism permit virtually no space for legitimate political opposition, classic Confucianism does in fact provide some scope. This illustrates, among other things, that there may be any number of ambiguities and contradictions in culturally oriented analyses if one looks carefully enough at the cultural tradition in question.

The penultimate section comprises a brief case study of how the PAP government has used a diffuse neo-Confucian ideology to deny legitimacy to political opposition.[3] Arguably, the almost obsessive denunciation of political opposition in Singapore betrays a certain weakness in the PAP government, and perhaps in the state itself, at least insofar as the PAP sees itself as the state and therefore regards challenges to itself as challenges to the very foundations of the state itself. This also has some important and obvious implications for democratic theory and practice, especially in terms of the extent to which the institutions of the state can reflect local cultural values and practices while still remaining 'essentially' democratic.

---

2 Contemporary studies, or uses, of Confucian philosophy are often called 'neo-Confucianist' by those who want to maintain a distinction between the study of classical Confucianism and some of its contemporary programmatic or ideological uses.

3 The discussion of Confucianism, its application in Singapore, and the implications for democratic theory and practice in this paper draw substantially on a previously published article (Lawson 1993b).

The Return of Culture

There is little doubt that the idea of culture has undergone a significant revitalisation in the post-Cold War era as an aid to the analysis of a range of social, political and economic phenomena, not only in comparative political studies but in international relations as well (see Lapid and Kratochwil, eds 1996). While some have viewed this development with scepticism, others have taken it so seriously as to posit cultural (or civilisational) difference as the 'central and most dangerous dimension of the emerging global politics' (Huntington 1996:13). Although many leading voices in the 'Asian values' debate would not necessarily endorse such alarmist and exaggerated views, their support of culture as a key foundational concept around which politics, economy and society revolves is just as deterministic. Similarly, questions such as 'what sort of structures and cultures facilitate obedience'[4] seem to assume in advance that culture is a decisive factor in determining political behaviour and attitudes.

One obvious effect of the new-found enthusiasm for culture has been to link the concept to almost every type of political, economic or social theory going around. In a critical review of some recent literature, Mazarr identifies several models which seek to establish such links. These include a model which holds that: 'Culture plays a critical role in determining the economic fates of nations, peoples and individuals because some cultures underwrite success better than others.' And another which assumes that: 'Culture serves as the dominant blueprint for social, economic and military structures and institutions, thus exercising a strong influence on the behaviour and prospects of nation-states in the world community' (Mazarr 1996:179, 181). If culture has indeed been the 'poor relation' of other explanations for the behaviour of states, such as structural approaches, then it certainly seems that its time has come (see Archer 1985 quoted in Migdal 1997:212).

Another important area of theorising that has been influenced by the culturalist trend is democratic theory. The word 'democracy', of course, names the apparently most desirable of all forms of government in the contemporary era. Since at least the end of World War II, there has scarcely been a government anywhere in the world whose leaders would call it anything other than democratic. This has led to the idea that democracy is an 'essentially contested concept' and cannot be pinned down to any one meaning (see Gallie 1956). In the post-Cold War era, the extent to which the concepts of both 'culture' and 'democracy' are entwined in political debates, or more especially harnessed to political causes, has become much more common.

During the Cold War, contestation over the 'meaning' of democracy was driven largely by ideological considerations revolving around the

---

4   Joel Migdal cites this question as being a central concern for comparative political science throughout the twentieth century (1997:208).

communist–liberal democratic polarities. It has been suggested that the dominance of ideological or doctrinal constructions of meaning tended to suppress alternative bases for formulations—most notably those involving the concept of culture (see Alston 1994:especially 5–6). On many occasions, however, cultural arguments would also be deployed in tandem with preferred ideological positions. The leaders of many one-party states in Africa during the Cold War era, for example, in addition to adopting a strong ideological position, frequently invoked the idea that one-partyism was a natural expression of authentic African cultural values, and democratic in its own unique way (Lawson 1993a). Arguments of this kind now also feature prominently in conservative élite discourses about democracy and human rights in Southeast Asia, as well as in the last remaining communist mega-state, China. These discourses are referred to collectively as the so-called 'Asian values' debate.[5]

The use of the geographical qualifier 'Asian' raises another important point. As I have argued elsewhere, broad statements of value, and the accompanying models of democracy that are often put forward by authoritarian state élites, do not simply reflect the usual range of concerns about sovereignty, national identity and domestic order versus external pressures and interference in the internal affairs of the state. In the Asian values debate, and others like it, the level of the state has been transcended, at least rhetorically, and a much broader site has been staked out by its proponents on a regional or civilisational scale—and this accords well with Huntington's general 'clash of civilizations' thesis. In terms of political models, the idea of 'Asian values' has also given rise to a number of culturally-derived, as well as geographically-oriented, qualifiers now attached to 'democracy' (Lawson 1995:7).

This is clearly evident in such projects as the construction and promotion of 'Asian democracy' which may be called a 'geocultural' model insofar as it purports to represent a broad geographical region in possession of certain unique cultural characteristics. This is despite the fact that the proponents of 'Asian democracy' are restricted largely to Southeast Asia—especially Singapore, Indonesia and Malaysia. As we shall see shortly, Singaporean élites, in particular, have attempted to project an image of their country as embodying the essence of 'Asianness' as well as being 'Asia's ideological champion' (Mortimer quoted in Ang and Stratton 1995:66). At a broader level, however, we look first at the context within which debates about culture and democracy have taken place in the post-Cold War era, as well as at some important definitional aspects of democracy itself.

---

5   There is now a huge (and ever-growing) literature on this topic. For an excellent overview and review of some of the most important contributions to this literature, see Dupont (1996).

Culture and Democracy

The practice of attaching qualifiers to 'democracy' is not new, and terms such as 'social democracy' and 'liberal democracy', not to mention 'organic democracy', 'guided democracy', 'presidential democracy' and 'selective democracy' are familiar enough. Such formulations were sometimes bolstered by reference to cultural values, but by and large they were more closely linked with other ideological positions. The latter embodied values which were usually regarded as good in terms of an assumed or hoped-for political and economic outcome rather than good by virtue of an explicit link to cultural authenticity. The geocultural model discussed here, however, while also justified at times by reference to economic development issues and imperatives, reflects a much more concerted effort to deploy the concept of culture as a basis for political legitimation and authentication in broader debates about democracy and democratisation, especially *vis-à-vis* Western models. It is important to note, then, that in addition to the regional orientation assumed by a geocultural model, a firm cultural border has been drawn most particularly between the 'West' and 'Asia'. This exercise reflects many of the features characteristic of Edward Said's classic formulation of 'Orientalism' (1978), but now in the inverted form of 'Occidentalism' (Lawson 1995:7; 1996).

These issues raise a number of questions about the procedural and substantive aspects of democratic politics and government. First, there is the question of how flexible the principles of democracy can be in practice and to what extent the institutionalisation of democracy can be adapted to fit particular circumstances. In turn, this prompts wider concerns about the cultural frameworks within which moral values are assumed to be embedded. Ethical relativism is an issue too, for democratic theory embodies an ethical view of political rule and, in its Western manifestations (both liberal and social), a strong normative and universalist orientation towards its implementation. These questions are of special importance when we consider the extent to which Western proponents of world-wide democratisation, or 'democratic enlargement', may simply be suffering from an overdose of ethnocentrism in their efforts to convert the entire world to their way of thinking.[6] For this may be interpreted as a form of epistemological imperialism resting on assumptions about the innate inferiority of alternative modes of political organisation and therefore carrying with it strong overtones of Western cultural superiority.[7]

Another set of issues, which is of more immediate definitional concern, arises from debates over the necessary and sufficient conditions for the practice of democratic politics, and we turn to these next. Here I argue

---

6   For a critical discussion of 'democratic enlargement' in the context of both 'democratic peace' studies and the 'Asian values' debate, see Tanji and Lawson (1997).

7   All these issues are dealt with in much greater detail in Lawson (1998).

that the almost universal rhetorical endorsement of democracy as the most desirable style of government has resulted not so much in the spread of actual democratic practices as it has in the conceptual stretching of the term so as to encompass an enormous variety of regimes, many of which are democratic in name only and which actively repudiate some of the most basic tenets of democratic theory and practice. This extends to countries, such as Singapore, whose governments operate under a constitution, where there is civilian supremacy over the military, where regular elections are held to return members of the legislature and the executive, and where there is widespread participation in such elections. These are some of the trappings of democratic politics, and must certainly be considered as necessary conditions, but they are hardly sufficient to establish Singapore as a substantively democratic polity.

The Conditions for Democracy

An important task for anyone attempting to confront issues of democracy and democratisation—beyond mere critique of authoritarian practices—is in establishing what features must be sustained in actual practice before a polity can claim reasonable approximation to the principles of democratic rule. Among the most commonly accepted primary institutional and procedural features are those associated with constitutionalism and the rule of law. In turn, these are underscored by an elected legislature and executive (as well as a separate, independent judiciary), supported by an electoral system which provides as nearly as possible for equality of voting power for every individual and which operates free from undue interference. These are usually accepted as the basic pre-requisites of contemporary representative democracies in mass polities. But of course it takes more to make a democracy than institutional structures, and for this reason they can only ever be described as necessary—and not sufficient—conditions for democratic government.

Implicit in these structures is the idea of mass participation in the political process, not just for show but as the ultimate arbiter of government rule and public policy. Contemporary revisionists might argue that democracy in these terms means little more than a competition between élites for the support of a majority of the mass.[8] But this view, if taken at face value, understates the extent to which these élites are in fact accountable for their conduct and are subject to the periodic judgement of the people. At the same time it must be acknowledged that opportunities for political participation do not automatically ensure a high level of such participation—nor do they necessarily ensure that government accountability is complete or even adequate. What can be said is that a measure of

---

8   And as Davis observes, the many departures of classical theory from reality have been pointed out in detail (1970:215).

procedural accountability is attained under democratic electoral practices, and that this constitutes one of the necessary (but by no means sufficient) conditions for the practice of democratic politics in mass polities.

This whole process rests on another necessary condition, and that is the presence of a constitutionally protected political opposition that is capable of providing an alternative government. This is one of the strongest enabling factors for the exercise of mass judgement. For without an alternative government, it is scarcely possible for the mass to judge, and to reject, an existing government. This simple fact is perhaps so obvious that it has escaped serious sustained analysis by many democratic theorists. Yet it is vital not only to the basis of theorising about democracy, but also to our understanding of some of the major obstacles to democratisation in places like Singapore. We shall therefore consider in more detail some of the relevant components of democratic theory that underscore the importance of constitutional political opposition.[9]

There are several strands of thought which together comprise the basis for justifying a form of constitutionally protected political opposition in contemporary mass polities. One of these derives from the notion that democratic systems award political power to governments on both a conditional and a temporary basis. The conditional element means that no government has the authority—moral or otherwise—to engage in *ultra vires* acts. Its powers are strictly limited by the doctrine of constitutionalism and in this sense it wields only conditional, qualified power—never absolute power. A democratic government is further constrained by the fact of its temporary tenure—it must always be subject to the periodic judgement of the people who may collectively choose to reject it in favour of some other contender for power. It is never the case, then, that governments enjoy permanent tenure in office. They must be prepared to give way to an alternative government (that is, to a political opposition) after a given period—if the people so decide. These are among the mechanisms that operate to protect the polity from exclusive claims to power and hence from authoritarian rule.

Another strand of democratic theory recognises not only the fact of the diversity of interests within any given society, and that these cannot be catered for adequately in a system which allows for the expression of only one set of interests, but also the intrinsic value of such diversity insofar as it provides the basis for wide-ranging critical public debate on political issues. This strand of thought has obviously been prominent within the Western liberal tradition. The same tradition, however, also has its less attractive aspects. These include an excessive emphasis on individualism

---

9   Discussion in this chapter is limited to constitutional oppositions for reasons of space. There are of course many other types of political opposition, both organised and informal, that play an important role in democratic politics. For further discussion see, especially, Rodan, ed. (1996); and for more detailed theorisation of constitutional political opposition, see Lawson (1993a).

at the expense of community-oriented perspectives on the one hand, and the *laissez-faire* economics of capitalist, free market ideology, which operates to the detriment of distributive justice, on the other (neither of which I have any desire to defend).

But these considerations should not obscure the point that without the freedom to organise political opposition against a government, and to have guarantees for the protection of opposition from persecution and, most important of all, to have constitutional provision for its possible succession to government if so chosen by an electorate, there is no sense in which a viable basis for the conduct of democratic politics in mass polities can be said to exist. In summary, the view taken here is that although democracy may encompass a plurality of forms and practices, reflecting a range of cultural and other values, it cannot mean everything and anything to all people—especially those in control of the apparatus of states which deny basic political rights to their citizens. These rights include the right of organised political oppositions to operate freely, and to replace political rulers through non-violent, constitutional means. This of course requires that political opposition is regarded—by both rulers and ruled—as legitimate. As foreshadowed earlier, the issue of the legitimacy of political opposition in Singapore has often been linked to discussions of cultural values—especially Confucian values. We shall therefore next consider some of the implications of Confucian thought for oppositional politics.

Oppositional Politics and Confucian Thought

Much has been written about the political salience of cultural values in the East Asian 'Confucian cultural area' which is generally taken to include China, Taiwan, the two Koreas, Vietnam, and Japan. In this area there is said to be little tolerance—at least amongst ruling elements—for the style of competitive politics usually associated with Western systems of government and opposition, and this is often related explicitly to the residues of Confucianism, even though it is acknowledged that its 'consummatory value system' no longer functions as an explicit social or political ideology (Moody 1988:1). A commonly-held view of the East Asian 'Confucian value system' has been that legitimate authority is essentially paternalistic as well as personal, and that this is widely accepted as a value by virtually all sectors of society. This kind of authority, it is argued, is not compatible with overt political criticism or oppositional activity. These practices are believed to be detrimental to social order and therefore should not be tolerated. Moreover, obedience to political authority, which is said to derive from values supporting the observance of roles and duties within the family, reinforced by filial respect for paternal authority, is said to make many confrontational

Western political practices unattractive—even abhorrent (see Pye 1985: 329–34; Bell 1995).

The apparent antipathy to oppositional politics in Confucian thought is related primarily to the idea that the political and social realms are essentially coterminous and that harmony, which is the basic principle for the right ordering of these realms depends ultimately on each and every individual acting correctly in an assigned role. These ideas fit the organic conception of the state implicit in Confucian thought, and underpin an uncompromisingly moralistic view of political power and the idea of rule by moral example. Conceived in this way, legitimate political power cannot be obtained through competition. Rather, it is bestowed on those individuals with the requisite status in accordance with the fundamental principles of a static, passive, paternalistic, and hierarchical order (see Pye 1985:41–3).

It has been argued that the Confucian view of power, and the general view of government that derives from it, renders the notion of compromise morally repugnant; that the belief in the superiority and duty of the educated man to lead undercuts ideas about the legitimacy of popular interests; and that the generally collectivist and organic conception of the state is much less favourable to action by individual citizens, especially with respect to the assertion of rights and interests (Cotton 1991a:320). Further, the primacy given in the Confucian approach to tradition—the 'Way of the Ancients' (Fingarette 1972:62) and the 'visions of the past' is such that individuals who dare challenge it are seen as exhibiting nothing but a 'self-serving effrontery in the face of the legitimate continuities of a received tradition' (Hall and Ames 1987:23). The stress on harmony in Confucian thought is also said to make the act of criticising those who hold political power anathema, since criticism is viewed as an act of disloyalty which threatens the integrity of the state and brings disorder and confusion. And since consensus is valued so highly as the basis of the political system, there is little room for the idea of legitimate conflict (Tamney 1991:402–3). This approach to power, politics, and government certainly seems antithetic to the give-and-take of competitive politics, as well as to the idea that people within a society or political community have different values and interests and are entitled to a political means of expressing them (Pye 1985:42).

Those familiar with the history of ideas in the West would have little difficulty in seeing the parallels between many elements of Confucian ideas about political power and those of classic conservative philosophy. Moreover, the traditional values of pre-modern Europe, which were also highly moralistic, were not markedly different from Confucian values, and European feudalism was certainly as personalistic in terms of relationships as anything in Confucian society (Moody 1988:10). This is supported, in part, by Tu's challenge to the assumption that Confucianism is inherently incompatible with modernity. He points out that the contrasts are not only overdrawn in many cases, but that closer inspection of the West's own complex experience shows the considerable strength of conservative (and anti-modernist) tendencies in the role of tradition in countries like Great Britain. He does, however, endorse the general idea of incommensurability between Confucian and Enlightenment values, arguing that 'the form of life characterised by Confucian ethics is significantly different from the distinctively modern Western Enlightenment mentality' (Tu 1989:95).

There is no doubting the many contradictions between important aspects of Confucian thought on the one hand, and the characteristic principles of contemporary democratic politics on the other, especially with respect to the idea of a legitimate, 'loyal', political opposition vying for political power, and acting as a permanent critic of government. But to claim that societies with a Confucian legacy are therefore incapable of developing a capacity for tolerance of any form of oppositional politics is to ignore not only key historical experiences of the West, as is evident in both evolutionary and revolutionary movements from autocratic to democratic forms, but some aspects of the Confucian tradition itself which, like most complex, long-standing traditions, contains any number of ambiguities. Classical Confucian thought may not appear to provide much scope for the kind of oppositional politics practised in contemporary democracies, but there are elements of the tradition which assign a valid place to criticism and which modify the idea that the 'mandate of heaven' is completely unassailable from below.

Many writers point out that the Confucian ruler could be criticised for behaving in an immoral fashion (although there was no moral justification for pursuing one's own interests against the ruler). Criticism, therefore, could be based on moral concerns even if it could not legitimately be *political* (Moody 1988:3). For example, the Confucian philosopher Hsun Tzu argues that although the enforcement of laws and morals usually requires unquestioning obedience, there are occasions on which such enforcement should be critically questioned and even resisted. 'In the case of a morally responsible minister, where the ruler has departed from *tao* [the way], it is quite proper for the minister to follow *tao* rather than his ruler' (cited in Cua 1985:64). In discussing the nature of power relationships between ruler–subject, father–son, husband–wife, and so forth, Tu also points out that the reciprocal nature of these relationships enjoins the stronger party to use power only in a morally informed fashion.

> The ruler must be righteous to enable the subject to be obedient. If the ruler is not righteous, the minister can offer criticism. If the ruler is dogmatic and authoritarian, the subject can revolt and choose a better one. The Book of Mencius considers revolution to be the right of the people (Tu 1984:24).

Similarly, Huang stresses that the practical and conceptual separation of political rulers and cultural élites from early Confucian times gave rise to a theoretical justification of the role of Confucian scholars in opposing political authorities as circumstances required (Huang 1987:1).[10] Glassman also points out that in the period of Confucian-Mandarin China, the emperor was held accountable for such matters as crop failure and outbreaks of banditry, and that criticism could be sought from court officials as well as lesser literati and peasants. On some occasions, the emperor was actually removed from office 'when deemed incompetent to overcome the problems besetting the nation' (Glassman 1991:197–8). Nonetheless, criticism had to be 'very carefully couched in a style of flattery and self-effacing caution', and petitioners were sometimes jailed, tortured, or executed at the 'whim or rage of the emperor'. But in many cases it seems that petitioners were honoured for bringing pressing problems to the attention of an otherwise insulated imperial court (1991:197–8). This does not mean, however, that there is an underlying liberal tradition in classical Confucian thought, for it clearly lacked such essential liberal notions as individual and human rights (Cotton 1991a: 320).[11] Most importantly, there was no institutional protection for critics (Moody 1988:3).

The main point is that the idea of legitimate criticism has some basis even in the body of thought which is held to be inimical to modern democratic practices and which is often regarded as a major impediment to democratisation. And as Friedman has pointed out, 'had China democratized before Europe, historians would have found that China's cultural heritage was uniquely democratic' (1994:27). None of this means that the task of institutionalising democratic opposition is a simple matter, nor that it is made easier merely by identifying one compatible aspect of a tradition which seems otherwise hostile to democratic precepts. Nonetheless, the political experience of Japan, South Korea and Taiwan suggests that the dynamics of political power and authority are not cast in a permanent cultural mould. Political ideas and political behaviour obviously do change— as do whole societies over time.

But even if Confucianism did constitute a rigid, unchanging tradition making it almost impossible for more liberal practices to gain widespread legitimacy, it is another thing to call Singapore a 'Confucian society'.[12] Some leading political commentators have certainly done so simply because the largest sector of the population is ethnically Chinese. In other words, the dominant Singaporean Chinese population have been portrayed as heirs to, and contemporary bearers of, a grand Confucian tradition.

---

10 Huang adds, however, that the concept was eliminated 'when the K'ang-hsi emperor successfully appropriated the long-aspired Confucian political ideal— the unity of power and truth'.

11 Cotton's comment is prompted by De Bary's attempt to identify a liberal tradition in China (De Bary 1983).

12 And indeed the same question could be asked of other countries in the actual 'Confucian cultural area'. After all, although Confucian thought has been important, it is scarcely the only body of thought to have made its mark on the area.

Contrary to this popular myth, the next section outlines some official attempts that have been made 'to reinvent Confucianism for a population never especially familiar with it' (Cotton 1991a:320). In many respects this is a classic case of the 'invention of tradition' which also raises some important and interesting points about the legitimising effect of 'authentic political culture'.

Confucius in Singapore

The government of Singapore has been tightly controlled by the People's Action Party for almost 40 years. Indeed, so comprehensive and pervasive is this control that one could well characterise Singapore as a paradigmatic case of fusion between state, regime, government and party in which many of the norms of democratic politics, especially those to do with the legitimacy of political opposition, have little place (Lawson 1993b). The PAP is well known for its hostile views on political opposition and its function in the political process. Indeed, PAP ideology has consistently depicted political opposition as a destructive and irresponsible force in Singaporean politics. Carolyn Choo's study shows clearly the extent to which the PAP has advocated, and enforced, measures to stifle and repress political opposition in Singapore since the party first came to power in 1959, especially through the Internal Security Act which allows, among other things, for detention without trial (1985:especially 38–75). So, although the political system operates with an elected parliament and legally 'free' political parties, the PAP has nonetheless used extra-parliamentary authoritarian devices to constrain challenges to its dominant position, thereby effectively institutionalising a one-party state under the façade of a constitutional parliamentary democracy (see Rodan 1993). A public speech delivered in 1971 by the then Foreign Minister epitomises some of the attitudes which support the Party's authoritarian approach, focusing specifically on political opposition.

> An opposition party consisting of bums, opportunists, and morons can endanger democracy and bring about chaos, disorder, and violence. This has happened and is happening in many countries. The same can happen under a one-party parliament of bums and crooks.

> Equally a one-party parliament can safeguard democracy and bring about peace, progress, and prosperity. Singapore has had a one-party parliament since 1968. If you forget theory and look at hard facts you will discover that though the People's Action Party has been in power for 12 years, its greater achievements in promoting the welfare of the people were under a one-party parliament (quoted in Chan 1976:228).

To oppose the PAP government in Singapore is not only to 'signify a lack of "Asianness"', to show that one is infected by Western individualism and permissiveness, [or] to prove that one is not really a Singaporean at heart' (Tremewan 1997:65); it is often to risk a great deal more. As Chua writes, to consider carrying out any form of political oppositional activity is to consider as well whether it is worth risking one's livelihood and perhaps even one's liberty. He notes that the PAP, 'in its determination to stay in power is unrelenting in keeping a close watch on the activities and words of oppositional individuals' and that members of opposition parties have often been prosecuted vigorously for offences such as defamation. He goes on to suggest that while such prosecutions are not necessarily illegal (or 'undemocratic'), and that of course no one is above the law, these cases are nonetheless 'often read as excessive "persecution" of individuals who hold opinions contrary to the regime' (Chua 1995:207–8).

Another observer has suggested that the definitive feature of authoritarianism in Singapore is the extent to which extra-parliamentary constraints have been imposed on opponents of the PAP. Rodan points out that fairly crude measures, such as detention or imprisonment have sometimes been used, but the PAP has commonly employed more sophisticated techniques 'that systematically obstruct counter views and institutionalise the PAP's ideology' (1993:77). These techniques have included the attempted 'Confucianisation' of Singapore through a program of educational indoctrination in schools, and an emphasis on Mandarin language training and usage, as well as through broader rhetorical exercises aimed especially at the Singaporean Chinese.[13]

As far back as the late 1970s, the leadership of the PAP acted on concerns about the 'cultural health' of the Chinese community which then constituted about 77 per cent of the population. 'Chineseness' itself was portrayed as a 'traditional culture encapsulated in Confucianism and Mandarin' which in turn were seen as embodying 'the values of discipline, respect for authority and commitment to the community' (Brown 1994: 93). As a means of counteracting unwelcome Western influences, a 'Speak Mandarin Campaign' was mounted along with a compulsory Mandarin language curriculum for Chinese school students. Mandarin, which was believed to be the most effective transmitter of Confucian values, was promoted as the authentic 'mother tongue' for Chinese Singaporeans despite the fact that fewer than one per cent actually spoke it as a first language. Rather, the most commonly spoken languages were dialects including Hokkein, Cantonese, Teochew, Hainanese and Hakka (Rahim 1996:8).[14] According to one commentator, the Mandarin

13 There are a number of critical implications for the Malay and Indian populations in Singapore that are not dealt with in this chapter. For an excellent short account of some of the issues, see Rahim (1996).
14 See also Clammer (1985), in which the percentages speaking these dialects in the year 1980 are given. Another commentator remarks that the artifice involved is underscored further by the fact that earlier official policy had been to promote the Malay language throughout the island not only because this would assist integration with Malaysia, but also because Malay was a common

language program has not been very successful. Not only has the use of dialects remained undiminished in many Chinese homes, but if these are being replaced by anything, it is the use of 'Singlish'—'a creatively hybrid and uniquely Singaporean version of English which is laced with Chinese, Malay, and Tamil expressions' (Ang and Stratton 1995:87)—and which the PAP regards with considerable distaste.

But the Mandarin language was not the only medium through which a Confucian ethos was to be nurtured, and it may indeed be seen as secondary to another kind of educational program. In 1983, the PAP government sponsored the foundation of the Institute of East Asian Philosophies (IEAP), the initial purpose of which was 'to advance the understanding of Confucian philosophy so that it can be reinterpreted and adapted to the needs of present society' (Tamney 1991:400). At much the same time the government also instituted a course on religious knowledge and Confucian ethics as part of the secondary school curriculum in Singapore. The texts for the course were commissioned especially for the purpose by the Ministry of Education. Prime Minister Lee Kuan Yew had again expressed considerable concern about too much 'Westernisation', and had stressed the need to promote traditional Asian values and virtues in school programs (Lu 1983:71). Once again, this concern seems to have been directed mainly towards the more numerous Chinese population whose significant numbers provide obvious grounds for treating Confucian moral values as the most important and influential in Singapore. It was also suggested that the Chinese population was 'more susceptible to other cultural influences' and that the Chinese, 'relative to other ethnic groups [were] actually moving away from their traditional values at a much faster pace' (Lu 1983:85).

In bringing Confucius 'home' to the Singaporean people, it seems that the PAP under Lee Kuan Yew had several purposes. First, Lee wished to reinforce the idea that oppositional politics as practised in the Western adversarial mode was virtually inconceivable in Singaporean society which should, instead, continue to strive for the Confucian ideals of consensus and harmony. 'Everything was re-ordered to "fit" the consensus model—one party, one press, one trade union movement, one dominant language, etc. In fact, his party came to represent all the elements in the society; his politics has embraced all to become a single entity' (Selvan 1990:271–3).[15] In this schema, state and society become an undifferentiated organic whole, although the PAP, as the state, is clearly the

language of communication often used by different dialect groups in speaking with each other (Cotton 1996:279).

15 Much of this sits oddly with Lee's criticism of communism which he condemns for its insistence on 'unquestioning obedience to the party line' without dissension or abstention, and with his favourable remarks on the tenets of democratic socialism which he says concede 'the right of opposition to challenge...values and therefore the right of the other parties displacing a democratic socialist in office' (Vasil 1984:183).

dominant organ. Another important point is that Lee's elevation of Confucianism as a focus of cultural identity and social unity not only underpinned the ideal of a uniform 'one people society', but was also held up in contrast to Western values, which were in turn denigrated and portrayed as a threat to social order (Vasil 1984:273).

While the Confucian ideal of the sage-emperor is obsolete in practical terms, the Singaporean texts nonetheless stressed the notion that governments are best led by ideal statesmen who are able to combine political power with philosophical wisdom (Tamney 1991:404). This idea has been strongly supported in public rhetoric as well. In a 1986 statement, Goh Chok Tong (then Deputy Prime Minister to Lee Kuan Yew), described the formal Singaporean political system as a British style of cabinet government on which had been superimposed 'a Confucian gentleman, a *junzi*, someone who is upright, morally beyond reproach, someone people can trust' (Chan 1993a:239). Moreover, the authority of the benevolent, paternalistic *junzi* can only be challenged if and when his 'good government', understood in terms of providing material well-being and political stability, fails in its essentials (Rahim 1996:7). Writing in 1993, Chan suggested that while Western democracies relied on checks and balances as well as oppositional forces to best control corruption and bad government, 'Singapore leaders have consistently argued...that finding "good men" (and women) is even more crucial'.'This, she maintains, has enabled Singapore to develop a tradition of corruption-free government since the PAP first came to power (Chan 1993b:15).[16]

The IEAP was ultimately unsuccessful in stimulating any real 'Confucianisation' of Singapore (and the Institute no longer exists in its original form). The Confucian ethics strand of the religious education program in schools—even though Confucianism is not a religion—was also a failure. Chua reports that the Confucian Ethics course was poorly subscribed and, after seven years of operation, its enrolment of just under eighteen per cent of eligible Chinese students compared very unfavourably with the almost 45 per cent electing to do Buddhist Studies and the 21 per cent choosing Bible Knowledge. It was eventually abandoned because it was also implicated, at least marginally, in the rise of religious tensions within Singapore (Chua 1995:29–31). More interesting, however, was the fact that the Ministry of Education was obliged to import a number of Confucian scholars from abroad to develop the appropriate texts, because Confucian ethics was a field in which there was virtually no existing expertise in Singapore, thereby underscoring the actual 'absence of Confucianism in Singapore's everyday life' (Chua 1995:159). Chua's description and analysis of the Chinese in Singapore highlights the essentially invented character of Confucianism there:

---

16 Singapore's corruption-free image, however, was tarnished recently when it was revealed that Lee Kuan Yew and his son had accepted significant discounts on the purchase of luxury condominiums.

First, as an immigrant population hewn from displaced peasantry of southern China, most Singaporean Chinese's understanding of Confucianism was at best a distilled folk version of familialism. Second, the educated amongst them at the time were likely to be influenced by the 'modernist' movements in post-1900 China, in which Confucianism was ridiculed and rejected rather than followed. Third, the most radical and active political elements in pre-independent Singapore were the Chinese population, across all classes...Finally, in the interests of generating a national culture, the [early] PAP government had standardised all school texts to local contents, eliminating references to any traditions (Chua 1995:28–9).

Chua concludes that in light of this counter-factual evidence, the interesting issue is not whether some weak version of Confucian ethics was (and is) alive among the Singaporean Chinese, but that the government had attempted, quite intentionally, to inculcate Confucianism as an ideological–moral device 'to shore up the existing state' (Chua 1995:29).

This brings to mind Geertz's remark, quoted by Migdal (this volume), that 'political authority still requires a cultural frame in which to define itself and advance its claims'. In light of the foregoing discussion, however, the questions that this begs are: which cultural frame, who chooses it, who is most privileged by its precepts, and who claims the authority to define political power within its field of reference? The first thing to concede is that not just any cultural frame will suit the purpose. For example, to use the 'cultural frame' of the Navajo people in the Singaporean context would not get the PAP very far, and would in fact make a laughing stock of them. Obviously, the cultural frame must be perceived to have some 'authenticity' in the local context and Confucianism, because it is associated with Chineseness, can be made to fit the bill in a way that a Navajo cultural frame could not. But while the Confucian cultural frame does have at least a superficial resonance with Singaporean society—or at least a significant part of it—and has allowed the PAP some scope to define claims to political authority within it, it remains more of a product of the PAP's instrumental purposes rather than a deeply ingrained feature of Singaporean society.

Of equal interest in any 'invention of tradition' exercise is the question of exactly what the 'invention' is constructed *against*, for such exercises never really take place in the absence of some kind of oppositional motif which is shown in a negative light. It has been pointed out, for example, that ancient Greek portrayals of 'barbarians' were very largely exercises in self-definition in as much as barbarians were depicted as the opposite, and infinitely inferior, contrast to the ideal Greek (see Hall 1989:ix). It seems clear enough that the invention of Confucianism in Singapore was carried out quite explicitly against the West in general, and Western notions of democratic politics in particular, and that this constitutes a prime instance of Occidentalism.

But despite all the evidence to the contrary, and the failure of the Confucian ethics programs, and ultimately the IEAP, the idea that Singapore is somehow a 'Confucian society' has passed into conventional wisdom, and assumptions there about 'the dominant Confucian culture of the Chinese population' (Chan 1993a:239) will no doubt continue to characterise conservative commentaries on culture and politics in Singapore. And naive observers, who do not think beyond stereotypes of 'Chineseness' being equated with Confucianism, may also unthinkingly assume that Singapore is essentially a Confucian culture. This is quite apart from the fact that the ethnic heritage of some 25 per cent of Singapore's population is not Chinese at all. The remainder of the population is made up of ethnic Indians, Sri Lankans and Malays, not to mention people with a hybrid ethnic heritage as well as thousands of other residents, including Bangladeshi and Indonesian labourers, Filipina maids, and European business people. If there is anything that characterises the diverse population of Singapore, then, it is its cosmopolitanism.

Apart from the Confucianisation program itself, one of the most interesting aspects of the exercise has been the attempt to revise, or re-theorise, democracy along Confucian lines. This was no mean task considering some of the important Confucian elements discussed earlier which appear to be quite antithetical to a number of the liberal and egalitarian principles embodied in democratic theory. Indeed, when the Head of the IEAP was asked what the greatest challenge to Confucianism today is, he apparently replied: 'Democracy' (Tamney 1991:399). According to one commentator, Confucian scholars of the IEAP remained ambivalent about the issue. In order to make Confucianism popular, they believed on the one hand that Confucianism must accommodate democratic ideology, yet they remained committed to the principal of harmony, rather than to legitimate conflict. They were equally ambivalent about the importance and place of a doctrine of human rights. Also discussed was the assumption on the part of many Westerners that the Western 'understanding of democracy is the only acceptable one, which position blinds them to an appreciation of the links between Confucianism and an Asian form of democracy' (Tamney 1991:404).

Others saw, or hoped for, a convergence of Eastern and Western forms such that a new, more 'universal' concept of democracy would emerge. One of the IEAP philosophers, Professor Wu Teh Yao, advocated a blending of Eastern consensual styles and Western styles in the formation of a hybrid polity called 'Consencracy'. He argued that this new concept reflected not merely the rule of the majority and a plurality of parties engaging in open debate and election, but embraced the idea that 'the genuine consent of the people going through the process of selection in a one-party state is also democratic'. He continued:

> Democracy understood in such a manner may be likened to the two sides of the same coin in government. In the Western parliamentary form it is arrived at through open debate from within and without; in an Eastern

form of democracy it is arrived at through closed debate within, with no opposition from without. In this dual and mixed form, democracy is synthesized to become a new polity which may be called CONSENCRACY (Wu 1979:57–8. Capitals in original.).

The idea of 'democracy Asian-style' in Singapore was further contrasted with Western forms of democracy in the following terms:

> Singaporeans must decide whether they want a system based on an *a priori* distrust of an elected government. They must ask themselves whether opposition politics *per se* is good. Do they want open confrontation or consensus-building as a means of settling disputes? Above all, Singaporeans must decide whether individual freedom should be put above the society's collective good.[17]

The notion of 'democracy Asian-style' may have an immediate appeal to those who favour a general move to democratisation but nonetheless shrink from asserting Eurocentric political ideals in 'alien' contexts. At a minimum, this position acknowledges that we do not live in a uniform, monochromatic world, and that there can be many variations on the democratic theme. At the same time, however, it is obvious that more rigid forms of relativism can operate as a powerful defence of authoritarianism. And it is ironic that most appeals to cultural relativism come from those who want to enforce political uniformity *within* a given society. In the case of the PAP in Singapore, ideological uniformity has clearly been sought at the cost of repressing opposing viewpoints.

Tu is therefore right to be concerned about the potential use of Confucianism as an ideological force underscoring coercive methods of control, and right in insisting that a healthy debate, whether directed towards the understanding of Confucian texts or any other system of ideas, should be understood in terms of a pluralistic (rather than relativistic) enterprise. He argues further that a lively interpretive tradition requires an evaluative process which selects a number of significant, competing interpretations for discussion. He stresses, however, that the state has no business in this process.

> When a state assumes the role of making such selections, it is often motivated by political considerations. A text will be interpreted along lines that support and reinforce its own ideological control. This possibility makes it all the more necessary to affirm more than one potential interpretation of a text. Such awareness will impede the state from monopolizing textual interpretation for its own ends. This is true not only of the Confucian tradition but of many other religious traditions as well (Tu 1984:30–1).

The question of the distinction between pluralism and relativism is clearly pertinent here. In brief, relativism of the kind discussed in this

---

17 Editorial comment in *Straits Times*, 13 May 1988, quoted in Tamney (1991: 405).

chapter may be taken as a stance which accords the same epistemological and normative status to competing systems of ideas about political institutions and values.[18] This kind of relativism provides the essential premise for rigidly deterministic claims such as: the liberal aspects of democratic institutions and values are valid and workable in the West because they are culturally embedded there, but cannot be expected to be valid and workable in other places where they are alien to the autochthonous culture or political tradition. Pluralism on the other hand denotes a stance whereby competing interpretations can be legitimately expressed, but are not necessarily accorded equal epistemological or normative status. In other words, pluralism allows that some interpretations may be better than others and therefore allows for the rejection of some interpretations as a sham. This does not amount to crude universalism and, with respect to democracy, it does not suggest that there is one, and only one, institutional form that can give expression to the values underlying democratic rule—although again, some may be better than others.[19]

Conclusion

The idea of culture has been used in Singapore as a political device which serves the purpose of upholding 'Asian' values in the face of alleged incursions of undesirable Western political values. This has provided an essential part of the justification for rejecting some key norms which underscore the theory and practice of modern democratic politics, namely, the norms associated with the operation of constitutional political opposition. One of the ironies of this in a place like Singapore is that the government, in opposing these norms, has attempted to use a system of thought which probably has no more cultural resonance with the local populace than many of the Western ideas which are said to be alien.[20] In this case the idea of culture is used as a rhetorical weapon in a battle which really has little to do with culture *per se*, but everything to do with the capacity of the PAP state to exercise political control within a system which bears only a superficial resemblance to democracy.

We must also consider what this means for broader state-in-society analyses as well as the assumptions that underpin ideas about 'strong' and 'weak' states. There is no question that the state in Singapore displays almost all the important characteristics normally associated with a strong

---

18 'Systems' is used here to denote the broad categories or paradigms of thought that are often posited in the form 'Western', 'Asian', 'Confucian', 'liberal–democratic', and so forth, and which are identified, in one way or another, with a general idea of 'culture'.

19 For further discussion of this, see Lawson (1995).

20 Describing Confucianism as a 'system of thought' is, in any case, problematic (see Cotton 1991b).

state. Looking at the definition provided in the introduction to this volume, it is obvious that the Singaporean state has the capacity to maintain social control and to ensure societal compliance with laws; it acts decisively and effectively in implementing policy; it provides basic services; and it manages and controls the national economy. What I have not included in this list of characteristics, however, are two other important items, namely, encouragement of societal participation in state institutions, and the retention of legitimacy. I have excluded these, not because they are entirely lacking in the case of Singapore, but because they are seriously compromised by the authoritarian and controlling nature of the PAP.

Adequate societal participation, on any reasonable account, must encompass legitimate oppositional activity, and it is quite clear that there is very little scope for this in Singapore. And arguably, it is difficult to test the legitimacy of the PAP's control of the state in the absence of reasonably free political oppositional activity. On the other hand, some may argue that the PAP's legitimacy is not what is really at issue, but rather the legitimacy of the state of Singapore itself. Here we could dig very deep into the whole issue of the distinctions between state, regime and government—which is obviously beyond the scope of this chapter. It must suffice to say that since the PAP regards itself as virtually synony-mous with the state, and has been primarily responsible for shaping the regime which provides the framework for state, party and society, questions concerning the legitimacy of the state must ultimately address the legitimacy of the PAP.

For the time being, the PAP seems eminently secure. In terms of its 'performance legitimacy' it has been extremely successful in bringing relatively high standards of living to its citizens with a minimum of government corruption. The streets are clean, the buses run on time, crime rates are low, and educational achievements impressive. On any index of material 'progress', Singapore must rate very high and there is no question that it is to the PAP's credit. In terms of leadership succession, too, the PAP—or more particularly Lee Kuan Yew—has acted very astutely in putting a successor in place long before Lee's capacity to lead was likely to be compromised by failing health or other causes. This contrasts markedly with the situation in Indonesia, and is a lesson well worth taking by Mohamad Mahathir in neighbouring Malaysia. Nonetheless, Lee Kuan Yew remains a vital linchpin for the entire system of PAP dominance and therefore for the political stability of the state. He is widely regarded as remaining the real power behind the throne, and many believe that it is his intolerance of any political opposition that has largely driven the recent campaigns to bankrupt opposition politicians via defamation proceedings in the courts. The real test of stability and/or PAP dominance, then, may well come with Lee's death.

Finally, let us return briefly to the question of culture and how it relates to issues of strength, weakness and state capacity. I hope enough has been said in the above discussion to demonstrate that there is very little substance in mystical explanations to do with ancient Confucian culture and values. If Singaporeans generally seem politically passive in the face of a strong party–state—notwithstanding a great deal of cynicism about the PAP and its rhetoric about Confucianism and Asian values more generally—this may be read as nothing much more than pragmatic acquiescence in a regime that has delivered many material goods, combined with an acute appreciation of the enormous risks to personal and material well-being that attend any involvement in political oppositional activity. In summary, the main lesson to be drawn from the discussion is this: If we are to ask such questions as 'why do the citizens of a state obey?', it simply will not do to point to a 'cultural factor' such as Confucianism and just accept that it facilitates obedience and conformist behaviour (see Migdal 1997:208). Instead, we must be concerned to examine the extent to which simple 'cultural explanations', especially when they are put forward by conservative state élites, actually obscure the most important dynamics of political power and control in state–society relations.

8 Weak States and the Environment in Indonesia and the Solomon Islands

PETER DAUVERGNE

Until the economic collapse that began in mid-1997 and the subsequent riots and student demonstrations that led to President Soeharto's resignation in May 1998, most scholars of Indonesia saw a strong, or at least a medium-strong state, especially in terms of policy formulation and control over non-state organisations. Almost all analysts have portrayed the Solomon Islands as weak since independence in 1978 (see Kabutaulaka and Dauvergne 1997). This chapter reflects on why Indonesia, until recently a seemingly strong state, and the Solomon Islands, an undeniably weak administrative state, have had such similar patterns of environmental mismanagement of commercial old-growth forests.[1] Log production is now about two times higher than sustainable levels in Indonesia. Until the crash in demand for tropical logs following the 1997 Asian financial crisis, log production was over three times higher than sustainable levels in the Solomon Islands. In both countries, the governments have revoked or diluted policies that threaten corporate profits. Loggers largely ignore

---

1 This chapter concentrates on the Indonesian state from the late 1960s to mid-1997, the same period that most of the information on forest management is drawn. For a summary of the literature on the Indonesian state, see MacIntyre (1990). He writes, 'while there is some serious dispute...as to the character of the state itself, there is in fact an underlying consensus that relations between state and society are massively tilted in the direction of the former' (1990:6). Neher, in a comparative book on Southeast Asia, writes: 'a strong, autonomous state has emerged in new order Indonesia. The state controls all aspects of political and economic life and has co-opted all institutions that could even potentially challenge the state' (Neher 1994:117). Most scholars have also recognised, however, that a critical weakness of the Indonesian state has been the lack of a clear heir-apparent to President Soeharto.

environmental rules and silvicultural practices, and make windfall legal and illegal profits. Commercial forests in Indonesia will certainly last longer; but this is largely a result of huge stocks, rather than better management.

A key reason for similar patterns of environmental mismanagement in Indonesia and the Solomon Islands is the incapacity and unwillingness of the state to control timber companies. In Indonesia, state control is undermined by élite attitudes, poor policies, insufficient institutional resources, and most importantly, pervasive patron–client links among state officials and timber operators. In the Solomon Islands, state capacity is undercut by weak state legal powers over forests, attitudes of decision makers, cultural pressures on state members, political instability, bad policies, inadequate bureaucratic resources, and to a lesser extent, ties among state officials and corporate executives. Yet, although the underlying reasons for low state capacity differ somewhat, the result is the same in both countries: timber companies operate with little, if any, state controls on environmental practices. This challenges the view of the Indonesian state as immutably strong over the last three decades, and suggests that scholars should use the labels 'weak' and 'strong' with great care, recognising that state capacity fluctuates across time and sectors.

It may strike some as odd to compare Indonesia—one of the world's largest economies, with a land area of about 190 million hectares, a population of 200 million, and an authoritarian government—with the Solomon Islands—one of the world's smallest economies, with a land area of around 2.8 million hectares, a population of about 375 000, and a democratic government. These countries also have distinct cultural and historical traditions. In addition, major differences exist between the timber sectors. Indonesia has around 100 million hectares of forest; the Solomon Islands has only 2.4 million hectares. The Indonesian state owns the primary forests and has the legal and political power to develop and implement national forest rules; in the Solomon Islands, land owners control most commercial forests and the state has fewer legal powers to develop national guidelines. Moreover, domestic firms dominate Indonesia's commercial timber industry, while multinational firms, mostly from Malaysia, dominate logging in the Solomon Islands. Despite all of these differences, however, important insights are gained by comparing two states with distinct foundations and levels of state capacity, yet such strikingly similar environmental patterns. In particular, it suggests that, even though specific political, demographic, cultural, historical, geographic, and economic factors lead to different underlying reasons for low state capacity, because environmental management of commercial timber is generally a low priority among development-oriented state officials, and because it generally provokes strong resistance from social forces that underpin the state, most states in the developing world, regardless of overall strength, will be weak environmental managers.

This chapter is divided into eight parts. The first section defines state, society, and capacity. The second and third sections outline the key features of the Indonesian and the Solomon Islands states, noting the inherent strengths of the Indonesian state from the late 1960s until mid-1997 and the integral weakness of the Solomon Islands state since independence. The fourth and fifth sections outline some key environmental and forest policies and legal powers in Indonesia and the Solomon Islands. The sixth and seventh sections assess the extent of state control over the environmental effects of commercial loggers. The final section reflects on the broader implications of this study for understanding state control over corporate environmental practices. Because the empirical evidence in this article relates to tropical forests, found almost exclusively in the developing world, generalisations are limited to developing countries. Future researchers, however, may well find these ideas useful for analysing environmental management in developed countries.

State–Society Relations and State Capacity

In the tradition of Weber, a state is an organisation that includes an executive, legislature, bureaucracy, courts, police, military, and in some cases schools and public corporations. A state is not monolithic, although some are more cohesive than others. A society is the arena in which state and non-state organisations compete over the official and unofficial rules of the game. States aim to control societies; non-state organisations aim to restructure states; and both states and non-state organisations aim to control the economy (market). Inevitably, to varying degrees, state agencies and non-state organisations shape the interaction and structure of each other. By definition, a state has a legitimate monopoly over the use of violence, and therefore has coercive tools to get individuals and groups within society to obey and conform. To preserve legitimacy and stability, a state also seeks to raise revenue, minimise internal and external threats, maintain internal cohesion and coordination, and mediate and deflect societal pressures and demands. State output is a result of contests and compromises across agencies and levels of the state, and with relevant non-state organisations in society.[2]

State capacity is the ability of the state to maintain social control, make policies, impose rules, provide basic services, and manage the national economy (including natural resources). A weak administrative state refers to a state that has particular problems providing essential services, such as education, health care, protection from random violence, and internal transportation and communication. Societal forces often undermine state capacity; but they can also enhance state technical ability and control

---

2 For similar conceptions of state–society relations, see Migdal (1988), Migdal, Kohli and Shue, eds (1994), and Grindle (1996).

(such as advice or support from business organisations). Strong state capacity requires coordinated actions among state agencies, technical competence, and a high level of state autonomy from societal pressures. It also involves a high level of legitimacy; in the long term simple coercion is insufficient. For logistical reasons, state capacity tends to decrease in areas far from the national capital (especially in unitary states).

State capacity is not static. The ability of states to make and enforce rules, maintain order, and manage economic resources varies depending on the level of societal opposition to state initiatives, the extent that non-state organisations capture or support agencies of the state, and the degree to which different components of the state undermine national policies. The content of state goals also has a critical impact on state capacity. Not all policies are equal. Some generate strong commitment from state leaders, technical advisers, and implementors, perhaps for ideological reasons, or perhaps to maintain stability or legitimacy. Other policies and official goals, however, function largely as a camouflage, perhaps to appease international and domestic critics, perhaps because implementation could undermine legitimacy and stability, or perhaps because few leaders or implementors really believe in these goals. For these reasons, state capacity varies across sectors and time and is best viewed on a continuum.

As the level of determination (comprising the attitudes and commitment of state leaders and officials) weakens and as societal resistance intensifies, state capacity to make and implement policies declines. As the level of state determination strengthens, and as societal resistance weakens (or when societal forces support state goals) state capacity to implement official policies rises. States like Indonesia will undoubtedly overwhelm societal forces on many issues, and are strong in these cases; but for some issues, especially ones that involve low levels of state determination and strong resistance from social groups that underpin the state itself, these states may well be unable to enforce official rules. On the other hand, states like the Solomon Islands clearly have great difficulty providing basic services and managing economic resources. Yet even in the Solomon Islands the state is strong in a few areas, such as maintaining adherence to criminal laws. Many states cluster along one end of the continuum, although few, if any, states display no examples of strength or weakness.

Environmental management is particularly prone to fall on the low end of the continuum. This occurs because environmental concerns tend to provoke low levels of state determination and high levels of societal resistance (which often translates into societal forces capturing state agencies). Some states are simply overwhelmed by corporate and economic pressures, contributing to ineffective policies, inadequate institutional resources, and diluted implementation. Unclear or weak state legal authority over particular resources can further undermine state capacity. In other cases, states have more control over policy formulation; but enforcement is non-existent. This does not presume that strong state capacity is *necessary* for effective environmental management—only that most states tend to be weak environmental managers. Communities may well be far stronger and more effective, although so far this has not occurred in the Solomon Islands.

The particular features of each country, state, economy, and society determine the extent of state control over non-state organisations and the extent that societal forces shape the state. These include geographic and demographic characteristics, political and legal systems, the national and local economies, the size and power of the coercive wing of the state (armed forces and police), the technical capacity of the bureaucracy, the culture, the legitimacy and cohesiveness of the state itself, the structure, size, and unity of non-state organisations, and the relative position of the state in the international system. The mix of these factors has contributed to a generally strong state in Indonesia (at least in terms of formulating policies and controlling societal forces) and a generally weak state in the Solomon Islands.

State Capacity in New Order Indonesia

Indonesia contains more than 300 ethnic groups and over 16 000 islands that stretch across about 5000 kilometres. Communication and transportation problems increase the difficulty of enforcing state rules and maintaining national social norms, especially compared to countries like Singapore. Nevertheless, until recently the New Order government had been remarkably adept at maintaining control and stability. Until the rapid depreciation of the rupiah that began in mid-1997, it was also reasonably successful in reducing poverty and promoting macro-economic growth. From the mid-1960s to the mid-1990s, gross domestic product increased on average by over five per cent per year. Perhaps even more impressive, the government improved health standards and lengthened life expectancy. In 1971, 132 of every 1000 children died before turning one; by 1992, this dropped to 65. From 1980 to 1990, life expectancy increased from fifty to 60 years (Neher 1994:115, 117).

After taking over from Sukarno in the mid-1960s, President Soeharto (a former general) gradually centralised and consolidated his control. Partly justified by the need for national integration and stability, the New Order government demolished the communist party, eliminated threats from factions within the military, filled the bureaucracy with loyal supporters, created a powerful and completely loyal government party (*Golkar*), sponsored corporatist business groups, maintained Indonesia's independence in the international state system, imposed the ideology of *Pancasila* (five principles of nationalism, belief in one god, democracy, humanity, and social justice) as the guide for all social organisation, and put tight controls on opposition political parties, radical religious movements, unions, student groups, the media, interest groups, and non-governmental organisations (NGOs). The president's control is further enhanced by his constitutional power to appoint regional governors and cabinet members and proclaim laws. Meanwhile, the power of regional governments is limited by the central government's control over revenues.[3]

The Indonesian Armed Forces (*Angkatan Bersenjata Republik Indonesia*, ABRI) is at the core of the New Order government. As Neher notes, 'In no other Southeast Asian nation, with the possible exception of Burma, has the military so pervasively intervened in politics' (1994:110). ABRI includes the army, navy, air force, and police, although the army dominates. It is the key coercive tool of the state, allowing the government to suppress potential threats, such as the 1996–97 riots and protests that surrounded the ouster of Megawati Sukarnoputri as chair of the opposition *Partai Demokrasi Indonesia* (Democratic Party). ABRI controls the national intelligence agency *Badan Intelijian Negara* (responsible for monitoring political dissent) and the Body for Coordinating National Stability (responsible for implementing martial law). It has both a military and socio-political role ('dual function' or *dwi fungsi*), allowing military officers to justify close supervision of non-military activities. It has links to the two main opposition parties, the *Partai Persatuan Pembangunan* and the *Partai Demokrasi Indonesia*, and it has 75 seats reserved in parliament (reduced from 100 in 1995) out of a total of 500 seats. It also has close ties to the ruling *Golkar* party. In addition, officers are appointed to positions in the civil service, state companies, and regional governments. Through its ten territorial commands, it monitors political activities in the outer islands; and through National Defence Institute courses it influences journalists and bureaucrats (Crouch 1988; Grant 1996:88–90).

The technical and financial resilience and expertise of the bureaucracy has allowed this wing of the state to dominate policy formulation. Little has changed since Karl Jackson noted in the late 1970s that 'national decisions are limited almost entirely to the employees of the state, particularly the officer corps and the highest levels of the bureaucracy, including especially the highly trained specialists known as the technocrats' (1978:3). Lucrative and vast oil reserves have also provided critical funds for bureaucratic initiatives and helped insulate the state from pressure from organised business groups.

The government carefully restricts NGO activities. The 1985 Law on Social Organisations (*Undang-undang Organisasi Kemasyarakatan*, Ormas) requires NGOs to accept *Pancasila* as their guiding principle, an

---

3   For background on state–society relations in the New Order, see Robison (1986), Nordholt (1987), Budiman, ed. (1990), Emmerson (1990), Brown (1994:chapter 4), Bourchier and Legge, eds (1995), Ramage (1995) and Winters (1996).

obligation that particularly threatens Muslim organisations. It also allows the government to guide and regulate NGO activities and disband any organisation that violates the principles of *Pancasila* (Grant 1996:68; Eldridge 1990:510–11).[4] Besides controlling NGOs, the government also censors the media. In 1994, for example, the government closed three magazines deemed too critical.

Particular cultural tendencies reinforce the control and preferences of state élites, including a popular acceptance of consensual decision making among senior officials, deference to age and seniority, and respect for self-control. Elite attitudes also have important implications for state capacity to protect the environment. Western-educated bureaucrats, especially the economic technocrats, have stressed economic development, often at all costs. These attitudes have shaped policy content, including the five-year plans (*Repelita*). With few technocrats committed to policies like conservation, reforestation and environmental protection, environmental management is generally a low priority in the bureaucratic hierarchy. As well, bureaucrats tend to dismiss NGOs that press for environmental reforms.[5]

Soeharto dominated the New Order period. But Indonesia was not a one-man state. Soeharto had to maintain the support and respect of senior military officers, bureaucrats, and politicians, as was convincingly revealed by his decision to resign on 21 May 1998. He maintained élite support in part by distributing lucrative patronage to reward followers (clients) and appease opponents. His family, especially his six children, are extraordinarily rich.[6] Military, political, and bureaucratic leaders at all levels of the state have also developed patron–client networks. These networks involve vertical, asymmetrical, reciprocal, and often material-based exchanges, where state officials provide contracts, licences, loans, or access to government services in exchange for gifts, money, support, or security.

Patron–client links have been especially important for ethnic Chinese. While Javanese dominate the military, bureaucracy, and polity, Indonesian Chinese—who only comprise about three per cent of the population—may account for 'as much as 70 per cent of all private economic activity' (Schwarz 1994:99).[7] A non-Chinese state member often performs the role of a patron (Ali) while an ethnic Chinese business leader acts as a client (Baba), although some rich Chinese also function as patrons. Ethnic

---

4   Eldridge is, however, quite optimistic about the influence of NGOs in Indonesia.
5   Based on personal interviews with bureaucrats from various departments, February/March 1994, and July/August 1997, Jakarta.
6   In 1996, Soeharto's children controlled business empires worth over US$6 billion (Sender 1996:57). Also, see Hiscock (1996:25, 29).
7   For details on Indonesian Chinese business leaders, see Schwarz (1994:98–132).

Chinese clients of Soeharto include the richest businessmen in the country, such as Bob Hasan, Prayogo Pangestu, and Liem Sioe Liong.

Patron–client links are a key avenue by which non-state organisations, especially corporate executives, interact and influence the state. Most studies of the 'patrimonial' Indonesian state presume that the particularistic, unsystematic, unorganised nature of these links translates into little coherent impact on state strength.[8] Yet the cumulative effects can, at least in some cases, have significant implications, especially for state capacity to enforce rules. When business clients support state initiatives these ties reinforce state goals. But when official state policies threaten corporate profits these ties often distort policies and undermine enforcement. Top state patrons support and protect business clients who break state rules. In addition, middle and lower-level state officials ignore regulations, or sometimes facilitate the illegal activities of clients and patrons. As a result, although Indonesia has displayed many characteristics of a strong state over the last three decades, in the case of commercial timber management, the cumulative effect of these links has debilitated state capacity.

State Capacity in the Solomon Islands Since Independence

Like Indonesia, the Solomon Islands is composed of numerous islands. Indonesia has, however, greater ethnic diversity, more distance between the islands, and over 500 times the population. Also unlike Indonesia, the Westminster-style parliamentary democracy in the Solomon Islands has not allowed any political figure to dominate, although former Prime Minister Solomon Mamaloni has ruled for much of the post-1978 independence period (1981–84, 1989–93, 1994–97).[9] NGOs, the media, and non-state social organisations also have far greater freedom in the Solomon Islands (Roughan 1994; 1997). In addition, the Solomon Islands does not have a conventional military; instead, the Police Field Force is responsible for security.

Compared to Indonesia, the Solomon Islands is a far weaker administrative state. The state has trouble providing basic services, including adequate roads, medical facilities, and public schools. It has even more problems handling macro-economic plans, monitoring multinational investors, and collecting taxes. State control is weakened by the large subsistence and semi-subsistence economies, which support about 85 per cent of the population. Although most people now rely more on the state, especially for hospitals, medical clinics, and schools, the majority still obtain basic needs, including food and shelter, without state support.

---

8   One exception is MacIntyre (1994).
9   The current Prime Minister, Bartholomew Ulufa'alu, took power in August 1997.

Bureaucratic agencies without adequate funds, computers, or trained personnel also undermine state administrative capacity. Political processes and norms further weaken the state. Compared to other Westminster parliamentary systems, political parties are fluid and unstable, contributing to constant political deals and jockeying. As Jeffrey Steeves aptly notes: 'In a political arena where instability and strife are endemic, medium- and long-term policy and program planning become early victims to calculations of political advantage' (1996:133).

State administrative capacity is further undercut by strong cultural pressure on politicians and bureaucrats to redistribute wealth to family and kin, contributing to extensive nepotism and 'corruption'. Traditional pressures on a leader to function as a 'big-man'—a status based on merit that is often obtained by accumulating and, more importantly, redistributing wealth—place heavy financial obligations on politicians. Constituents often expect politicians to act as a traditional big-man, arranging feasts, paying school fees, and deferring funeral costs. These traditional pressures also influence bureaucrats, although bureaucrats are generally only expected to support family members. As a result, however, both bureaucrats and politicians are highly susceptible to bribes; as well, these obligations tend to weaken loyalty to national or state goals.

Other competing identities and loyalties further weaken state capacity. Many state officials identify more with family, kin, tribes, or *wantok* groups (people who speak the same language) than with the state. For this reason, state officials will sacrifice state goals and revenue to support their kin, tribe, or *wantok* group. Recipients of state services often perceive these as a gift from their political representative or well-placed relative, further undermining state capacity to control social groups. Because people expect so little from the state, however, this also allows the state to evade criticism and crises of legitimacy, even when administrative services are appalling (Kabutaulaka and Dauvergne 1997).[10]

As in Indonesia, élite attitudes that support economic development and downgrade environmental concerns contribute to low state determination to develop and enforce stringent environmental legislation. Informal and semi-traditional power relations that involve the exchange or redistribution of material goods by state members to societal supporters also contribute to distorted policies, lower state revenues, and weak enforcement. But informal links between state officials and loggers are markedly different in the Solomon Islands. Here, most ties are between state members and foreign business executives; as a result, they tend to be short-term arrangements—mostly one-time bribes, gifts, and perks. They are not part of any social grouping that could be considered a patron–client network, although these one-time deals do distort state policies and

---

10 Of course, some improvements have occurred in the Solomon Islands over the last two decades, such as lower infant mortality rates (Saadah, Heywood and Morris 1995:23).

undercut state enforcement. An even more important difference, however, is that the Solomon Islands state simply does not have the bureaucratic resources, international clout, legal powers, or technical competence to control multinational investors. The next two sections outline some of the basic forest and environment policies in Indonesia and the Solomon Islands, focusing in particular on state legal control over timber management.

The State, Policies, and Forests in Indonesia

Forests likely cover between 90 to 110 million hectares of Indonesia, although the government claims that 143 million hectares exist. The government has set aside 64 million hectares for selective logging (known as production forest). Most of these forests are on the outer islands of Kalimantan, Sulawesi, Sumatra, and New Guinea (in Irian Jaya). The Indonesian state has exclusive control over primary forests. Various sections of the bureaucracy shape forest management. With a staff of around 50 000, the Ministry of Forestry sets annual allowable harvests, and monitors and enforces cutting and silvicultural guidelines. The Ministry of Trade and Industry supports timber processing. And the State Ministry for the Environment coordinates environmental management, assesses the environmental effects of logging proposals, and monitors reforestation. More indirectly, Finance, Agriculture, Transmigration, Public Works, and Energy and Mines also influence forest management.

The 1967 Basic Forestry Law forms the core of forest rules. The 1989 Indonesian Selective Cutting and Replanting System (TPTI), along with various amendments, regulates loggers. Companies must submit annual harvest estimates, and five-year and 35-year management plans. The government also charges a non-refundable reforestation fee of US$22 per cubic metre of harvested logs. In addition, companies are supposed to provide one to five per cent of profits to support community development near their logging site. Some of Indonesia's forest management rules have clear structural defects. For example, the government issues twenty-year licences to log concessions on a 35-year cycle. Inappropriate tax structures and government subsidies have also led to the development of far too many plywood plants and sawmills, creating a chronic shortage of logs and strong incentives for illegal loggers. In addition, insufficient forest fees and taxes have left the government capturing remarkably little economic rent, although higher reforestation fees have increased the government's share of timber rents in recent years. The government could certainly improve policies, although as we will see later, an even greater problem is inadequate enforcement of current regulations.

The State, Policies, and Forests in the Solomon Islands

Forests cover about 85 per cent of the Solomon Islands.[11] Most forests are on steep slopes and small islands, and commercial logging is only appropriate or viable on about 480 000 hectares. Customary land owners control around 87 per cent of land area; the rest is owned privately or controlled by the government. In the mid-1990s, about 80 per cent of logging occurred on customary land. The 1969 Forest and Timber Act is the core of national forest legislation in the Solomon Islands. This has been amended several times and was renamed the Forest Resources and Timber Utilisation Act in 1984. The main state agency responsible for forest management is the forestry division of the Ministry of Forests, Environment and Conservation. The Ministry of Finance issues log export licences and grants companies exemptions on export taxes. The Foreign Investment Board approves applications and sets minimum financial, employment, and infrastructure development criteria for foreign investors. The Division of Inland Revenue is responsible for collecting taxes. There are serious problems with the structure and content of forest legislation. No consolidated text exists and it is often quite difficult to uncover timber management rules (see Fingleton 1989; Corrin 1992; Montgomery 1995: 74–6; and Ells 1996:9–11).

Serious flaws also exist with government policies to capture timber rents. Four main fees are imposed on foreign loggers: log export taxes, royalties to land owners, provincial forest charges, and corporate taxes on royalty payments and profits. Inconsistent log export taxes, tax breaks for 'reforestation programs' and 'community development', and partial or full tax exemptions on log exports to promote processing by land owner companies (including one for the company Somma, linked to former Prime Minister Mamaloni) have allowed companies to make windfall profits. Even though log exports account for about half of government export earnings, the government captures only a relatively small portion of timber revenues. State agencies responsible for monitoring multinational timber investors also have insufficient financial and technical resources. The Ministry of Forests, Environment and Conservation does not have enough forest officers to monitor logging sites and timber exports. The Division of Inland Revenue also has limited powers to prevent corporate schemes to evade taxes (Price Waterhouse 1995:39–40).

The extent of forest area, state financial and technical resources, state legal powers, government policies, and land ownership all shape state capacity to manage forests. In Indonesia, the state has the full legal right to manage forests. In the Solomon Islands, the state must work closely with land owners, and does not have the legal power to exert firm control. The Indonesian state also has much greater institutional assets to manage

11 Portions of the sections on forest policies and timber companies in the Solomon Islands draw on Dauvergne (1998a).

forests and control social forces, although Indonesia certainly has a more difficult task, needing to cover a much larger area. Both countries have structural problems with policies, although overall Indonesia has a more elaborate policy framework. Yet, as the next section documents, despite Indonesia's apparent strength, little difference exists between state control of domestic companies in Indonesia and state control of multinational investors in the Solomon Islands.

The State and Timber Companies in Indonesia

Before the mid-1960s, logging on the outer islands of Indonesia was limited to small-scale operations. The 1967 Foreign Capital Investment Law created favourable conditions for multinational investors, sparking a logging boom, especially in Kalimantan. By 1980, log production was five times higher than in 1968.[12] Over this time, investors made substantial profits, partly from generous tax breaks and cheap timber rights, and partly by ignoring reforestation, operating unsustainable sites, avoiding investments in processing plants, and evading taxes. Throughout the 1970s, the government became increasingly annoyed with uncooperative multinational firms, especially their reluctance to invest in processing.

Before 1971, most foreign investors held 100 per cent ownership. Starting in the early 1970s, the government began to push investors to accept joint venture partners. By 1975, the government no longer accepted foreign investments in logging, restricting investors to processing ventures. In 1977, the government imposed a mandatory deposit on log exports to support processing. The following year, the government doubled the log export tax to increase government revenues and further encourage processing. Companies that resisted pressure to invest in processing had their concession area reduced; particularly recalcitrant companies had their licences revoked. By the end of the 1970s, foreign firms began to withdraw, partially in response to signs of even further government restrictions.[13]

Despite strong opposition from the World Bank and powerful developed countries, the government gradually banned log exports from 1980 to 1985. State capacity to restrict foreign timber investors and impose the log export ban was remarkably strong. This partially reflected the growing capability and assertiveness of the state at this time. State capacity, however, was also significantly strengthened by the support of domestic

---

12 Unless otherwise noted, data on Indonesian log, sawnwood, and plywood production and exports prior to 1990 are calculated from Food and Agriculture Organisation (FAO), various yearbooks. Data from 1990 to 1997 are calculated from the International Tropical Timber Organisation (1995, 1996, 1997, and 1998).

13 For a discussion of this period, see Gillis (1987 and 1988), and Dauvergne (1997a:chapter 3).

business leaders whose financial opportunities and control were greatly enhanced by the ban. Supported by state subsidies, Indonesia's sawnwood and plywood industries expanded quickly in the 1980s. In 1979, sawnwood production was less than 3.5 million cubic metres; by 1988 it had gone over 10 million cubic metres. In 1980, plywood production was only around one million cubic metres; by 1992 it also went over 10 million cubic metres.

The sawnwood and plywood industries have remained strong in the 1990s. From 1990 to 1997, Indonesia's annual sawnwood production averaged more than 7.5 million cubic metres. Over this period, annual plywood production averaged over 9 million cubic metres. The Indonesian Wood Panel Association (Apkindo) had guided the expansion of the plywood industry until the government agreed to dismantle controls on plywood in February 1998 as part of a loan deal with the International Monetary Fund (IMF).[14] Under Bob Hasan, Apkindo issued export licences, set export prices, controlled shipping and insurance companies for plywood exporters, managed total plywood production volumes, and targeted export destinations. To break open foreign markets, Apkindo established marketing wings, including Nippindo for Japan and Indo Kor Panels for Korea. Through these marketing arms, Apkindo flooded overseas markets with high-quality plywood sold well below world market prices. Because Apkindo controlled export licences, plywood companies had little choice but to follow Apkindo's orders. By the early 1990s, Apkindo had managed to capture about three-quarters of world trade in tropical plywood, although fierce Malaysian competition reduced this to around two-thirds in the mid-1990s.[15]

Domestic corporate control in the 1980s and 1990s has contributed to even higher national production levels than in the 1970s. Based on data from the International Tropical Timber Organisation (ITTO), average log production from 1990 to 1997 was around 34 million cubic metres, over 13 million cubic metres higher than average log production in the 1970s. Log production may well be even higher than the ITTO figures. A 1996 World Bank study claimed that log production was around 40 million cubic metres. Including illegal logging and smuggling, NGO experts estimate that annual log production is more likely around 44 million cubic metres, two times higher than a recent World Bank estimate of sustainable yield. Damage is compounded by bad harvesting practices, and by illegal

---

14 It is not yet clear how this agreement will reshape the plywood industry. For example, Apkindo's shipping company simply changed its name on 1 February 1998 and then 'recommended' that Apkindo members continue to use its services. This 'recommendation' was widely viewed as an order. On 30 March 1998, the government revoked Apkindo's monopoly rights over plywood exports, in theory restricting Apkindo to supplying assistance and information. Nevertheless, informal controls may continue.

15 For further details on the structure and role of Apkindo, see Dauvergne (1997b).

cutting in national parks and conservation areas. At the current rate of destructive logging, the expansive primary forests of Indonesia could disappear in three decades ('Timber' 1994).

Ties among state members and timber executives distort forest policies and undercut enforcement. Bob Hasan is the most powerful timber businessman. He is close friends with Soeharto. He is chairman of Nusamba (*Nusantara Ampera Bakti*), an investment company controlled by Soeharto's foundations. He was chairman of Apkindo until Soeharto appointed him as the Minister of Trade and Industry in March 1998. He also has the rights to log two million hectares. Another powerful Indonesian business leader is Prayogo Pangestu, the largest timber operator in Asia. He controls 5.5 million hectares of forests and employs 55 000 people. He is also the world's largest tropical plywood exporter. Like Hasan, Prayogo has close ties to the Soeharto family. He is partners with Soeharto's daughter Siti Hardiyanti Rukmana (Tutut) in a huge pulp and paper mill. As well, he has made substantial donations to Soeharto-family charities and bailed out poor investments by Soeharto and senior military officers. With such powerful connections, it is not surprising that his Barito Pacific Group of companies has received substantial state loans, leaving the group with one of the heaviest debts in the country (see Schwarz 1992:44; Pura 1993; Pura, Duthi and Borsuk 1994; and Schwarz 1994).

During the timber boom in the late 1960s, Soeharto handed out timber licences to reward loyal military officers, appease potential opponents, and bolster the military budget. By 1978, the central and regional military commands controlled over a dozen timber companies. Today, the military is still an active timber operator, although apparently less so than in the 1970s. For example, the armed forces owns 51 per cent of the International Timber Corporation of Indonesia (Soeharto's son Bambang Trihatmodjo controls 34 per cent, and Hasan owns fifteen per cent). This company operates a 600 000 hectare concession in East Kalimantan, the largest in Indonesia. The timber company P.T. Yamaker, which logs a site near the Sabah border in East Kalimantan, also has close army ties. One insider claims that convoys of trucks smuggle logs into Sabah.[16]

Within the context of high-level military, political, bureaucratic, and business ties to the timber industry, poorly paid forest officers appear to routinely ignore corporate misconduct in exchange for cash, gifts, or career opportunities. Inadequate staff, limited environmental training, insufficient institutional resources, and huge and remote logging sites further hamper efforts to monitor and enforce forest management rules. A member of the Indonesian NGO Network for Forest Conservation (SKEPHI) is scathing: 'None of Indonesia's logging companies obey the

---

16 Confidential interview, senior Indonesian official, Jakarta, 3 March 1994. For further details on the International Timber Corporation of Indonesia, see International Timber Corporation Indonesia (1992), Rush (1991), and Pura (1990).

rules' (quoted in Schwarz 1992:45). Even the Ministry of Forestry admits that few loggers have followed the rules. Not surprisingly, the current campaign to reduce illegal and destructive logging has confronted powerful resistance and has had limited effects. In a rather understated way, in 1996 the *Jakarta Post* noted, 'in recent years, the ministry [of forestry] has tightened supervision to prevent illegal logging, and over-logging by concessionaires, but the move has so far resulted mostly in distorted log markets' ('Importing Logs' 1996).

Protected and aided by key political, military, customs, and tax officials, timber companies also forge export, transportation, and harvest documents to evade royalties, taxes, and reforestation fees. The Indonesian NGO Forum for the Environment (WALHI) and the Indonesian Legal Aid Foundation (YLBHI) estimate that in the 1980s the government only collected 30 per cent of reforestation fees. Even these limited reforestation funds do not always support timber plantations. For example, in late 1996 Soeharto authorised a Rp250 billion transfer from the reforestation fund to Kiani Kertas, a pulp company controlled by Hasan (Saragosa 1997). Even more remarkable, the IMF revealed in early 1998 that the government did not use reforestation funds to tackle the 1997 forest fires because these funds had been allocated to Indonesia's national car project, controlled by Soeharto's youngest son.

State control over timber companies strengthened incrementally after Djamaludin Suryohadikusumo became Forestry Minister in 1993. By the end of 1993, the government had revoked 60 timber licences. By early 1994, the government had assumed control of twenty per cent of the shares of twelve concession holders and 100 per cent of the shares of another twelve with poor management records. State companies now manage around eleven per cent of Indonesia's forests. The government has also fined several companies. These efforts, however, have had little impact on aggregate log production. The most powerful firms have tended to avoid this 'crackdown', or in some cases they have simply ignored state sanctions. For example, in late 1996, Forestry Minister Djamaludin refused to renew 60 timber licences of companies with poor management records. In April 1997, however, the forestry department discovered that these companies simply kept operating. More recently, the plantation companies that illegally set the 1997 forest fires in Kalimantan and Sumatra went largely unpunished (Dauvergne 1998b).

The State and Timber Companies in the Solomon Islands

Multinational companies have dominated logging in the Solomon Islands.[17] The history can be divided into three periods: 1963–81, 1981–

---

17 This section only examines multinational timber investors. In 1995, land owner companies accounted for nine per cent of log exports, although even here most had contracts with multinational firms.

90, and 1990–98. In the first period, three foreign loggers controlled the industry: Levers Pacific Timber, a subsidiary of United Africa Company; the Australian firm, Allardyce Lumber Company; and the US-funded Kalena Lumber Company. Levers Pacific Timber was the largest logger, accounting for two-thirds to three-quarters of total production. During this time, most logging occurred on government owned or leased land, primarily in Western province. Although environmental rules and management were limited, annual log production only averaged around 260 000 cubic metres, below the theoretical sustainable level.

This changed in the early 1980s. Under the first Mamaloni government, the number of licences quadrupled and foreign firms moved into Guadalcanal, Malaita, and Makira-Ulawa. Although many of these were small operations, log production escalated, especially on customary land. From 1981 to 1986, annual log production exceeded sustainable levels (based on Frazer 1997:44–52). The increase in licences and log production, the move to customary land, and the spread to more islands stretched state capacity to monitor and regulate foreign timber investors. The withdrawal of Levers Pacific Timber temporarily relieved pressure on the forests and state capacity, and aggregate production again fell below a sustainable level at the end of the 1980s.

Starting in 1991, however, an influx of Malaysian investors significantly altered the timber sector. Logging licences have proliferated, often with highly favourable terms for investors. State officials have succumbed to corporate pressures (and sometimes bribes), stalling environmental reforms, eroding implementation of forest management rules, and leading to generous tax breaks. In this context, the state and communities are even less able to monitor and control foreign loggers than in the 1980s. In 1995, log production from natural forests was 826 000 cubic metres, over two times higher than in 1991. In 1996, despite strong domestic and international criticism, log production remained at about the same level (CBSI 1997:16). At this rate, loggers would have depleted commercial forests in thirteen years; if the rate had continued to increase, this would have occurred in less than a decade (Montgomery 1995:75).[18] Since mid-1997, however, the Asian financial crisis has contributed to a sharp drop in international timber prices and demand for Solomon Islands logs, slowing at least temporarily this looming environmental disaster.[19]

---

18 Unless otherwise noted, data on log production in the Solomon Islands are calculated from the *1995 Forestry Review*, an unofficial report published in 1996, based on figures from the Timber Control Unit Project of the Ministry of Forests, Environment and Conservation, Solomon Islands Government (supplied to the author by a government official in the Solomon Islands in July 1996); and *Forestry Review Update 1996* (June), an unofficial government report that builds on the *1995 Forestry Review* (supplied by a government official in the Solomon Islands in July 1996).

19 Since coming to power in August 1997, the Ulufa'alu government has made ambitious announcements about reforming the logging industry in the

As mentioned earlier, because customary land owners control most forest areas in the Solomon Islands, the state has fewer legal powers to 'manage' commercial forests than in countries where the state owns the primary forests. The powers that the Solomon Islands state does hold—in particular the power to regulate foreign investment and approve logging licences—had little impact on aggressive investors during the Mamaloni governments of 1989–93 and 1994–97. The process of obtaining a logging licence illustrates the constraints on, and options for, the state. To obtain a logging licence, a company first submits an application to the national government. If approved, the application is then forwarded to the relevant provincial government and Area Council. A Timber Rights Hearing, which includes land owners, Area Council members, and provincial officials determines who owns the timber, whether the owners are willing to sell their rights, how owners will share profits, and the role of the provincial government. If the parties agree to logging, a public notice must be issued with sufficient time for objections. After this, the Area Council forwards a Certificate of Recommendation and Land Ownership to the forestry division. Company officials and land owner representatives then publicly negotiate a Standard Logging Agreement (a provincial representative and a forest division representative act as observers). In theory, the forest division is supposed to monitor negotiations, ensuring that proper procedures are followed, that legal appeals are settled, and that the final logging agreement and the Area Council certificate are consistent. Assuming that the process is acceptable, the Commissioner of Forests then issues a licence to the applicant. If procedural disputes arise, or if the agreement is breached, the matter is referred to the High Court.

This process appears to provide several opportunities for the state to intervene and reject a logger's application. But in practice the government does not effectively monitor negotiations. Far too many logging licences have been approved for foreign investors, sometimes even before they make formal agreements with land owners, giving them licences without access rights. Although unlikely, if all of these licences became active, loggers could harvest four million cubic metres a year, depleting commercial timber in only three years (Economic Insights 1994b:54; Baird 1996:23; Ells 1996:10–11).

Land owner and corporate negotiations for timber rights and licences are often long and acrimonious. Although delays have frustrated some investors, inadequate state supervision, ambiguous laws, corrupt and divided community negotiators, corporate bribes, corporate funding of Area Council (Timber Rights) meetings, and highly trained corporate negotiators have generally allowed multinational timber companies to negotiate favourable agreements. For example, the Standard Logging Agreement and the Forest Act recommend a royalty rate of 17.5 per cent of free-on-

---

Solomon Islands. As of May 1998, the concrete outcome of these proposals is still unclear. For a discussion of these proposals, see Dauvergne (1998a).

board (FOB) value. Yet the average royalty rate in 1994 was only 11.5 per cent of FOB value. Moreover, despite favourable agreements, timber investors have distorted or broken many agreements with land owners. They have ignored verbal and written promises to provide 'lasting development', such as roads, bridges, medical clinics, and schools. They have often left behind far more damage than land owners expect, disrupting traditional food sources, polluting rivers, and violating sacred sites. And they have evaded timber royalty payments (Bennett 1995:262; Frazer 1997:51; Price Waterhouse 1995:23; Ells 1996:11, 16; *Sol-Tree Nius* 2 February 1995:3; Fingleton 1994:21).

Corporations have also pressured and bribed some key politicians and bureaucrats to create a favourable policy climate for investors and reverse reforms that threaten profits. The most visible example occurred during Prime Minister Billy Hilly's government from 1993 to 1994. The Hilly government initiated reforms to lower log production and strengthen state control over foreign timber investors. The government raised log export taxes, and increased efforts to verify log export prices, grades, and species. The government also began work on new national forest legislation, proclaimed plans to ban log exports in 1997, and floated the idea of hiring a foreign company to strengthen surveillance and compliance. These moves to control timber investors were quickly thwarted. In October 1994, Hilly's government fell after a series of defections and resignations. According to former Minister of Forests, Environment and Conservation Joses Tuhanuku (1993–94), this was 'the making of foreign logging companies' (1995:69). From 1994 to 1997, environmental protection and control over foreign investors weakened even further under Prime Minister Mamaloni. The government decreased log export taxes, postponed the log export ban until at least 1999, removed foreign advisers, abolished moves to strengthen surveillance of foreign operations, and agreed to cancel four forestry aid projects, including the Timber Control Unit Project (created in 1993 with the support of Australian aid to monitor log grades, species, volumes, and prices).

Foreign loggers have largely ignored environmental rules outlined in Standard Logging Agreements. According to these agreements, companies should supply land owners with logging and road plans, obey the River Waters Act, follow proper skidding practices, clean up work areas, restrict logging to safe distances from waterways and to stipulated species and sizes, follow cutting and removal rules, and construct roads and bridges according to government guidelines. Some corporate groups, such as Malaysia's Kumpulan Emas, have little logging experience. Others, especially from Sarawak Malaysia, have terrible records at home (Dauvergne 1997a:chapter 4). In the Solomon Islands, weak state administrative capacity, limited state legal powers, remote logging sites, and few provincial and community resources allow loggers to operate with little scrutiny and almost no restraints. Tuhanuku writes: 'During my time as Minister, foreign logging companies persistently showed a blatant disregard for the nation's laws, regulations and policy of the government of the day' (1995:69). Companies log areas outside their licence, damage or cut under-sized and protected trees, build temporary and inappropriate roads and bridges, leave pools of stagnant water that spread malaria, pollute and disrupt food and water sources, disregard reforestation duties, and ignore obligations to consult with land owners. A study of a logging site operated by the Malaysian company Silvania concluded: 'The degree of canopy removal and soil disturbance was the most extensive seen by the authors in any logging operation in tropical rainforest in any country' (quoted in Forests Monitor 1996:7). Phillip Montgomery argues:

> To come back and re-cut the Solomons forest in 50 years and get equivalent sorts of yields to what they are now producing means that everything has to be done correctly now. The reality is that there is no adherence at all to a silvicultural regime that will allow this to occur. Many of the harvesting operations are still poorly planned and poorly managed' (1995:74).

The *1995 Forestry Review*, an unofficial internal government document, is even harsher: 'forest practices in many locations [in the Solomon Islands] are amongst the worst in the world' (for further details, see South Pacific Regional Environment Programme 1992:25–6; Greenpeace Pacific 1995).

Besides dismal environmental practices, foreign loggers have pressured and enticed state officials to provide generous tax breaks. For example, the *Solomon Star* reported that from 1993 to 1995 Integrated Forest Industries distributed SI$7 million and supplied generous perks to government ministers and powerful bureaucrats. Not surprisingly, Integrated Forest Industries paid no taxes in 1995. In that year, according to the *1995 Forestry Review*, as a result of tax breaks, combined with lower international prices and lower export taxes, government revenue captured by the log export tax fell by SI$12.6 million, even though log exports jumped by 88 000 cubic metres.

Securing tax breaks is only one means that loggers use to increase and maintain profits. They also evade royalty payments, log export taxes, and corporate taxes on profits. Companies forge species names and log grades, conceal high-grade logs in low-grade shipments, and simply under-record prices to lower log export taxes (which in turn lowers recorded profits). According to Ron Duncan, schemes to under-record log export prices in 1993 may have cost the Solomon Islands government up to SI$94 million (1994:xvii). Price Waterhouse estimates that 'the declared FOB value is...25 percent to 30 percent under-recorded' (1995:ii). The *1995 Forestry Review* claims that most firms 'should have at least been able to achieve the prices realised by Somma of SI$458 as the Makira logs are generally smaller and of lower quality to those on other concessions'.[20] Yet in that year, all foreign loggers reported far lower average log export prices, decreasing the overall average export price to a mere SI$366. A 1995 report by the Solomon Islands Central Bank and the Timber Control Unit also uncovered evidence of underpricing of log exports. After calculating for reasonable shipping and insurance costs, this report found that the average Japanese import price of Solomon Islands logs in 1994 was US$33.90 per cubic metre higher than the declared export price; in Korea, it was US$32 per cubic metre higher.[21]

Conclusion: Environmental Degradation and Weak States

This study reveals that scholars must use labels such as strong and weak states prudently. A seemingly strong state can be quite weak in some areas. The underlying reasons for strong and weak capacities also shift over time and across sectors. In Indonesia, for example, state capacity to control loggers was fairly strong in the 1970s when the industry was dominated by multinational corporations. With the support of domestic business leaders, with alternative revenue sources, and with a high level of state determination, the state managed to restrict foreign investments, develop and impose policies to promote domestic processing, and strictly enforce a log export ban. State action was so firm that by the mid-1980s most multinationals had simply withdrawn from the timber sector.

State members in Indonesia are now far less committed to policies that promote sustainable management than they were to policies in the 1970s to control foreign investors and diversify the economy. This in part reflects attitudes, as well as competition for resources within the state which undercut funding and support for environmental concerns. Even more importantly, however, state capacity has been debilitated by close personal and financial links between political leaders and timber executives, and among middle and lower-level state officials and timber operators. In this context, destructive loggers have pushed production well over sustainable levels, the state has only captured a fraction of timber rents, and state moves to reform timber management have largely failed. This demonstrates that just because a state has significant autonomy from formal social groups and tight controls over non-state organisations (such as labour, business, political parties, the media, and NGOs) does not mean that the state can necessarily enforce official rules that challenge the profits or goals of diffuse social forces that underpin the state. Severing

---

20 Somma had less incentive to under declare log export prices because the government exempted it from 96 per cent of the log export tax.

21 Agent fees in places like Singapore and Hong Kong may account for about US$5 of this difference (Mulholland and Simbe 1995:2). For greater detail on the environmental and economic impact of multinational investors in the Solomon Islands since 1990, see Dauvergne (1997c).

ties with these diffuse groups—such as patrons turning against clients—could undermine the very foundation of the state. These otherwise strong states will be especially weak when state determination is low and resistance from powerful societal members is high, a characteristic situation for the environmental management of natural resources. Indonesia also demonstrates that just because a state dominates policy formulation does not mean that the policies will be well constructed or well enforced.

As in Indonesia, state capacity to control the environmental practices of loggers has decreased in the Solomon Islands over the last two decades. In the 1960s and 1970s, with only three large foreign loggers, and with most logging on state owned or leased land, the state was able to maintain a reasonable level of control, and log production remained below sustainable levels. During the 1980s and 1990s, however, national-level timber management in the Solomon Islands became more difficult as the number of logging licences shot up, as loggers spread to more islands and to customary land, as Malaysian investors flooded the country, as the government became increasingly dependent on log export revenues, and as production went well over sustainable levels.

Compared to Indonesia, patron–client ties between business leaders and state officials are less important for explaining low state capacity to manage timber in the Solomon Islands. It is more a result of political instability, inadequate technical and financial resources, conflicting loyalties of state members, legal constraints on state actions, and straightforward corporate bribes and pressure. For these reasons, combined with large subsistence and informal economies, and the relatively weak position of the Solomon Islands in the international system, in most areas, state capacity in the Solomon Islands has been consistently and significantly lower than in Indonesia. Yet, despite markedly different state structures and overall capacities, and different historical, institutional, cultural, geographic, demographic, political, and economic settings, both countries are now confronted with the same irresolvable crisis: inappropriate forest and environmental policies, unsustainable and destructive logging, widespread degradation, limited reforestation, inadequate timber rents, and a state that has little, if any, control over corporate practices.

This finding suggests that, although each state has distinct foundations of state capacity, and although state capacity can shift over time, it is reasonable to hypothesise that when valuable commercial forests exist, and when a developing state is confronted by aggressive corporations that provide vital state revenue or crucial personal support for state members, then the state will exert weak control over corporate environmental practices—a hypothesis that is reasonably extrapolated to other resource sectors, and perhaps to environmental management generally. Searching the tropical world it is certainly easy to find state policies and rhetoric that support sustainable development and environmental protection, often employing an almost hegemonic global environmental language (Dauvergne 1997d). But the commitment of state officials seems minimal and it is difficult to find any examples of tight state control over the environmental practices of loggers. For example, as timber investors (mostly from Malaysia) flooded Papua New Guinea in the late 1980s and early 1990s, log production more than doubled, from 1.45 million cubic metres in 1990 to 3.5 million cubic metres in 1994. Although total production fell to about three million cubic metres in 1995, these loggers are still leaving behind widespread environmental degradation (Filer 1997b). Guyana provides another example of weak state control over the environmental management of timber firms. In 1989, the government had only leased about seventeen per cent of the 14 million hectares of suitable commercial forest area. Yet by 1994, the government had leased well over half of this area and further proposals are still under review. These investors (again, mostly from Malaysia) are quickly pushing up production with few environmental controls. From 1992 to 1994, log production more than doubled, from 151 000 cubic metres to 403 000 cubic metres. In 1995, it increased again to 456 000 cubic metres. Over the next decade, it will escalate even further as Malaysian operations reach capacity (Colchester 1994; Sizer 1996).

In some ways, it is not surprising that Papua New Guinea and Guyana—which like the Solomon Islands are weak administrative states—have little control over the environmental practices of loggers. What is perhaps more illuminating (and alarming) is that logging practices are just as bad in states with a similar overall capacity as Indonesia had at the height of its powers (such as the Malaysian state of Sarawak), or with a greater overall capacity (such as Burma). In Sarawak, where timber exports underpin the economy, destructive loggers are linked to top political patrons, including Chief Minister Taib, and protected and assisted by middle-and-lower level state officials. In this context, despite government promises to improve forest management in the early 1990s, annual log production from 1990 to 1995 averaged almost 18 million cubic metres, over two times higher than sustainable levels. At this rate, loggers will destroy the primary forests of Sarawak in less than a decade (Dauvergne 1997a:chapter 4).

The Burmese state has strengthened environmental policies and tightened control over environmental management since the military coup in September 1988. For example, the government created a National Commission for Environmental Affairs in 1990, issued a new Forest Law in late 1992, and proclaimed the Wild Life, Natural Forests and Preservation Law in 1994. One of the government's most important environmental initiatives is the move to 'green' the central Dry Zone. This strong state determination to develop and enforce new environmental policies appears motivated primarily by a desire to control outlying social groups, not by a genuine desire to implement sustainable development. The campaign to green the central Dry Zone is led by three senior military officers, committees of loyal bureaucrats and military officers coordinate the project, and mass 'public participation' provides the work force (that is, free labour). In many areas, however, commercial forest management is, according to Raymond Bryant, 'business-as-usual'. The state, for example, allowed Thai loggers to over-log and destroy wide areas from 1989 to 1993,[22] and is now supporting unsustainable logging in the Kachin State and the Pegu Yoma. In these cases, the Burmese government is sacrificing environmental concerns to provide supporters with lucrative timber patronage. According to Bryant:

> In the process, claims of sustainable development in the forestry sector appear as hollow in Burma as they do in Indonesia, the country upon which Burmese political and economic development appears to be increasingly modeled (1996:355–6).

The inherent weakness of states to control the environmental effects of loggers does not bode well for the future of the world's tropical old-growth forests, especially as aggressive investors continue to move into increasingly isolated areas with few administrative structures, such as Laos, Cambodia, Surinam, Brazil, Cameroon, Democratic Republic of Congo (formerly Zaire), Belize, and Gabon. These countries could well be headed toward logging industries similar to the ones in Indonesia, Sarawak, Papua New Guinea, and the Solomon Islands, and just beginning in Guyana. If this does happen, and the pattern of weak state control over the practices of loggers continues, then all of these countries will likely end up with widespread deforestation, as has already occurred in the once lush countries of Thailand and the Philippines.

---

22 In late 1993, with the Burmese government less dependent on logging revenue, with less military need to remove forest cover, and with many areas near the Thai border already cleared, the government cancelled the agreements with Thai loggers. With government support, however, logging still occurs in this area, although production is now lower (Bryant 1996:354).

9 Land Regimes and State Strengths and Weaknesses in the Philippines and Vietnam

BENEDICT J. TRIA KERKVLIET

How and in what sense are the states in Vietnam and the Philippines strong or weak is the main question of this paper. I want to consider the abilities and inabilities of states in these two countries to formulate and carry out policies and the relationship of states to other parts of society. My main theme is the difficulty of making overall, broad generalisations about a state's strength. An assessment needs to take into consideration particular policies, perspectives, and components of strength–weakness.

The main similarity between the Philippines and Vietnam that is important for my study is that in both, a major political issue over several decades has been how agricultural land should be governed. This is the policy area I want to emphasise. The political systems in the two nations since independence from colonialism in the mid-twentieth century are substantially different. The Philippines is more democratic in the sense that citizens may rather readily organise and publicly espouse and promote their particular interests. Restrictions against this are numerous in Vietnam.

Literature on Philippine and Vietnam State–Society Relations

Most analysts of Philippine politics agree that the state, since the country's independence from colonial rule in 1946, has been relatively 'weak'. It has been unable to set down policies for industrialisation, economic development, or other objectives and carry them through to implementation largely because it has lacked sufficient autonomy from powerful oligarchies and foreign influences (especially from the United States), has a poorly developed bureaucracy, and has leaders who are more prone to pursue narrow, personalistic and familial interests rather than broader societal ones. Even the authoritarian regime of Ferdinand Marcos (1972–86), which initially vowed to fashion a 'developmental state', soon proved to be unable or uncommitted to accomplish that goal.[1] One dissenter is Sidel (1995a:chapters 1, 2). The Philippine state may not be a 'developmental state', he says, but it is a strong state in other respects. Its leaders have been able to use agencies of the state to get people in society to do what they ask of them.

Scholarly assessments of Vietnam's state since independence are divided. Some see the state as rather impervious to outside influences and pressures, possessing a coherent bureaucracy that can transmit and implement policy from the centre to the hinterlands, and can mobilise resources to carry out major social, economic, and political projects and programs. Porter, for instance, argues that major decisions in Vietnam 'are made entirely *within* the bureaucracy and are influenced by it rather than by extra bureaucratic forces in the society—whether parliamentary parties, interest groups, or mass movements'. A small group of Communist party officials determine major policies; implementation involves dynamic interaction between the central level and local party cadres (Porter 1993:101). Migdal rates Vietnam as one of the handful of 'Third World' countries with a state that is 'high on the continuum of "stateness"', meaning 'the ability of state leaders to use the agencies of the state to get people in the society to do what they want them to do' (1988:xiii, 267).

Other analysts, however, argue that the bureaucracy, Communist Party, and other elements of the state in Vietnam are far less able to coordinate programs and implement policies than the strong state view would require (Woodside 1979; Thrift and Forbes 1986:81–3, 101–4). Fforde and de Vylder go so far as to conclude, on account of the huge distortions between what the state wanted and what actually happened, that the state was 'weak' in the 1960s and 1970s. In effect, because the state was unable to prevent the rise of opposition to its programs, it failed to carry out rapid urban industrialisation, collectivise production, control the marketing of goods and services, and implement other components of the centrally planned political economy that the Communist Party's leadership envisioned (Fforde and de Vylder 1996:4, 56–69). Since the late 1970s and early 1980s, after backing away from that program and endorsing 'market socialism', the 'highly decentralized' character of the state and the limited ability of the central government to control local authorities have become more apparent, according to Melanie Beresford (1994?:13–14).[2] Along

---

1 For a sampling of the literature on the Philippine state, see Rivera (1994: especially chapters 5–6), McCoy (1994:10–19), Villacorta (1994). Also see Wurfel (1988:56, 327).

2 I should add that Beresford also argues that the weak, decentralised character of Vietnam's state is not due to a strong civil society. Local interests defying central state authority, she emphasises, are not necessarily the same as civil society.

with those market reforms, Fforde and Seneque find that 'a strong inter-
locking "triangle"' of interests in local areas has emerged to frustrate state
development programs and policies, a situation similar to the 'triangle of
accommodation' by which Migdal explains how most Third World states
are weakened (Fforde and Seneque 1995:130, 132; Migdal 1988:chapter
7).

I will not in this chapter argue which of these interpretations of
Vietnam and the Philippines is accurate. My purpose is to indicate uneasi-
ness with accepting entirely any one of these interpretations. All have
merit, but no single one is sufficient, at least in terms of my understanding
of relations between the state and the rural majority in each country. To
proceed, I need to discuss a few pertinent concepts.

Concepts: Drawing on Migdal

I am comfortable for now to think of 'the state' in terms similar to those
made by Migdal and Skocpol, who in turn draw on Weber, among other
authors (Migdal 1988:19–20; Skocpol 1979:29–31; Migdal 1994). The
state encompasses policy making, administrative, policing, and military
organisations with a central leadership. It attempts to make binding rules
for a national society, monopolise the authoritative use of violence, and
defend itself and the nation's territory against domestic and international
rivals or intruders. Although 'state' is a singular noun, the state is rarely a
singular actor; the degree of coherence among the organisations within it
varies over time and from one state to another. Also, while the state is
different from society, it is not separable from it (Migdal 1994:26). A state
is a creation of society yet is not the same as society and has helped to
shape what society is. Confusing, yes. But this manner of thinking is more
helpful, I submit, than treating the state and society as separate.

Migdal assesses the strength of a state in terms of its leaders' abilities
to get people to do what state policies and laws require of them. Doing so
necessitates social control, which means to subordinate what people would
otherwise be inclined to do to the behaviour prescribed by the state's
rulers. High levels of social control enable states to mobilise their populations, collect taxes and other resources from society, have sufficient
autonomy from other organisations to decide on and implement state
programs, monopolise coercion to prevent other groups in society from
obstructing the state's authority, and stand up to external foes (Migdal
1988:xiii, 22, 32).

An important feature of Migdal's conceptualisation of strength is that
social control—what he calls the 'currency' over which organisations in
society fight and which the state seeks to dominate—is graduated along a
scale of increasing comprehensiveness and, hence, strength. The 'most
elementary' level of social control, he says, is 'compliance'—getting
people to conform to its demands. A step higher and stronger is 'par-

ticipation' involving 'voluntary use of and action in state-run or state-authorised institutions'. The 'most potent factor accounting for strength of the state' is legitimation, which is also more 'inclusive than either compliance or participation. It is an acceptance, even approbation, of the state's rules of the game its social control, as true and right' (1988:32–3).

I accept Migdal's compliance, participation, and legitimation as components of strength, though I do not necessarily see them as ascending levels. Legitimacy need not come only after sectors of society comply with and then get involved in a state program. It may occur before either one of the other two. How these components come together and in what sequence requires investigation and analysis.

Migdal does not elaborate much about legitimation and legitimacy, perhaps because most of his book is about states that are more on the weak end of the strong–weak continuum, whose leaders have considerable difficulty getting compliance and whose policies and laws are frequently undermined by, among other forces, the 'politics of survival' and 'triangles of accommodation'.

To me, political legitimacy is a mixture of competence, reciprocity, abiding by the rules, and the appropriate use of coercion or force.[3] People in every society have some minimal expectations from a political authority, such as the state. They would usually expect, for example, state authorities to be able to maintain peace and order and protect citizens from foreign invaders and turmoil. Beyond the minimal are other considerations, such as contributing to, or raising, people's material well-being. Reciprocity refers to the extent to which the state or other political authority give something of benefit back to people who, for their part, give support or at least acquiescence, pay taxes, and so on. Abiding by the rules pertains to upholding tacit or explicit understandings about how authorities should govern and how to choose those who are to govern. All political authority, all states, use coercion and force, but within acceptable or tolerable limits. Exceeding those bounds runs into the realm of illegitimate use of political power.

Assessments of legitimacy can vary from one sector of society to another according to ethnicity, class, region, religion, or other social, economic, cultural, or philosophical considerations and predilections. Like beauty and other intangibles, legitimacy is in the eyes of the beholder. This adds to difficulties of determining how much legitimacy an authority has. Nevertheless, with Migdal, I think legitimacy is a quality that must be taken into consideration when assessing political strength of a state and its relations with society.

In addition to bearing in mind the different components of strength that were just discussed, I see two additional dimensions that need to be kept in mind when assessing strength and weaknesses of a state and state-

---

3   I am drawing on two books by Moore (1969:54–61 and 1978:15–30). Some of these elements overlap with those discussed by Alagappa (1995:14–26).

society relations. These two are not apparent in Migdal's writings. One is policy area—the particular laws, programs, or points of contention. Few if any states are uniformly strong, or weak, on all policy making, administrative, policing, or military fronts. A state may be an effective tax collector, for example, but a weak implementor of policies against racial or religious discrimination. Even the same function might be strong in certain parts of the country or on certain aspects of society but weak in other areas. Policing and law enforcement, for instance, might be vigilant and strict in some regions but weak in frontier zones, or effectively stop violations of building codes but be poor in countering drug rings.

A second is perspective. What appears to be a strength from one vantage point may be a weakness when seen from another. What one group or sector of society sees as strong could be seen as weakness by another. Not carrying through with a policy agenda and changing course can be seen as weakness from the perspective of those who favoured it or would have benefited from it but a strength by those who opposed that policy and favour the new course.

I want now to take these three dimensions—components of strength, policy area, and perspective—to analyse aspects of state–society relations in the Philippines and Vietnam. The policy area that interests me concerns land regimes, that is, how land is governed—who may use it, do what with it, and with what rights and obligations. I am emphasising the perspectives of small farmers, peasants, and agricultural workers, especially in the lowlands, for whom securing land to farm has been a major concern in recent decades.[4] In order to do this, I need first to outline major features of land regimes in the two countries in the late colonial period (1910s to the 1930s) and then since independence (post-1940s).[5]

Land Regimes

A major theme in the rural Philippines and Vietnam has been contending values about how land should be governed. The land regime preferred by many Filipino and Vietnamese peasants, agricultural workers, and other small agrarian producers—villagers, for short—has often been at odds with what more powerful interests and groups, including the state, have wanted. The resulting friction and contestation have brought about modest, incremental progress in the Philippine countryside in the sense that more villagers have somewhat greater and more secure access to land in recent decades than they did at the beginning of this century. In

---

4   I say this knowing it is impossible to generalise accurately about these groups and their perceptions. Nevertheless, I believe I can do so less *in*accurately than to talk about entire populations of both countries.

5   For this outline I am drawing on a longer discussion in Kerkvliet (1997). I thank the Centre for Asian Studies, Amsterdam, for permission to use that material here.

Vietnam, the results of these struggles have been considerably more favourable for most villagers as far as access to land is concerned, but the process has also been far more violent than in the Philippines.

Land regimes in the Philippines and Vietnam during the late colonial period were very similar. Each shared three central principles.[6] First, both the United States and French colonial states emphasised and protected private land. A person or other legal entity could personally own land and buy and sell it as one would a bag of rice or article of clothing. The Spanish had already institutionalised this idea in many parts of the Philippines before the United States took over at the turn of the century. In Vietnam, private land ownership was somewhat less pervasive as it was mingled with and modified by other land arrangements, particularly communal ownership and common land rights.

Second, both colonial states endorsed the idea that how much land someone owned was a matter for individuals, not the state, to decide, a stance that permitted land to be concentrated in the hands of a few people. Whether a person had no land or a thousand hectares was of little or no legal concern to colonial rulers in either country. Hence, neither state restricted how much land a Filipino or Vietnamese individual, family, or company could own.[7] In Vietnam, French citizens and companies, too, could own unlimited amounts. The situation was similar in the Philippines, although United States' law did restrict how much land certain foreign entities could own.[8]

Third, the state usually recognised only ownership that had been duly legalised by its rules and regulations governing land registration, deeds, bills of sale, taxes, and so on. Other bases for claiming ownership, such as common law and local practices, were rarely accepted by these colonial states.

A key feature of both colonial states, which dovetails with the three principles underlying the dominant land regime in each, is that they were far more partial to wealthy people, large land owners, and other social–economic élites than to villagers. American and French colonial officials actively sought support from the gentry and made policies accordingly.[9]

---

6   For Vietnam, see Ngo (1973), Murray (1980:55–95, 374–472), Fforde (1983), Bassford (1985), Pham (1985:chapters 2–4). For the Philippines, see McLennan (1980:chapters 7–9), Larkin (1993:chapter 3), Fegan (1982), Edgerton (1982).

7   Limits specified in US law on how much 'public land' a person or corporation could acquire and in French Vietnam on how large 'land concessions' could be did not prevent individuals and companies from accumulating land in other ways.

8   The United States' colonial regime did break up several huge estates owned by certain religious orders within the Catholic Church.

9   In 1936, the General Inspector of Agriculture for the French colonies, Yves Henry, referred to this stance as the '"client" policy of basing French domination on the support of a minority for which the best land, ample credit and

One manifestation was allowing, even encouraging, large holdings. Another was a legal system biased to large land owners and others with money and influence.

This dominant land regime had numerous adverse consequences for a large proportion of rural Filipinos and Vietnamese. Not that village life before US and French rule was idyllic or even better; in some respects these colonial states were accelerating processes already in motion before they arrived. In any event, colonial land regimes posed immense challenges for a large proportion of villagers in the 1920s and 1930s. Often they were caught up in protracted struggles to acquire or keep fields to farm whether as owners or tenants. Their claims to land, terms of its use, tenancy conditions, and credit arrangements were often contested and undermined by more powerful interests, including the courts, police, and other agencies of the state. Conflicts over land became particularly intense in the 1920s and 1930s on account of sharp shifts in class relations in favour of large land holders, the diminishing frontiers for new land, volatile economic conditions, and the emergence of peasant organisations, among other reasons.[10] Violent uprisings erupted as Filipino and Vietnamese peasants took last gasp steps to protest against not having enough to support their families, a predicament frequently linked to precarious or non-existent access to farm land.

In Vietnam, bitter conflicts over access to land, how it should be used and allocated, and the distribution of grain and other produce from the land contributed directly to a revolutionary war against French colonial rule. Of course, nationalism and the desire for independence were also important. Still, for a large proportion of Vietnamese villagers, the prospect of having access to land, retrieving land that had been taken from them or their communities, and improving their standard of living (especially staving off starvation) were as important as replacing French rulers with Vietnamese ones.

During and following Vietnam's war for independence (1945–1954) and then its war for reunification (1960s–1975), the Communist Party-dominated state of Vietnam overthrew the colonial land regime. This, what we might call, 'land revolution' stretched over decades and was complicated by many factors, most notably the partitioning of the country from 1954 to 1975, during which the Communist Party's state authority was restricted mainly to the northern half of the country. The land revolution involved three stages. The first two—land redistribution and

---

influential position were reserved'. That policy plus 'concentrating entirely on the large-scale development of the rice fields', he went on, led to the establishment in Cochinchina of 'a plutocracy of large and medium-scale landowners holding about 80 percent of the rice fields' (quoted in International Labour Office 1975:193).

10 A sample of relevant literature includes Scott (1976:88–9, 126ff), Popkin (1979:chapters 5–6), Hy (1985), Sturdevant (1976:chapters 9, 11, 12), Kerkvliet (1977:chapter 2), and Connolly (1992).

collectivisation of land and agricultural production—had been envisioned by the Communist Party leadership since the 1950s, if not earlier. The third—decollectivisation and reassigning land to households—was an afterthought, which only dawned on the leadership as it confronted numerous, increasingly insurmountable problems, especially in the late 1970s. One major problem was swelling opposition among villagers to collectivisation.

By 1956, nearly all land in north Vietnam had been redistributed more-or-less equally, benefiting over 70 per cent of the north's rural population (Truong 1987:35). Without paying any compensation in return, authorities had taken fields from landlords deemed to be abusive and from others with more than their fair share and gave that land to villagers who had none or very little. It was a tumultuous process, pitting people against each other and resulting in many unjustified punishments, including killings, excesses that later Communist Party leaders tried to rectify.

In the south, the Vietnamese–United States government, based in Saigon for most of the 1954–75 period, embraced a land regime largely in line with that of the French before. The Saigon government had no effective tenancy reforms and, until 1970, showed little commitment to addressing grievances of poor rural people, a stance that alienated it from villagers in many parts of the south (Sansom 1970:66–9, 228–45; Callison 1983:46–51, 74–8). The land redistribution program, which began in 1970, was too late to significantly affect the course of the war. On the other hand, the war in the south against the Vietnamese–United States government and for reunification won considerable support among many villagers. Their leaders continued to press for better tenancy conditions and land redistribution. After the country was reunited in 1975–76, the Communist Party government of the newly named Socialist Republic of Vietnam continued land redistribution in the south. It outlawed tenancy and reduced the proportion of southern villagers with no farm land from twenty per cent in 1968 to about six per cent in 1978 (Nguyen 1990:48, 149).[11]

---

11 I have not yet found sufficient material on the land distribution situation in south Vietnam at the end of the war in 1975. Vietnamese scholars estimate that by 1965, 1.3 million hectares in areas where the National Liberation Front (NLF) had significant influence or control had been put in the hands of the peasantry (*ruong dat ve tay nong dan*). This included land that landlords had abandoned, owners had donated, and the revolutionary movement had confiscated, as well as that which peasants had converted from waste land to farm land. Adding that to the approximately 750 000 hectares that peasants already had as of 1945 brings to 2.1 million hectares, out of roughly 3 million in south Vietnam, that tillers of land controlled (*lam chu ruong*), though not necessarily 'owned' (Lam 1985:101–2).The land reform that the Vietnamese–United States government began to implement in 1970 resulted in 1.14 million hectares being distributed according to Callison (1983:327); Nguyen (1990: 144) mentions a figure of one million. Unclear, however, is how much of this

The second stage was collectivisation, which the Communist Party began in the north in the late 1950s and in the south in the late 1970s. To the Party's leadership, collectivised agricultural production was a vital part of creating a socialist country in which individualistic or family-based production, private property, and non-state markets would have only minor roles in an otherwise centrally planned, state-dominated political economy. Collectivised farming, overseen by managers of state-initiated rural cooperatives, would also, according to the Communist Party's leaders, minimise inequalities and especially prevent land from being reconcentrated into the hands of a small number of owners.

By the early 1960s, most agricultural land in northern Vietnam was collectivised and managed by the state cooperatives and, at least on paper, villagers worked in production brigades for the cooperative, having only small gardens and ponds to grow things on their own.

While most villagers went along with collectivisation and some genuinely embraced it, many had doubts. Vietnamese villagers had no tradition of collectivised farming. And after obtaining fields of their own during the land redistribution of the 1950s, many, perhaps most, families were reluctant to surrender them to the cooperatives. By the mid-1960s, disaffection toward collectivised production and agricultural cooperatives was common in many parts of rural north Vietnam. Promised improvements in living conditions had failed to occur, not just because of the war with the United States, though that certainly made difficult conditions worse.[12] Many rural people had concluded that collectivised farming was a major cause of impoverishment.

Nevertheless, so far as researchers have thus far been able to learn, villagers in the north during the 1960s and 1970s did not organise nor openly protest against the state's program. There were several plausible reasons, two of which should be noted here. During Vietnam's war against the United States and for reunification, the state regarded cooperatives as integral to the war effort. Consequently, anyone openly opposing collec-

---

area overlapped with land the NLF had already redistributed and hence is included in the figures referred to above.

12 An indication of hardship is that in north Vietnam the consumption of staple food (*luong thuc*, rice plus, primarily, sweet potato, cassava, and corn) peaked at 192 kilograms/person annually in 1957–59—after land redistribution and during the initial years of cooperatives and collectivised farming. Then in 1959–60 it dropped slightly to 189 kilograms/person and between 1961 and 1965 it fell precipitously to 160 kilograms/person annually, barely equal to the minimum calorie level for adequate nutrition established at that time. Thereafter, it sank well below that minimum level (Vietnam 1989:138, 143). (These measures are rice equivalents; i.e., 160 kilograms/person means staple foods equal to 160 kilograms of rice [*gao*].) Per capita production of staple food peaked at 318 kilograms in 1961, fell to 304 in 1965, then to 274 in 1966, and continued downward for several more years (Vietnam 1991:87). (These figures are paddy [*thoc*] equivalents.)

tivised farming risked being seen as unpatriotic. Second, it was illegal for people to form associations or organisations outside those authorised by the state. The military, police, and Communist Party guarded against signs of public disorder and protest.

Unable or unwilling to openly oppose the collectivised land regime and cooperatives, Vietnamese villagers in the north came to terms with and modified the system as best they could in order to meet their livelihood and other needs. In the process, they greatly distorted the collective system in many areas, frequently frustrating officials who were trying to make villagers use land in accordance with state rules and to extract the amounts of grain and other produce that state agencies expected. When officials began to impose cooperatives and collectivisation in the south after 1976, they encountered more direct, though still low keyed resistance from villagers there (see Ngo 1988 and 1980; Beresford 1989:109–61).

Such protracted, usually everyday type of resistance through and around official channels in the north and later in the south contributed to significant food shortages in urban areas, and other serious economic problems. These and other pressures pushed national leaders to begin gradual reforms in the late 1970s and accelerate the change in the 1980s (see Fforde 1989:especially 203–5; Chu et al. 1992:especially 78–9; and Kerkvliet 1995:396–418).

The result was the re-allocation of land to individual farming families—the third stage of Vietnam's land revolution. The maximum holding allowed by the 1993 land law is three hectares for annually cropped land (growing rice, corn, vegetables, and so on), and the limit may be lowered by local authorities (Vietnam 1993). Individuals do not own land but have the right to use it for fixed periods of time, making it possible at anniversary dates of use rights for villages to readjust the allocations among households in order to assure land to all who want to farm and minimise inequalities. A few people have managed to circumvent official legal limits (Smith 1995:34, 37; Dang 1995:167–8). But by and large, at least thus far, farm land is distributed remarkably evenly.

The Philippines, since independence in 1946, has had no land revolution. Far from it. The land regime inherited from the United States colonial era has changed only at the margins, despite persistent and often intensive pressure and protests from organisations of villagers and their urban allies for agrarian reform. No laws limit how much land a person or company can own if no tenants farm it. In 1988, less than six per cent of all owners had half of all agricultural land in the country; less than two per cent owned roughly 36 per cent of it (Putzel 1992:29, Table 1.9). The proportion of all farms operated by tenant farmers has declined only slightly, from 35 per cent in 1939 to 32 per cent in 1991.[13] Meanwhile,

---

13 Based on data in Philippines (1941:970), and Philippines (1991:8). Because reporting methods in 1991 were somewhat different from those in 1939, I have had to assume, in an effort to make comparisons, that half of the 852 592

the proportion of completely landless people has doubled from around fifteen per cent of agricultural population in the 1950s to about 30 per cent in the 1980s (based on material in Aguilar 1983:347–9; Kerkvliet 1987:205). Having no land to farm—not even as tenants—nor better alternatives, these villagers rely primarily on seasonal work in the fields of owners and tenants. Typically, they are among the poorest rural Filipinos.

Among the few notable modifications in the land regime, resulting from pressures for changes and various agrarian reform laws, is that the Philippine state has gradually limited how much land an owner can have tenant farmed, although until 1988 the laws exempted land producing sugar cane and several other crops.[14] Another improvement, from the point of view of most villagers, is that new laws and better enforcement have given tenants in many areas a firmer grip on the land they till. Third, leasehold tenancy has increased from four per cent of all tenants in 1960 to eleven per cent in 1991 nation wide. In some regions, leasehold tenancy is now more prevalent than share tenancy (Hayami, Quisumbing and Adriano 1990:87–8). While both forms of tenancy have negative features, leasehold is now generally better than share tenancy because rents are much less and the resulting net incomes for the tenants are usually higher.

But these improvements are modest compared to the major land redistribution and other agrarian reforms for which hundreds, if not thousands of organisations of peasants and other advocates have lobbied, demonstrated, and protested in the Philippines since the 1940s. And they do little to accommodate the values underpinning villagers' demands and views about who have rights to land (Kerkvliet 1993:especially 474–9).

One prominent reason for minimal change in the land regime is that national and local élites, whose members generally hold many key positions in the state, generally have a vested interest in the status quo. This helps to explain why they have never developed much concern or regard for the desire of small farmers, peasants, and agrarian workers to have secure access to land. In particular, and in striking contrast to Vietnam, independence from the United States' colonial rule came about in a peaceful, negotiated manner. The politically and economically dominant classes in Philippine society who pressed for independence did not need nor seek nor want extensive support from the peasantry. And no major political event since has pushed a significant proportion of the élites to ally with villagers. The state, consequently, has continued to remain relatively aloof from the needs of the rural majority.

Second, the United States government, until recently, greatly influenced Philippine policy on land, among other matters. And the prevailing

---

farms reported in 1991 as having multiple ways to access land involved tenancy in one form or another and that the other half involved ownership of some kind.
14 The limit was 300 hectares according to a 1955 law, modified to 75 hectares in 1963, then 24 hectares in 1971, and five hectares in 1988.

stance of the United States, from one administration to another, despite some dissent within those administrations, was to oppose restructuring the land regime.[15]

Third, although villagers share many interests, they are also divided by regional differences and economic sectors (rice, sugar, coconut, and so on). Even in the same village, peasants who own land are not necessarily united with tenants trying to get better tenancy conditions, and tenants frequently see agricultural workers as competitors for land. Poor villagers often seek linkages to better off people, a feature of political life that weakens agrarian reform organisations and their ability to translate membership numbers into votes to elect people who will push for better land policies.

Fourth, few peasant and agricultural workers' organisations survive more than a few years. Most wither and die due to insufficient funding, internal fighting, and other reasons. In particular, intimidation and outright repression by government authorities and opponents of agrarian reforms have crippled efforts to build sustained, national organisations for agrarian reform.[16] The few which have lasted several years are usually regionally based. Only a small number have had a national following, and those have eventually suffered either major splits or collapsed.[17] Rarely, even among the regional ones, have these organisations been able to make land reform an election issue.

State Strengths and Weaknesses

Taking land from those who had more than they could personally farm and redistributing it to others with none or very little demonstrated the Vietnam state's resolve to favour villagers and its strength to carry out that program. For many among the landed élite, the state's actions and possibly the state itself were illegitimate, and in that respect, using the components of strength outlined earlier, the Vietnam state was weakened. To many landless and small land holding rural families, however, the Communist Party's state had considerable legitimacy particularly because of its policies to reduce tenants' rents and then redistribute land to those actually farming it, even though some cadres had used excessive coercion

---

15 See Monk's insightful study (1990).

16 Consider, for example, the violence and intimidation against the *Pambansang Kaisahan ng mga Magbubukid* (National Union of Peasants) in 1945–48, *Malayang Samahang Magsasaka* (Free Farmers Union) in 1968–72, and the *Kaisahang Magsasaka ng Pilipinas* (Philippine Peasant Union) in 1987–94.

17 I am thinking here especially of the Federation of Free Farmers (FFF) and the Congress for a People's Agrarian Reform (CPAR).

and violence during the land reform (Vasavakul 1995:266).[18] And considering it came to power through mass-based armed revolutionary struggle, the state leadership saw that having these rural people on their side was crucial.

Being seen as a strong state helped its leaders make some headway in the second stage of Vietnam's land revolution, collectivisation. In particular, the legitimacy the state had earned in the eyes of a large proportion of villagers through its ability to fight for Vietnam's independence and reunification, its land redistribution program, and other policies benefiting the rural majority (in education, health, and cultural matters) helped the new Communist Party-dominated state to get rural people to comply with collectivisation, at least up to a point. Rather than compliance being a stepping stone to legitimacy, as Migdal's argument would suggest, political legitimacy in this case came first and helped Vietnam's leadership to get involvement among many rural people who were sceptical of, even opposed to, collectivised farming.

As the war for reunification ended and the country was reunited, Vietnam's state leadership redoubled its efforts to enlarge the size of collectivised farming units, extend collectivisation to the southern half of the country, and press villagers to participate more fully in the state's socialist model. But the leaders encountered more determined resistance and foot dragging among villagers.

Had Vietnam's leadership somehow managed to bulldoze ahead, pushing its vision of how land should be consolidated and farmed collectively, it may have succeeded in implementing more of its socialist blueprint. Instead, it backed away from collectivised farming, behaviour that can, indeed, be seen as a sign of weakness if an assessment of strength emphasises getting people to subordinate their own preferences to what the state prescribes without regard for legitimacy. This, I think, is what Fforde and de Vylder do. Passages in Migdal's writings can lead one to a similar conclusion about Vietnam.[19]

Had Vietnam's leadership pressed ahead, the risks of greatly alienating a major proportion of the rural population would have risen markedly. Such insistence might well have provoked considerable agrarian unrest, directly threatening the regime's ability to maintain peace and order. In other words, it might have cost the state its legitimacy in the eyes of significant sectors of society, thereby undermining its strength.

---

18 As Vasavakul says (265–6), land to the tiller and having enough food to eat and clothes to wear were what many rural people understood socialism to mean.

19 All states, Migdal writes, must engage in explicit or covert bargaining with interests in society. But in strong states, the bargaining results in only 'limited' distortions of what policy makers intended. When the distortions are 'major', Migdal says, the state is weak (1988:238).

Rather than that course, the Communist Party in effect bargained and negotiated with villagers from the mid-1970s into the 1980s, accommodating more and more of their preference for family-based farming, among other things, to the point that ultimately the state abandoned collectivised farming and reallocated land to individual households. The state's turn around helped bring peasants closer to getting the secure access to land for which they had long been struggling and helped the state to recover its flagging legitimacy in the eyes of many villagers. Bargaining and negotiation between the state and villagers were not signs of weakness but of strength. It was also an indication of the Vietnam state's capacity to govern.[20]

In the Philippines, from the point of view of the rural majority interested in securing land for farming, the state is unable or unwilling to follow through on the agrarian reform promises its leaders have often made. Frequently it is even incapable of enforcing the modest agrarian reform laws already in the books on account of administrators succumbing to pressures from those opposed to reforms. At the same time, the Philippine state conveys to rural Filipinos a considerable degree of strength. It has been able to resist and withstand persistent pressures from the countryside for more extensive changes in the nation's land regime. Put another way, the state has been able to make villagers comply with the prevailing land regime despite their many objections to it and desires to change it.

Neither the state's weaknesses nor strengths are beneficial to the rural majority; indeed, often the rural majority are the worse for both. Yet despite this situation, the state's legitimacy in the eyes of most villagers remains more or less intact, and hence so does that component of the state's strength. In other words, unlike in Vietnam, the Philippine state's policies regarding the country's land regime do not appear to have much bearing on the state's legitimacy as far as most villagers are concerned.

Because the Philippine state did not emerge from a popular, agrarian revolution to obtain independence from colonial rule, questions regarding legitimacy or illegitimacy of the post-colonial state and its particular governments have not been closely linked in the minds of most villagers to the prevailing land regime. This is one major reason for the basis of state legitimacy in the Philippines being different from Vietnam's.

Political legitimacy in the Philippines, I am inclined to conclude, is more closely associated with democratic institutions and processes, however imperfectly they may be used there. Arguably, other considerations also bear on matters of legitimacy in Philippine politics, but the land

---

20 Among the qualities of a 'capable state', says Grindle, is the ability to 'be responsive to the demands and pressures of societal groups', having 'responsive political leaders and administrators' and permitting 'societal participation in decision making' (1996:7–8).

regime by itself, or as a principal factor, is not particularly significant.[21] This conclusion is based in part on an analysis of two political legitimacy crises in the country.[22]

The Huk rebellion (1946–early 1950s) emerged from an agrarian reform movement and considerable rural unrest. But the failure of the national government to pass far reaching land tenure legislation or to implement existing tenancy laws was not what drove peasants and their supporters to rebellion. They ultimately rebelled mainly because of tremendous state repression and violence against their organisations and leaders and because the national government flagrantly violated the rules of elections and other democratic processes between 1946 and 1951. These actions included, for example, authorities in 1946 kidnapping and murdering a popular leader of a major peasant organisation and in the same year refusing to allow congressmen from central Luzon, who had been elected by a ground-swell of village voters, to take their seats in the House of Representatives. For many supporters, the rebels were trying to defend villagers against an illicit government that had trampled their rights to organise and had been repressive way beyond the pale of their toleration. After subsequent elections proved to be more democratic, a new government (Ramon Magsaysay's) that permitted dissent and public debate on agrarian issues had been elected and seemed likely to push for additional tenancy reforms, and the rapacious behaviour of the military had abated, the rebellion subsided as well (Kerkvliet 1977:143–55, 260–2).

The second legitimacy crisis involved the Marcos regime. When Ferdinand Marcos and his domestic and US supporters dumped several democratic institutions to impose martial law in 1972, he promised fundamental changes in the land regime that would benefit tenants, small land owners, and agricultural workers. This vow contributed to initial widespread support in rural areas for the abrupt changes, just as Marcos's promises of economic growth and a higher standard of living for the majority influenced many other Filipinos to conditionally accept the replacement of democratic political institutions with this new authoritarian state.[23]

---

21 For an analysis of political legitimacy in this archipelago, see Sidel (1995b: especially 140–9), and Thompson (1995:29–32, 74, 170–2, 184).

22 I am excluding the Muslim separatist movement, which periodically has burst into rebellion, and is a third political crisis in which legitimacy has been a significant issue. Unlike the two I am going to discuss, however, this one challenged the legitimacy of the very idea of the Philippine nation. Hence, it is fundamentally different from the other two, which accepted the nation but challenged the legitimacy of those governing it and how they used state institutions.

23 At the same time, however, other Filipinos regarded the Marcos regime as illegitimate, a view that influenced some to go underground and even join the New People's Army.

From the late 1970s and early 1980s, however, the legitimacy of this new political system was increasingly questioned, culminating in a mass uprising in 1986 that brought it down. But its limited accomplishments in agrarian reform seem to have played a minor role in that struggle. What brought Marcos' rule into disrepute for a broad spectrum of Filipinos was massive corruption, economic misery, spreading civil war due in large measure to military abuses and repression, and gross violations of elections and other democratic institutions it claimed to be revitalising (see Thompson 1995:chapters 4–8; de Dios 1988; Diokno 1988; and Almendral 1988). In short, Marcos and his allies violated all aspects of legitimate authority. The regime had been incompetent, served society very badly, disregarded laws and rules, and relied excessively on violence and coercion to perpetuate its rule.

Conclusion

My main point with regard to analysing state strengths and weaknesses in relation to society is the need to consider policy area, perspective, and the components that constitute strength. Such analyses lend to a more nuanced understanding than do analyses lacking a break down of this kind. The Philippine state is typically portrayed as weak. An analysis along the lines I have pursued suggests that the situation is more complex. Vietnam's state is also said by some analysts to be weak, although others have deemed it strong. The approach I am suggesting helps one to appreciate why assessments can be so different.

I have emphasised in this examination of Vietnam and the Philippines since independence:

• the perspective of rural villagers for whom having secure access to land in order to farm and support their families has been a major concern;

• land regimes, the area where state policies and villagers' interests have frequently intersected; and

• components of state strength, especially legitimacy.

The Philippine state has tried to preserve the land regime that prevailed during the American colonial period in the first half of the twentieth century. In so doing it has staved off considerable pressures from tenants, landless agricultural families, and other villagers to divide land more equitably and make other reforms that would be beneficial to the majority of rural landless and near-landless. By prevailing over those pressures, the state has managed to get a large proportion of rural people to live within the bounds of that dominant land regime despite their preferences for an alternative system and their attempts to overhaul it. In other words, the state has constrained the rural majority to comply with and participate in this land regime, demonstrating strength in terms that Migdal has stressed.

Where the Philippine state has clearly been weak, in the eyes of Filipino villagers, is implementing well the reforms in the land regime that have become law. Pressures from land reform movements have resulted in modifications to the prevailing land regime. When implemented, those changes have given tenants firmer claims to their farms and other benefits. Too often, however, state agencies have failed to implement the laws, allowing instead large land owners, landlords, and other opponents of reforms to subvert the reforms.

While the struggle of villagers to reform the land regime has challenged the validity and fairness of that system of land use and distribution and has been punctuated by major confrontations between opponents of the land regime and the state, villagers' alternative vision for land has not led them to question the legitimacy of the Philippine state. In other words, villagers have not linked their dispute with the dominant land regime to the state's legitimacy. Hence, in that sense, too, the state has strength from the perspective of most villagers. The state's legitimacy and its right to set policy has been linked more clearly to democratic processes and methods of deciding who has the right to govern. Periodic gross violations of democratic rules of governance have seriously weakened the state and aroused Filipinos, including many villagers, to protest and to demand reinstatement of democratic processes.

In Vietnam, on the other hand, such democratic institutions and processes have not been linked to the legitimacy of the Communist Party-dominated state as far as most villagers are concerned. But the land regime has been. Overturning the pre-independence land regime in order to distribute land more or less equally to all farming villagers has been a major source of legitimacy—and hence strength—of the state in the eyes of rural Vietnamese. The state tried to capitalise on that strength when it attempted to collectivise land that it had previously distributed to villagers. Villagers' hesitancy, reluctance, and opposition to collectivisation— though rarely openly expressed or organised, in part because the state severely restricted any public criticism of its policies—created major obstacles for the state's plan. When pressing villagers to fully comply with collectivised farming, the state demonstrated a certain strength but at the same time undermined its legitimacy in the countryside. By ultimately coming to terms with villagers' preference for household based farming, abandoning collectivisation, and reallocating farm land to individual villager households, the state forsook its plan—a sign of weakness to some—but bolstered its legitimacy, and thus strength, in the eyes of most rural people.

References

Aguilar Jr, Filomeno V., 1983. 'The Agrarian Proletariat in the Rice Growing Areas of the Philippines', *Philippine Studies* 31:347–9.

Ahrne, Göran, 1990. *Agency and Organization: Towards an Organization Theory of Society* (London: Sage).

—— 1994. *Social Organizations: Interaction Inside, Outside and Between Organizations* (Thousand Oaks, CA: Sage Publications).

Alagappa, Muthiah, 1995. 'The Anatomy of Legitimacy', in Muthiah Alagappa, ed., *Political Legitimacy in Southeast Asia: The Quest for Moral Authority* (Stanford, CA: Stanford University Press).

Alasia, Sam, 1997. 'Party Politics and Government in Solomon Islands', State Society and Governance in Melanesia Discussion Paper 97/7 (Canberra: Research School of Pacific and Asian Studies, Australian National University).

Almendral, Gemma Nemenzo, 1988. 'The Fall of the Regime', in Aurora Javate-de Dios, Petronilo Bn. Daroy and Lorna Kalaw-Tirol, eds, *Dictatorship and Revolution: Roots of People's Power* (Metro Manila: Conspectus).

Alston, Philip, 1994. 'The Best Interests Principle: Towards a Reconciliation of Culture and Human Rights', in Philip Alston, ed., *The Best Interests of the Child: Reconciling Culture and Human Rights* (Oxford: Clarendon Press).

Anderson, B. O'G., 1983. *Imagined Communities: Reflections on the Origin and Spread of Nationalism* (London: Verso).

—— 1990. *Language and Power: Exploring Political Cultures in Indonesia* (Ithaca, NY: Cornell University Press).

Ang, Ien and Jon Stratton, 1995. 'The Singapore Way of Multiculturalism: Western Concepts/Asian Cultures', *Sojourn* 10, 1:65–89.

Archer, Margaret S., 1985. 'The Myth of Cultural Unity', *British Journal of Sociology* 36:333–53.

Asian Development Bank, 1996. *Strategies for the Pacific: Policies and Programs for Sustainable Growth* (Manila: Office of Pacific Operation, ADB).

Asia–Pacific Action Group, 1990. *The Barnett Report: A Summary of the Report of the Commission of Inquiry into Aspects of the Timber*

175

Industry in Papua New Guinea (Hobart: Asia–Pacific Action Group).

Baird, Nicola, 1996. 'In a Jungle of Vested Interests', *Financial Times* 15 January.

Barker, Rodney, 1990. *Political Legitimacy and the State* (Oxford: Clarendon Press).

Barnett, Michael N., 1998. *Dialogues in Arab Politics: Negotiations in Regional Order* (New York: Columbia University Press).

Bassford, John L., 1985. Land Development Policy in Cochinchina under the French, 1865–1925, PhD Dissertation 1984 (Ann Arbor, MI: University of Hawaii, [xerox] University Microfilms).

Bell, Daniel A., 1995. 'Democracy in Confucian Societies: The Challenge of Justification', in Daniel A. Bell, David Brown, Kanishka Jayasuriya and David Martin Jones, eds, *Towards Illiberal Democracy in Pacific Asia* (London: Macmillan).

Benda, Harry J., 1972. 'The Pattern of Administrative Reforms in the Closing Years of Dutch Rule in Indonesia', in *Continuity and Change in Southeast Asia: Collected Journal Articles of Harry J. Benda* (New Haven, Conn: Yale University Southeast Asia Studies Monograph Series No. 18). Originally published in 1966, in *Journal of Asian Studies* 25.

Benhabib, Seyla, 1992. *Situating the Self: Gender, Community and Post-modernism in Contemporary Ethics* (New York: Routledge).

Bennett, Judith A., 1995. 'Forestry, Public Land, and the Colonial Legacy in the Solomon Islands', *The Contemporary Pacific* 7, 2: 243–75.

Beresford, Melanie, 1989. *National Unification and Economic Development in Vietnam* (London: Macmillan).

———— 1994(?). Interpretation of the Vietnamese Economic Reforms 1979–85, unpublished:13–14.

Berndt, Ronald M., 1962. *Excess and Restraint: Social Control Among a New Guinea Mountain People* (Chicago: University of Chicago Press).

Bolongaita, Emil P., 1995. 'Presidential Versus Parliamentary Democracy: Rethinking Philippine Plans for Parliamentary Reforms', *Philippine Studies* 43, 1:105–23.

Bonnell, Susanne, 1994. *Dilemmas of Development—Social Change in Porgera: 1989–1993. A Report to Porgera Joint Venture*, Report No. 2 (Thornlands, Queensland: Porgera Social Monitoring Programme, Subada Consulting Pty Ltd, August).

Bourchier, David and John Legge, eds, 1995. *Democracy in Indonesia: 1950s and 1990s*, Monash Papers on Southeast Asia No. 31 (Clayton, Victoria: Centre of Southeast Asian Studies, Monash University).

Boutilier, J., 1982. 'The Government is the District Officer: An Historical Analysis of District Officers as Middlemen in the British Solomon Islands Protectorate 1893–1943', in William R. Rodman and Dorothy Ayers Counts, eds, *Middlemen and Brokers in Oceania*, ASAO Monograph 9 (Ann Arbor, MI: University of Michigan Press).

Bratton, Michael, 1989. 'Beyond the State: Civil Society and Associational Life in Africa', *World Politics* 41, 3:407–30.

Bresnan, John, 1993. *Managing Indonesia: The Modern Political Economy* (New York: Columbia University Press).

Brigham, John, 1996. *The Constitution of Interests: Beyond the Politics of Rights* (New York: New York University Press).

Brown, David, 1994. *The State and Ethnic Politics in Southeast Asia* (London: Routledge).

Brunton, Brian and Duncan Colquhoun-Kerr, 1985. *The Annotated Constitution of Papua New Guinea* (Port Moresby: University of Papua New Guinea Press).

Bryant, Raymond L., 1996. 'The Greening of Burma: Political Rhetoric or Sustainable Development?' *Pacific Affairs* 69, 3:341–60.

Bryson, Scott S., 1991. *The Chastised Stage: Bourgeois Drama and the Exercise of Power* (Saratoga, CA: Anma Libri).

Budiman, Arief, ed., 1990. *State and Civil Society in Indonesia*, Monash Papers on Southeast Asia No. 22 (Clayton, Victoria: Centre of Southeast Asian Studies, Monash University).

Burke, Edmund, 1969. *Reflections on the Revolution in France*, edited by C. C. O'Brien (London: Penguin).

Calhoun, Craig, ed., 1996. *Habermas and the Public Sphere* (Cambridge, MA: MIT Press).

Callison, Charles Stuart, 1983. *Land-to-the-Tiller in the Mekong Delta: Economic, Social, and Political Effects of Land Reform in Four Villages of South Vietnam* (Berkeley, CA: Center for South and Southeast Asian Studies, University of California).

Calvert, Peter, ed., 1987. *The Process of Political Succession* (London: Macmillan).

Camilleri, Joseph A. and Jim Falk, 1992. *The End of Sovereignty?: The Politics of a Shrinking and Fragmenting World* (Brookfield, VT: Edward Elgar).

Carbonell-Catilo, Ma. Aurora, Josie H. de Leon and Eleanor E. Nicolas, 1985. *Manipulated Elections* (Manila, no publisher cited).

Carroll, J.J., 1994. 'Glimpses into Philippine Political Culture: Gleanings from the Ateneo Public Opinion Survey Data', *Pilipinas* 22:47–61.

CBSI, Central Bank of the Solomon Islands, 1997. *Annual Report* (Honiara: Central Bank of the Solomon Islands).

Cederman, Lars-Erik, 1997. *Emergent Actors in World Politics: How States and Nations Develop and Dissolve* (Princeton, NJ: Princeton University Press).

Chan Heng Chee, 1976. *The Dynamics of One Party Dominance: The PAP at Grass-roots* (Singapore: Singapore University Press).

——— 1993a. 'Singapore: Coping with Vulnerability', in James W. Morley, ed., *Driven by Growth: Political Change in the Asia–Pacific Region* (Armonk, NY: M.E. Sharpe).

——— 1993b. 'Democracy: An Asian Perspective', in Robert Bartley, Chan Heng Chee, Samuel P. Huntington and Shijuro Ogato, *Democracy and Capitalism: Asian and American Perspectives* (Singapore: Institute of Southeast Asian Studies).

Chanock, Martin, 1985. *Law, Custom, and Social Order: The Colonial Experience in Malawi and Zambia* (New York: Cambridge University Press).

Chazan, N., 1994. 'Engaging the State: Associational Life in Sub-Saharan Africa', in Joel S. Migdal, Atul Kohli and Vivienne Shue, eds, *State Power and Social Forces: Domination and Transformation in the Third World* (Cambridge/New York: Cambridge University Press).

Che Man, Wan Kadir, 1990. *Muslim Separatism: The Moros of Southern Philippines and the Malays of Southern Thailand* (Singapore: Oxford University Press).

Choo, Carolyn, 1985. *Singapore: The PAP and the Problem of Political Succession* (Selangor: Pelanduk Publications).

Chowning, Ann, 1977. *An Introduction to the Peoples and Cultures of Melanesia*, 2nd edn (Menlo Park, CA: Cummings Publishing Company).

Chu Van Lam, Nguyen Thai Nguyen, Phung Huu Phu, Tran Quan Toan, and Dang Tho Xuong, 1992. *Hop Tac Hoa Nong Nghiep Viet Nam: Lich Su, Van De, Trien Vong* [Agricultural Cooperativiza-

tion in Vietnam: History, Problems, and Prospects] (Hanoi: NXB
Su That).

Chua Beng-Huat, 1995. *Communitarian Ideology and Democracy in
Singapore* (London: Routledge).

Clammer, John, 1985. *Singapore: Ideology, Society and Culture*
(Singapore: Chopmen Press).

Clapham, Christopher, 1985. *Third World Politics: An Introduction*
(London: Croom Helm).

———— 1996. *Africa and the International System: The Politics of State
Survival* (Cambridge: Cambridge University Press).

Clark, Jeffrey, 1993. 'Gold, Sex and Pollution: Male Illness and Myth at
Mt Kare, Papua New Guinea', *American Ethnologist* 20, 4:742–
57.

———— 1997. 'Imagining the State, or Tribalism and the Arts of Memory
in the Highlands of Papua New Guinea', in Ton Otto and Nicholas
Thomas, eds, *Narratives of Nation in the South Pacific*
(Amsterdam: Harwood Academic Publishers).

Clastres, Pierre, 1974. *Society Against the State: Essays in Political
Anthropology*, translated by Robert Hurley in collaboration with
Abe Stein (New York: Zone).

Clifford, William, Louise Morauta and Barry Stuart, 1984. *Law and Order
in Papua New Guinea*, Vols I and II (Port Moresby: Institute of
National Affairs and Institute of Applied Social and Economic
Research).

Colchester, Marcus, 1994. 'The New Sultans: Asian Loggers Move in on
Guyana's Forests', *Ecologist* 24, March/April:45–52.

Cole, Rodney V., ed., 1993. *Pacific 2010: Challenging the Future*, Pacific
Policy Paper 9 (Canberra: National Centre for Development
Studies, Australian National University).

Combs, James E., 1980. *Dimensions of Political Drama* (Santa Monica,
CA: Goodyear Publishing).

Connell, John, 1997. *Papua New Guinea. The Struggle for Development*
(London: Routledge).

———— and John P. Lea, 1993. *Pacific 2010: Planning the Future:
Melanesian Cities in 2010*, Pacific Policy Paper 11 (Canberra:
National Centre for Development Studies, The Australian National
University).

Connolly, Michael J., 1992. *Church Lands and Peasant Unrest in the Philippines: Agrarian Conflict in 20th-Century Luzon* (Loyola Heights: Ateneo de Manila University Press).

Corral, V.P., 1993. 'Sectoral Representatives in the Eighth Congress: A Documentation', *Congressional Studies Journal* 1, 1:6–102.

Corrigan, Philip and Derek Sayer, 1985. *The Great Arch: English State Formation as Cultural Revolution* (Oxford: Blackwell).

Corrin, Jennifer, 1992. Abrogation of the Rights of Customary Land Owners by the Forest Resources and Timber Utilization Act, unpublished interest group paper, South Pacific Legal Studies, ALTA 47th Annual Conference, 9–12 July.

Cotton, James, 1991a. 'The Limits to Liberalization in Industrializing Asia: Three Views of the State', *Pacific Affairs* 64, 3:311–27.

——— 1991b. 'On the Identity of "Confucianism": Theory or Practice?', *Political Theory Newsletter* 3, 2:113–21.

——— 1996. 'State and Society in Singapore', *Pacific Review* 9, 2:278–83.

Cover, Robert, 1995a. 'The Folktales of Justice: Tales of Jurisdiction', in Martha Minow, Michael Ryan and Austin Sarat, eds, *Narrative, Violence, and the Law: The Essays of Robert Cover* (Ann Arbor, MI: University of Michigan Press).

——— 1995b. 'Nomos and Narrative', in Martha Minow, Michael Ryan and Austin Sarat, eds, *Narrative, Violence, and the Law: The Essays of Robert Cover* (Ann Arbor, MI: University of Michigan Press).

Cribb, Robert, 1992. *Historical Dictionary of Indonesia* (Metuchen, NJ, and London: Scarecrow Press).

Crouch, Harold, 1978. *The Army and Politics in Indonesia* (Ithaca, NY: Cornell University Press).

——— 1979. 'Patrimonialism and Military Rule in Indonesia', *World Politics* 31, 4:571–87.

——— 1988. *The Army and Politics in Indonesia*, rev. edn (Ithaca, NY: Cornell University Press).

Cua, Antonio S., 1985. *Ethical Argumentation: A Study in Hsun Tzu's Moral Epistemology* (Honolulu: University of Hawaii Press).

Dalglish, Peter and Mark Connolly, 1992. *Too Much Time, Too Little Money: The Challenge of Urban Street Youth in Papua New Guinea* (Toronto: Street Kids International).

Dang Phong, 1995. 'Aspects of Agricultural Economy and Rural Life in 1993', in Benedict J. Tria Kerkvliet and Doug J. Porter, eds, *Vietnam's Rural Transformation* (Boulder, CO/Singapore: Westview Press/Institute for Southeast Asian Studies).

Dauvergne, Peter, 1997a. *Shadows in the Forest: Japan and the Politics of Timber in Southeast Asia* (Cambridge, MA: MIT Press).

────── 1997b. 'Japanese Trade and Deforestation in Southeast Asia', in Rodolphe De Koninck and Christine Veilleux, eds, *Southeast Asia and Globalization: New Domains of Analysis/ L'Asie du Sud-Est face à la mondialisation: les nouveaux champs d'anlayse* (Québec: GÉRAC, Université Laval).

────── 1997c. 'Corporate Power in the Forests of the Solomon Islands', Working Paper No. 1997/6 (Canberra: Department of International Relations, Research School of Pacific and Asian Studies, Australian National University, October).

────── 1997d. 'Globalisation and Deforestation in the Asia–Pacific', Working Paper No. 1997/7 (Canberra: Department of International Relations, Research School of Pacific and Asian Studies, Australian National University).

────── 1998a. 'Reforming Multinational Loggers in Solomon Islands', *Pacific Economic Bulletin* 13, 1:110–19.

────── 1998b. 'The Political Economy of Indonesia's 1997 Forest Fires', *Australian Journal of International Affairs* 52, 1:13–17.

Davis, Lane, 1970. 'The Cost of the New Realism', reprinted in Henry S. Kariel, ed., *Frontiers of Democratic Theory* (New York: Random House).

De Bary, Wm. Theodore, 1983. *The Liberal Tradition in China* (Hong Kong: Chinese University Press).

de Dios, Emmanuel S., 1988. 'The Erosion of the Dictatorship', in Aurora Javate-de Dios, Petronilo Bn. Daroy and Lorna Kalaw-Tirol, eds, *Dictatorship and Revolution: Roots of People's Power* (Metro Manila: Conspectus).

────── and R.V. Fabella, 1996. *Choice, Growth and Economic Development: Emerging and Enduring* (Manila: University of the Philippines Press).

Derham, David P., 1960. *Report on the System for the Administration of Justice in the Territory of Papua and New Guinea* (Canberra: Department of Territories).

Di Palma, Giuseppe, 1990. *To Craft Democracies: An Essay on Democratic Transition* (Berkeley, CA: University of California Press).

Diamond, L., 1994. 'Rethinking Civil Society. Toward Democratic Consolidation', *Journal of Democracy* 5, 3:4–17.

Dickson-Waiko, A.N., 1994. A Woman's Place is in the Struggle: Feminism and Nationalism in the Philippines, PhD Dissertation (Canberra: Australian National University).

DiMaggio, Paul, 1989. 'Foreword', in Marshall W. Meyer and Lynne G. Zucker, *Permanently Failing Organizations* (Newbury Park, CA: Sage).

Dinnen, Sinclair, 1996. 'Violence, Security and the 1992 Election', in Yaw Saffu, ed., *The 1992 PNG Election: Change and Continuity in Electoral Politics*, Political and Social Change Monograph 23 (Canberra: Australian National University).

——— 1997. 'Restorative Justice in Papua New Guinea', *International Journal of the Sociology of Law* 25, 3:245–62.

——— Ron May and Anthony J. Regan, eds, 1997. *Challenging the State: The Sandline Affair in Papua New Guinea* (Canberra: National Centre for Development Studies and Department of Political and Social Change, Research School of Pacific and Asian Studies, Australian National University).

Diokno, Ma. Serena I., 1988. 'Unity and Struggle', in Aurora Javate-de Dios, Petronilo Bn. Daroy and Lorna Kalaw-Tirol, eds, *Dictatorship and Revolution: Roots of People's Power* (Metro Manila: Conspectus).

Dorney, Sean, 1990. *Papua New Guinea: People, Politics and History Since 1975* (Sydney: Random House).

Doronila, Amando, 1992. *The State, Economic Transformation, and Political Change in the Philippines, 1946–1972* (Singapore: Oxford University Press).

Duchacek, Ivo D., Daniel Latouche and Garth Stevenson, 1988. *Perforated Sovereignties and International Relations: Transsovereign Contacts of Subnational Governments* (New York: Greenwood Press).

Duncan, Ron, 1994. *Melanesian Forestry Sector Study*, International Development Issues, no. 36 (Canberra: Australian International Development Assistance Bureau).

Dunn, John, ed., 1995. *Contemporary Crisis of the Nation State?* (Cambridge, MA: Blackwell).

Dupont, Alan, 1996. 'Is There an "Asian Way"?', *Survival* 38, 2:13–33.

Durkheim, E., 1915. *Elementary Forms of Religious Life* (London: Allen & Unwin).

Dyson, Kenneth H.F., 1980. *The State Tradition in Western Europe: A Study of an Idea and an Institution* (Oxford: Martin Robertson).

Economic Insights, 1994a. 'Papua New Guinea: The Role of the Government in Economic Development' (Canberra: Australian International Development Assistance Bureau).

────── 1994b. *The Solomon Islands Economy: Achieving Sustainable Economic Development* (Canberra: Australian Agency for International Development, Economic Insights).

Edelman, Murray, 1971. *Politics as Symbolic Action: Mass Arousal and Quiescence* (Chicago: Markham).

────── 1988. *Constructing the Political Spectacle* (Chicago: The University of Chicago Press).

Edgell, Stephen, Sandra Walklate and Gareth Williams, eds, 1995. *Debating the Future of the Public Sphere* (Brookfield, VT: Avebury).

Edgerton, Ronald K., 1982. 'Frontier Society on the Bukidnon Plateau, 1970–1941', in Alfred W. McCoy and Ed. C. de Jesus, eds, *Philippine Social History* (Honolulu: University Press of Hawaii).

Ekeh, P.P., 1975. 'Colonialism and the Two Publics in Africa: A Theoretical Statement', *Comparative Studies in Society and History* 17:91–112.

Eldridge, Philip, 1990. 'NGOs and the State in Indonesia', in Arief Budiman, ed., *State and Civil Society in Indonesia* (Clayton, Victoria: Centre of Southeast Asian Studies, Monash University).

Ells, Philip, 1996. 'Logging and Legal Access in Solomon Islands' (Ely, Cambridgeshire: Forest Monitor Limited, July).

Emmerson, Donald K., 1990. Beyond Zanzibar: Area Studies, Comparative Politics, and the 'Strength' of the State in Indonesia, paper prepared for a panel on The Strength of the State in Southeast Asia, Association for Asian Studies, Chicago, 6–8 April.

Engel, Laurie, 1994. 'The Australian Aid Program and its Role in Supporting PNG's Law and Order Policies', in A. Thompson, ed., *Papua New Guinea: Issues for Australian Security Planners* (Canberra: Australian Defence Studies Centre, Australian Defence Force Academy).

Engelstein, Laura, 1988. 'Gender and the Juridical Subject: Prostitution and Rape in Nineteenth-Century Russian Criminal Codes', *Journal of Modern History* 60, 3:458–95.

Epstein, A.L., 1972. 'Indigenous Law', in *The Encyclopaedia of Papua and New Guinea*, 2:631–4 (Melbourne: Melbourne University

Press in association with the University of Papua and New Guinea).

Erfani, Julie A., 1995. *The Paradox of the Mexican State: Rereading Sovereignty from Independence to NAFTA* (Boulder, CO: Lynne Rienner).

Esherick, Joseph W., and Jeffrey N. Wasserstrom, 1990. 'Acting Out Democracy: Political Theater in Modern China', *Journal of Asian Studies* 49, 4:835–65.

Evans, Peter B., 1995. *Embedded Autonomy: States and Industrial Transformation* (Princeton, NJ: Princeton University Press).

———, Dietrich Rueschemeyer and Theda Skocpol, eds, 1985. *Bringing the State Back In* (Cambridge/New York: Cambridge University Press).

Fegan, Brian, 1982. 'The Social History of a Central Luzon Barrio', in Alfred W. McCoy and Ed. C. de Jesus, eds, *Philippine Social History* (Honolulu: University Press of Hawaii).

Feil, D. K., 1987. *The Evolution of Highland Papua New Guinea Societies* (Cambridge: Cambridge University Press).

Feith, Herbert, 1962. *The Decline of Constitutional Democracy in Indonesia* (Ithaca, NY: Cornell University Press).

Fforde, Adam, 1983. 'The Historical Background to Agricultural Collectivisation in North Vietnam: The Changing Role of "Corporate Economic Power"', Birkbeck Discussion Paper No. 148 (London: Birkbeck College, University of London).

——— 1989. *The Agrarian Question in North Vietnam, 1974–1979: A Study of Cooperator Resistance to State Policy* (Armonk, NY: ME Sharpe).

——— and Stefan de Vylder, 1996. *From Plan to Market: The Economic Transition in Vietnam* (Boulder, CO: Westview Press).

——— and Steve Seneque, 1995. 'The Economy and the Countryside: The Relevance of Rural Development Policies', in Benedict J. Tria Kerkvliet and Doug J.Porter, eds, *Vietnam's Rural Transformation* (Boulder, CO/Singapore: Westview Press/Institute for Southeast Asian Studies).

Fiji, 1996. *The Fiji Islands: Towards a United Future*, Report of the Fiji Constitution Review Commission 1996, Parliamentary Paper No. 34 of 1996.

Filer, Colin, 1990. 'The Bougainville Rebellion, the Mining Industry and the Process of Social Disintegration in Papua New Guinea', in R.J.

May and Matthew Spriggs, eds, *The Bougainville Crisis* (Bathurst, NSW: Crawford House Press).

—— 1997a. 'Compensation, Rent and Power in Papua New Guinea', in Susan Toft, ed., *Compensation for Resource Development in Papua New Guinea* (Canberra: National Centre for Development Studies, Australian National University, Pacific Policy Paper 24, and the Law Reform Commission of Papua New Guinea, Monograph No. 6).

—— 1997b. 'A Statistical Profile of Papua New Guinea's Log Export Industry,' in Colin Filer, ed., *The Political Economy of Forest Management in Papua New Guinea*, Monograph 32 (London/ Boroko: IIED and National Research Institute).

Fingarette, Herbert, 1972. *Confucius: The Secular as Sacred* (New York: Harper & Row).

Fingleton, James S., 1989. *Assistance in the Revision of Forestry Policy and Legislation*, First Report to the Government of the Solomon Islands on Forestry Legislation, TCP/SOI/8851 (A), Consultancy Report No. 2 (Rome: Food and Agriculture Organization, January).

Fingleton, Jim, 1994. 'Forest Resource Management in the South Pacific: Logging Your Way to Development', *Development Bulletin* 31, July:19–22.

Finkel, Norman J., 1995. *Commonsense Justice: Jurors' Notions of the Law* (Cambridge, MA: Harvard University Press).

Finnemore, Martha, 1996. *National Interests in International Society* (Ithaca, NY: Cornell University Press).

Fishman, Robert M., 1990. 'Rethinking State and Regime: Southern Europe's Transition to Democracy', *World Politics* 42, 3:422–40.

Fitzpatrick, Peter, 1984. 'Law and Societies', *Osgoode Hall Law Journal* 22, 1:115–38.

Forests Monitor, 1996. Kumpulan Emas Berhad and its Involvement in the Solomon Islands, draft briefing document, April.

Foster, Robert J., 1992. 'Taking Care of Public Telephones: Moral Education and Nation-State Formation in Papua New Guinea', *Public Culture* 4, 2:31–45.

—— 1996. 'State Ritual: Ethnographic Notes on Voting in the Namatanai Electorate', in Yaw Saffu, ed., *The 1992 PNG Election: Change and Continuity in Electoral Politics*, Political and Social Change Monograph 23 (Canberra: Australian National University).

186

Frazer, Ian, 1997. 'The Struggle for Control of Solomon Island Forests', *The Contemporary Pacific* 9, 1:39–72.

Friedman, Edward, 1994. 'Democratization: Generalizing the East Asian Experience', in Edward Friedman, ed., *The Politics of Democratization: Generalizing East Asian Experiences* (Boulder, CO: Westview Press).

Friedman, Lawrence M., 1990. *The Republic of Choice: Law, Authority, and Culture* (Cambridge, MA: Harvard University Press).

Fry, Greg, 1997. 'Framing the Islands: Knowledge and Power in Changing Australian Images of "The South Pacific"', *The Contemporary Pacific: A Journal of Island Affairs* 9, 2:305–44.

Galanter, Mark, 1981. 'Justice in Many Rooms: Courts, Private Ordering, and Indigenous Law', *Journal of Legal Pluralism and Unofficial Law* 19:1–47.

Gallie, W.B., 1956. 'Essentially Contested Concepts', *Proceedings of the Aristotelian Society* 56:167–98.

Gammage, Bill, 1996. 'Police and Power During Contact in the New Guinea Highlands', in Hal Levine and Anton Ploeg, eds, *Work in Progress: Essays in New Guinea Highlands Ethnography in Honour of Paula Brown Glick* (Frankfurt: Peter Lang).

Geertz, Clifford, 1960. *The Religion of Java* (Glencoe, Ill: The Free Press).

——— 1980. *Negara: The Theatre State in Nineteenth Century Bali* (Princeton, NJ: Princeton University Press).

——— 1983. *Local Knowledge: Further Essays in Interpretive Anthropology* (New York: Basic Books).

Gillis, Malcolm, 1987. 'Multinational Enterprises and Environmental and Resource Management Issues in the Indonesian Tropical Forest Sector', in Charles S. Pearson, ed., *Multinational Corporations, Environment, and the Third World: Business Matters* (Durham, NC: Duke University Press).

——— 1988. 'Indonesia: Public Policies, Resource Management, and the Tropical Forest', in Malcolm Gillis and Robert Repetto, eds, *Public Policies and the Misuse of Forest Resources* (Cambridge: Cambridge University Press).

Glassman, Ronald M., 1991. *China in Transition: Communism, Capitalism, and Democracy* (New York: Praeger).

Goddard, M., 1995. 'The Rascal Road: Crime, Prestige and Development in Papua New Guinea', *The Contemporary Pacific* 7, 1:55–80.

Golay, Frank H., 1961. *The Philippines: Public Policy and National Economic Development* (Ithaca, NY: Cornell University Press).

Goldring, J., 1978. *The Constitution of Papua New Guinea: A Study in Legal Nationalism* (Sydney: Law Book Company).

Gordon, Robert J., 1983. 'The Decline of the Kiapdom and the Resurgence of "Tribal Fighting" in Enga', *Oceania* 53, 3:205–23.

―――― and Mervyn J. Meggitt, 1985. *Law and Order in the New Guinea Highlands: Encounters with Enga* (Hanover, VT: University Press of New England).

Gottlieb, Gidon, 1993. *Nations Against State: A New Approach to Ethnic Conflicts and the Decline of Sovereignty* (New York: Council on Foreign Relations Press).

Goulbourne, Harry, ed., 1979. *Politics and State in the Third World* (London: Macmillan).

Grant, Bruce, 1996. *Indonesia*, 3rd edn (Carlton, Victoria: Melbourne University Press).

Greenpeace Pacific, 1995. 'Pavuvu Island Logging, Russell Is Group, Central Province, Solomon Islands', Greenpeace Pacific, Environmental Impact Report, November.

Griffin, J., 1988. 'A Barbaric Report', *Times of PNG* 25–31 August.

Griffin, James, Hank N. Nelson and Stewart Firth, 1979. *Papua New Guinea: A Political History* (Melbourne: Heinemann Educational Australia).

Grindle, Merilee S., 1996. *Challenging the State: Crisis and Innovation in Latin America and Africa* (Cambridge: Cambridge University Press).

Guehenno, Jean-Marie, 1995. *The End of the Nation-State* (Minneapolis: University of Minnesota Press).

Gulbrandsen, Ornulf, 1996. 'Living Their Lives in Courts: The Counter-Hegemonic Force of the Tsawana Kgotla in a Colonial Context', in Olivia Harris, ed., *Inside and Outside the Law* (New York: Routledge).

Gutierrez, E., I. Torrente and N. Garcia, 1992. *All in the Family: A Study of Elites and Power Relations in the Philippines* (Quezon City: Ateneo Center for Social Policy and Public Affairs).

Habermas, Jürgen, 1987. *The Theory of Communicative Action*, Vol. 2, *Lifeworld and System: A Critique of Functionalist Reason* (Boston: Beacon Press).

———— 1991. *The Structural Transformation of the Public Sphere: An Inquiry into a Category of Bourgeois Society* (Cambridge, MA: MIT Press).

Hall, David L. and Roger T. Ames, 1987. *Thinking Through Confucius* (Albany, NY: State University of New York Press).

Hall, Edith, 1989. *Inventing the Barbarian: Greek Self-Definition Through Tragedy* (Oxford: Clarendon Press).

Hall, John A., 1986. 'Introduction', in John A. Hall, ed., *States in History* (Oxford: Basil Blackwell).

Hannan, Michael T. and John Freeman, 1977. 'The Population Ecology of Organizations', *American Journal of Sociology* 82, 5:929–64.

Harris, Bruce M., 1988. *The Rise of Rascalism: Action and Reaction in the Evolution of Rascal Gangs*, Discussion Paper No. 54 (Port Moresby: Institute of Applied Social and Economic Research).

Hawes, G., 1992. 'Marcos, His Cronies and the Philippines' Failure to Develop', in R. McVey, ed., *Southeast Asian Capitalists*, Studies on Southeast Asia (Ithaca, NY: Southeast Asia Program, Cornell University).

Hayami, Yujiro, Ma. Agnes R. Quisumbing, and Lourdes S. Adriano, 1990. *Toward an Alternative Land Reform Paradigm* (Manila: Ateneo de Manila University Press).

Hayes, G., 1995. Book Review (R.V. Cole, ed., *Pacific 2010: Challenging the Future*), *The Contemporary Pacific: A Journal of Island Affairs* 7, 1:191–4.

Hefner, Robert W., 1993. 'Islam, State, and Civil Society: ICMI and the Struggle for the Indonesian Middle Class', *Indonesia* 56:1–35.

Henningham, Stephan, 1995. *The Pacific Island States: Security and Sovereignty in the Post-Cold War World* (New York: St Martins Press).

Hindson, Paul and Tim Gray, 1988. *Burke's Dramatic Theory of Politics* (Brookfield, VT: Avebury).

Hiscock, Geoff, 1996. 'Wealth Sprouts on Suharto Family Tree', *Australian* 10 October.

Huang Chin-Shing, 1987. *The Price of Having a Sage-Emperor: The Unity of Politics and Culture*, Occasional Paper and Monograph Series No. 10 (Singapore: Institute of East Asian Philosophies).

Huet, Marie-Hélène, 1982. *Rehearsing the Revolution: The Staging of Marat's Death 1793–1797*, translated by Robert Hurley (Berkeley, CA: University of California Press).

Hunt, Lynn Avery, 1992. *The Family Romance of the French Revolution* (Berkeley, CA: University of California Press).

Huntington, Samuel P., 1996. *The Clash of Civilizations and the Remaking of World Order* (New York: Simon & Schuster).

Hutchcroft, Paul D., 1991. 'Oligarchs and Cronies in the Philippine State: The Politics of Patrimonial Plunder', *World Politics* 43, 3:410–50.

Hutchful, Eboe, 1995–96. 'The Civil Society Debate in Africa', *International Journal* 51, 1:54–77.

Hy Van Luong, 1985. 'Agrarian Unrest from an Anthropological Perspective: The Case of Vietnam', *Comparative Politics* 17, 2:153–74.

IDEA, 1997. *Voter Turnout from 1945 to 1997: A Global Report* (Stockholm: International Institute for Democracy and Electoral Assistance).

'Importing Logs', 1996. *Jakarta Post* 17 January. Reuters News Briefing.

Ingebritsen, Christine, 1998. *The Nordic States and European Unity* (Ithaca, NY: Cornell University Press).

International Labour Office, 1975. *Labour Conditions in Indo-China* (Nendeln: Kraus Reprint, first published Geneva, 1938).

International Timber Corporation Indonesia (ITCI), 1992. *P.T. International Timber Corporation Indonesia* (Jakarta: ITCI).

International Tropical Timber Organization (ITTO), 1995. *Annual Review and Assessment of the World Tropical Timber Situation: 1993–1994* (Yokohama: ITTO).

———— 1996. *Annual Review and Assessment of the World Tropical Timber Situation: 1995* (Yokohama: ITTO).

———— 1997. *Annual Review and Assessment of the World Tropical Timber Situation: 1996* (Yokohama: ITTO).

———— 1998. *Annual Review and Assessment of the World Tropical Timber Situation: 1997* (Yokohama: ITTO).

Jackson, Karl D., 1978. 'Bureaucratic Polity: A Theoretical Framework for the Analysis of Power and Communications in Indonesia', in Karl D. Jackson and Lucian W. Pye, eds, *Political Power and Communications in Indonesia* (Berkeley, CA: University of California).

Jackson, Robert H., 1990. *Quasi-States: Sovereignty, International Relations and the Third World* (Cambridge/New York: Cambridge University Press).

190

Jackson, Robert H. and Carl G. Rosberg, 1982. 'Why Africa's Weak States Persist: The Empirical and the Juridical in Statehood', *World Politics* 35, 1:1–24.

Kabutaulaka, Tarcisius and Peter Dauvergne, 1997. The Weak State in the Solomon Islands, unpublished paper, presented at a workshop on Weak and Strong States in Melanesia and Southeast Asia, 13 August, Australian National University, Canberra.

Kahin, George McT., 1952. *Nationalism and Revolution in Indonesia* (Ithaca, NY: Cornell University Press).

Kaplan, Robert, 1997. *The Ends of the Earth: From Togo to Turkmenistan, from Iran to Cambodia, A Journey to the Frontiers of Anarchy* (New York: Knopf).

Katzenstein, Peter, ed., 1996. *Culture of National Security: Norms and Identity in World Politics* (New York: Columbia University Press).

——— 1997. *Tamed Power* (Ithaca, NY: Cornell University Press).

Keller, Edmond J. and Donald Rothchild, 1996. *Africa in the New International Order: Rethinking State Sovereignty and Regional Security* (Boulder, CO: Lynne Rienner).

Kerkvliet, Benedict J. Tria, 1977. *The Huk Rebellion* (Berkeley, CA: University of California Press).

——— 1987. 'Peasants and Agrarian Workers: Implications for United States Policy', in Carl Landé, ed., *Rebuilding a Nation: Philippine Challenges and American Policy* (Washington, DC: Washington Institute for Values in Public Policy).

——— 1990. *Everyday Politics in the Philippines. Class and Status Relations in a Central Luzon Village* (Berkeley, CA: University of California Press).

——— 1993. 'Claiming the Land: Take-overs by Villagers in the Philippines with Comparisons to Indonesia, Peru, Portugal, and Russia', *Journal of Peasant Studies* 20, 3:459–93.

——— 1995. 'Village–State Relations in Vietnam: The Effect of Everyday Politics on Decollectivization', *Journal of Asian Studies* 54, 2:396–418.

——— 1997. *Land Struggles and Land Regimes in the Philippines and Vietnam during the Twentieth Century* (Amsterdam: Centre for Asian Studies).

King, David, 1992. 'The Demise of the Small Towns and Outstations of Papua New Guinea: Trends in Urban Census Populations and Growth from 1966 to 1990', *Yagl-Ambu* 16, 3:17–33.

King, Peter, Wendy Lee and Vincent Warakai, 1985. *From Rhetoric To Reality: Papua New Guinea's Eight Point Plan and National Goals after a Decade* (Port Moresby: University of Papua New Guinea Press).

Kituai, August, 1988. 'Innovation and Intrusion: Villagers and Policemen in Papua New Guinea', *Journal of Pacific History* 23, 2:156–66.

———— 1993. My Gun, My Brother: Experiences of Papua New Guinea Policemen 1920–1960, PhD Thesis (Canberra: Australian National University).

Klotz, Audie, 1995. *Norms in International Relations: The Struggle against Apartheid* (Ithaca, NY: Cornell University Press).

Koelble, Thomas A., 1995. 'The New Institutionalism in Political Science and Sociology', *Comparative Politics* 27, 2:231–43.

Krasner, Stephen D., 1988. 'Sovereignty: An Institutional Perspective', *Comparative Political Studies* 21, 1:66–94.

Kuehls, Thom, 1996. *Beyond Sovereign Territory: The Space of Eco-politics* (Minneapolis: University of Minnesota Press).

Laitin, David D., 1986. *Hegemony and Culture: Politics and Religious Change Among the Yoruba* (Chicago: University of Chicago Press).

Lam Quan Huyen, 1985. *Cach Mang Ruong Dat o Mien Nam Viet Nam* [Land Revolution in South Vietnam] (Hanoi: NXB Khoa Hoc Xa Hoi).

Landé, Carl H., 1965. *Leaders, Factions and Parties: The Structure of Philippine Politics*, Monograph Series No. 6 (New Haven, CT: Yale University Southeast Asian Studies).

———— 1987. 'Introduction: Retrospect and Prospect', in Carl H. Landé, ed., *Rebuilding a Nation: Philippine Challenges and American Policy* (Washington, DC: Washington Institute Press).

———— 1996. *Post-Marcos Politics: A Geographical and Statistical Analysis of the 1992 Presidential Election* (New York/Singapore: St Martins Press/Institute of Southeast Asian Studies).

Lapid, Yosef and Friedrich Kratochwil, eds, 1996. *The Return of Culture and Identity in IR Theory* (Boulder, CO: Lynne Rienner).

Larkin, John A., 1993. *Sugar and the Origins of Modern Philippine Society* (Berkeley, CA: University of California Press).

Larmour, Peter, 1990. 'Public Choice in Melanesia: Community, Bureaucracy and the Market in Land Management' *Public Administration and Development* 10:53–68.

—— 1992. 'States and Societies in the Pacific Islands', *Pacific Studies* 15, 1:99–121.

—— 1998. 'Corruption and Governance in the South Pacific', *Pacific Studies* 20, 3:1–17.

—— ed., 1991. *Decentralisation and Customary Land Registration in Papua New Guinea*, Monograph 27 (Port Moresby: National Research Institute).

Latouche, S., 1987. 'The Ethical Implications of Development: A Philosophic Reflection on an Economic Process', in S. Stratigos and P. Hughes, eds, *The Ethics of Development: The Pacific in the 21st Century*, Volume 1 (Port Moresby: University of Papua New Guinea Press).

Lawson, Stephanie, 1991. 'Some Conceptual and Empirical Issues in the Study of Regime Change', Regime Change and Regime Maintenance in Asia and the Pacific, Discussion Paper No. 3 (Canberra: Department of Political and Social Change, Research School of Pacific Studies, Australian National University).

—— 1993a. 'Conceptual Issues in the Comparative Study of Regime Change and Democratization', *Comparative Politics* 25, 2:183–205.

—— 1993b. 'Institutionalizing Peaceful Conflict: Political Opposition and the Challenge of Democratization in Asia', *Australian Journal of International Affairs* 47, 1:15–30.

—— 1995. 'Occidentalising Democracy', *Pacific Research* 8, 4:7–9.

—— 1996. 'Cultural Relativism and Democracy: Political Myths About "Asia" and the "West"', in Richard Robison, ed., *Pathways to Asia: The Politics of Engagement* (Sydney: Allen & Unwin).

—— 1998. 'Democracy and the Problem of Cultural Relativism: Normative Issues for International Politics', *Global Society* 12, 2:251–270.

Lev, Daniel, S., 1966. *The Transition to Guided Democracy: Indonesian Politics 1957–1959* (Ithaca, NY: Modern Indonesia Project, Cornell University).

Liddle, R. William, 1996. 'The Islamic Turn in Indonesia: A Political Explanation', *Journal of Asian Studies* 55, 3:613–34.

Lowry, Robert, 1996. *The Armed Forces of Indonesia* (Sydney: Allen & Unwin).

Lu, Martin, 1983. *Confucianism: Its Relevance to Modern Society* (Singapore: Federal Publications).

Lyons, Gene M. and Michael Mastanduno, eds, 1995. *Beyond Westphalia? State Sovereignty and International Intervention* (Baltimore, MD: Johns Hopkins University Press).

MacFarling, Ian, 1996. *The Dual Function of the Indonesian Armed Forces: Military Politics in Indonesia* (Canberra: Australian Defence Studies Centre, Australian Defence Forces Academy).

Machado, K.G., 1972. 'Changing Patterns of Leadership Recruitment and the Emergence of the Professional Politician in Philippine Local Politics', *Philippine Journal of Public Administration* 16, 2:147–69.

MacIntyre, Andrew, 1990. *Business and Politics in Indonesia* (Sydney: Allen & Unwin).

——— 1992. 'Politics and the Reorientation of Economic Policy in Indonesia', in Andrew J. MacIntyre and Kanishka Jayasuriya, eds, *The Dynamics of Economic Policy Reform in South-east Asia and the South-west Pacific* (Singapore: Oxford University Press).

——— 1993. 'The Politics of Finance in Indonesia: Command, Confusion, and Competition', in Stephan Haggard, Chung H. Lee and Sylvia Maxfield, eds, *The Politics of Finance in Developing Countries* (Ithaca, NY: Cornell University Press).

——— 1994. 'Business, Government and Development: Northeast and Southeast Asian Comparisons', and 'Power, Prosperity and Patrimonialism: Business and Government in Indonesia', in Andrew MacIntyre, ed., *Business and Government in Industrializing Asia* (Ithaca, NY: Cornell University Press).

Mackenzie, A., 1987. 'People Power or Palace Coup: The Fall of Marcos', in Mark Turner, ed., *Regime Change in the Philippines. The Legitimation of the Aquino Government*, Political and Social Change Monograph 7 (Canberra: Australian National University).

Mair, Lucy P., 1948. *Australia in New Guinea* (London: Christophers).

Mann, Michael, 1986. 'The Autonomous Power of the State: Its Origins, Mechanisms and Results', in John A. Hall, ed., *States in History* (Oxford: Basil Blackwell).

March, James G. and Johan P. Olsen, 1989. *Rediscovering Institutions: The Organizational Basis of Politics* (New York: Free Press).

Marty, Martin E., 1997. *The One and the Many: America's Struggle for the Common Good* (Cambridge, MA: Harvard University Press).

May, R.J., 1984. 'Class, Ethnicity, Regionalism and Political Parties', in R.J. May, ed., *Social Stratification in Papua New Guinea*, Working Paper No. 5 (Canberra: Department of Political and Social

Change, Research School of Pacific Studies, Australian National University).

—— 1989. 'People Power and Powerful People: Regime Change and Regime Maintenance in the Asia–Pacific Region', in R.J. May and William J. O'Malley, eds, *Observing Change in Asia. Essays in Honour of J.A.C. Mackie* (Bathurst, NSW: Crawford House Press).

—— 1990. 'The Moro Movement in Southern Philippines', in K.M. de Silva, S. Kiribamune and C.R. de Silva, eds, *Asian Panorama: Essays in Asian History, Past and Present* (New Delhi: Vikas Publishing House).

—— 1996. 'The Situation on Bougainville: Implications for Papua New Guinea, Australia and the Region', *Current Issues Brief No. 9 1996–97* (Canberra: Parliamentary Research Service).

—— 1997. 'Des promesses à la crise: économie politique de la Papouasie-Nouvelle Guinée', *Révue Tiers Monde* 38, 149:139–56.

—— ed., 1982. *Micronationalist Movements in Papua New Guinea*, Political and Social Change Monograph 1 (Canberra: Australian National University).

—— and S. Tupouniua, 1980. 'The Politics of Small Island States', in R.T. Shand, ed., *The Island States of the Pacific and Indian Oceans: Anatomy of Development*, Monograph No. 23 (Canberra: Development Studies Centre, Australian National University).

—— and A.J. Regan with A. Ley, eds, 1997. *Political Decentralisation in a New State: The Experience of Provincial Government in Papua New Guinea* (Bathurst, NSW: Crawford House Publishing).

—— and V. Selochan, eds, 1998. *The Military and Democracy in Asia and the Pacific* (Bathurst, NSW: Crawford House Publishing).

Mazarr, Michael J., 1996. 'Culture and International Relations: A Review Essay', *Washington Quarterly* 19, 2:177–97.

McCoy, Alfred W., 1994. '"An Anarchy of Families": The Historiography of State and Family in the Philippines', in Alfred W. McCoy, ed., *An Anarchy of Families: State and Family in the Philippines* (Quezon City: Ateneo de Manila University Press).

McLennan, Marshall S., 1980. *The Central Luzon Plain: Land and Society on the Inland Frontier* (Manila: Alemar-Phoenix Publishing House).

Meyer, John W. and Brian Rowan, 1977. 'Institutionalized Organizations: Formal Structure as Myth and Ceremony', *American Journal of Sociology* 83, 2:340–63.

Meyer, Marshall W. and Lynne G. Zucker, 1989. *Permanently Failing Organizations* (Newbury Park, CA: Sage).

Migdal, Joel S., 1987. 'Strong States, Weak States: Power and Accommodation', in Myron Weiner and Samuel P. Huntington, eds, *Understanding Political Development* (Boston: Little, Brown).

—— 1988. *Strong Societies and Weak States: State–Society Relations and State Capabilities in the Third World* (Princeton, NJ: Princeton University Press).

—— 1994. 'The State in Society: An Approach to Struggles for Domination', in Joel S. Migdal, Atul Kohli and Vivienne Shue, eds, *State Power and Social Forces: Domination and Transformation in the Third World* (Cambridge/New York: Cambridge University Press).

—— 1997. 'Studying the State', in Mark Irving Lichbach and Alan S. Zuckerman, eds, *Comparative Politics. Rationality, Culture and Structure* (Cambridge/New York: Cambridge University Press).

——, Atul Kohli and Vivienne Shue, eds, 1994. *State Power and Social Forces: Domination and Transformation in the Third World* (Cambridge/New York: Cambridge University Press).

Miranda, F.B., 1993. 'Democratization in the Philippines: Recent Developments, Trends and Prospects', *Asian Journal of Political Science* 1, 1:85–112.

Monk, Paul, 1990. *Truth and Power: Robert S. Hardie and Land Reform Debates in the Philippines, 1950–1987* (Clayton, Victoria: Centre of Southeast Asian Studies, Monash University).

Montgomery, Phillip, 1995. 'Forestry in Solomon Islands', *Pacific Economic Bulletin* 10, December:74–6.

Moody Jr, Peter R., 1988. *Political Opposition in Post-Confucian Society* (New York: Praeger).

Moore Jr, Barrington, 1969. *Reflections on the Causes of Human Misery and Upon Certain Proposals to Eliminate Them* (Boston: Beacon Press).

—— 1978. *Injustice: The Social Bases of Obedience and Revolt* (White Plains, NY: M.E. Sharpe).

Morauta, Louise, 1980. 'Permanent Urban Residents in PNG: Problems and Prospects', in Proceedings of the 1979 Waigani Seminar on Urbanisation (Port Moresby: University of Papua New Guinea).

Mulholland, Seamus and Gane Simbe, 1995. *Report of Visit to Japan and Korea by TCUP Commercial Unit Manager and CBSI Foreign*

Exchange Manager 26 March to 8 April 1995, internal report, May.

Murray, Martin J., 1980. *The Development of Capitalism in Colonial Indochina, 1870–1940* (Berkeley, CA: University of California Press).

Nanau, Gordon, 1998. 'Decentralisation Reform in Solomon Islands', in Peter Larmour, ed., *Governance and Reform in the South Pacific* (Canberra: National Centre for Development Studies, Australian National University).

Navari, Cornelia, 1991. 'Introduction: The State as a Contested Concept in International Relations', in Cornelia Navari, ed., *The Condition of States* (Milton Keynes: Open University Press).

Neher, Clark D., 1994. *Southeast Asia in the New International Era*, 2nd edn (Boulder, CO: Westview Press).

Nenta, R., 1996. Papua New Guinea: Security and Defence in the Nineties and Beyond 2000, Conference Proceedings, Sydney, 28 June.

Newberg, Paula R., 1995. *Judging the State: Courts and Constitutional Politics in Pakistan* (New York: Cambridge University Press).

Ngo Vinh Long, 1973. *Before the Revolution: The Vietnamese Peasants under the French* (Cambridge, MA: MIT Press).

—— 1980. 'View from the Village', *Indochina Issues* 12, December:1, 4–7.

—— 1988. 'Some Aspects of Cooperativization in the Mekong Delta', in David Marr and Christine P. White, eds, *Postwar Vietnam: Dilemmas in Socialist Development* (Ithaca, NY: Southeast Asia Program, Cornell University Press).

Nguyen Thu Sa, 1990. 'Van de Ruong Dat o Dong Bang Song Cuu Long' [The Matter of Land in the Mekong Delta], in *Mien Nam trong Su Nghiep Doi Moi cua Ca Nuoc* (TP Ho Chi Minh: NXB Khoa Hoc Xa Hoi).

Nordholt, N.G. Schulte, 1987. *State–Citizen Relations in Suharto's Indonesia: Kawula-Gusti* (Rotterdam: Comparative Asian Studies Programme, Erasmus University).

NSO, 1993. *National Population Census—Final Figures. Census Division: Population* (Port Moresby: National Statistical Office).

O'Donnell, Guillermo and Philippe C. Schmitter, 1986. *Transitions from Authoritarian Rule: Tentative Conclusions about Uncertain Democracies* (Baltimore, MD: Johns Hopkins University Press).

Offe, Claus, 1996. *Modernity and the State: East, West* (Cambridge, MA: MIT Press).

Ohmae, Kenichi, 1995. *The End of the Nation-State: The Rise of Regional Economies* (New York: Free Press).

Oldenburg, Ray, 1989. *The Great Good Place: Cafés, Coffee Shops, Community Centers, Beauty Parlors, General Stores, Bars, Hangouts and How They Get You Through the Day* (New York: Paragon House).

Oram, Nigel, 1973. 'Law and Order: Maximum Participation at all Levels', *New Guinea* January:4–22.

——— 1976. *Colonial Town to Melanesian City: Port Moresby 1884–1974* (Canberra: Australian National University Press).

Osiel, Mark J., 1995. 'Dialogue with Dictators: Judicial Resistance in Argentina and Brazil', *Law and Social Inquiry* 20, 2:481–560.

Panglaykim, J. and Heinz Arndt, 1966. 'Survey of Recent Developments', *Bulletin of Indonesian Economic Studies* 4, June:1–35.

Parry, G.L., 1972. 'Organised Juvenile Crime in Port Moresby', *South Pacific Bulletin* 22, 1:43–44, 60.

Pham Cao Duong, 1985. *Vietnamese Peasants Under French Domination, 1861–1945* (Berkeley, CA: Center for South and Southeast Asian Studies, University of California).

Philippines, Commission of the Census, 1941. *Census of the Philippines, 1939*, vol. 2, *Summary for the Philippines and General Report* (Manila).

Philippines, National Statistics Office, 1991. *1991 Census of Agriculture*, vol. 1, Philippine summary (Manila).

Pirie, P., 1995. Book Review (R.V. Cole, ed., *Pacific 2010: Challenging the Future*), *The Contemporary Pacific: A Journal of Island Affairs* 7, 1:188–91.

PNG, 1973. *Report of the Committee Investigating Tribal Fighting in the Highlands* [Paney Report] (Port Moresby: Government Printer).

PNGCMP, Papua New Guinea Chamber of Mines and Petroleum, 1991. The Law and Order Crisis—Effects on the Mining and Petroleum Industry, paper for the National Crime Summit, Port Moresby, 12 February.

Popkin, Samuel L., 1979. *The Rational Peasant: The Political Economy of Rural Society in Vietnam* (Berkeley, CA: University of California Press).

198

Porter, Gareth, 1993. *Vietnam: The Politics of Bureaucratic Socialism* (Ithaca, NY: Cornell University Press).

Pospisil, Leopold, 1979. 'Legally Induced Culture Change in New Guinea', in Sandra B. Burman and Barbara E. Harrell-Bond, eds, *The Imposition of Law* (New York: Academic Press).

Price Waterhouse, Economic Studies and Strategies Unit, 1995. *Forestry Taxation and Domestic Processing Study*, Final Draft Report, Report for the Solomon Islands Government, Ministry of Finance, and the Ministry of Forests, Environment and Conservation (December).

Pulea, Mere, 1986. *The Family, Law and Population in the Pacific Islands* (Suva: Institute of Pacific Studies).

Pura, Raphael, 1990. 'Rapid Loss of Forest Worries Indonesia', *Asian Wall Street Journal* 3 February.

—— 1993. 'Timber Tycoon Confronts His Critics', *Asian Wall Street Journal* 27 August:1, 8.

——, Stephen Duthi, and Richard Borsuk, 1994. 'Plywood Tycoon May Purchase Malaysian Firm', *Asian Wall Street Journal* 3 February:1, 4.

Putnam, Robert D., 1993. 'What Makes Democracy Work?' *National Civic Review* 82, 2:101–7.

—— 1995a. 'Bowling Alone: America's Declining Social Capital', *Current* 373:3–10.

—— 1995b. 'Tuning in, Tuning Out: The Strange Disappearance of Social Capital in America', *PS: Political Science and Politics* 28, 4:664–83.

Putzel, James, 1992. *A Captive Land: The Politics of Agrarian Reform in the Philippines* (New York: Catholic Institute for International Relations, London and Monthly Review Press).

Pye, Lucian W. with Mary W. Pye, 1985. *Asian Power and Politics: The Cultural Dimensions of Authority* (Cambridge, MA: Belknap Press).

Rahim, Lily, 1996. In Search of the 'Asian Way': Cultural Nationalism and the Reinvention of Identity in Singapore and Malaysia, paper presented at the Conference on The Future of Nationalism and the State, Department of Government, University of Sydney, 15–17 July.

Ramage, Douglas E., 1995. *Politics in Indonesia: Democracy, Islam and the Ideology of Tolerance* (London: Routledge).

Reay, Marie, 1987. 'Laying Down the Law in Their Own Fashion', in L.L. Langness and T.E. Hayes, eds, *Anthropology in the High Valleys* (Novato, CA: Chandler and Sharp).

Reed, Stephen W., 1943. *The Making of Modern New Guinea* (Philadelphia: American Philosophical Society).

Regan, A.J., 1997. 'The Operation of the Provincial Government System', in R.J. May and A.J. Regan with Allison Ley, eds, *Political Decentralisation in a New State: The Experience of Provincial Government in a New State* (Bathurst, NSW: Crawford House Publishing).

Reilly, Ben, 1996. 'The Effects of the Electoral System in Papua New Guinea', in Yaw Saffu, ed., *The 1992 PNG Election: Change and Continuity in Electoral Politics*, Political and Social Change Monograph 23 (Canberra: The Australian National University).

Rivera, Temario C., 1994. *Landlords and Capitalists: Class, Family and State in Philippine Manufacturing* (Quezon City: UP Center for Integrative and Development Studies and University of the Philippines Press).

———— 1996. *State of the Nation. Philippines* (Singapore: Institute of Southeast Asian Studies).

Robison, Richard, 1986. *Indonesia: The Rise of Capital* (Sydney/London: Allen & Unwin).

Rodan, Garry, 1993. 'Preserving the One-Party State in Contemporary Singapore', in Kevin Hewison, Richard Robison and Garry Rodan, eds, *Southeast Asia in the 1990s: Authoritarianism, Democracy and Capitalism* (Sydney: Allen & Unwin).

————, ed., 1996. *Political Oppositions in Industrializing Asia* (London: Routledge).

Rosenau, James N., 1988. 'The State in an Era of Cascading Politics: Wavering Concept, Widening Competence, Withering Colossus, or Weathering Change?' *Comparative Political Studies* 21, 1:13–44.

Roughan, John, 1994. 'Solomon Islands Nongovernment Organizations: Major Environmental Actors', in Fay Alailima, Werner vom Busch, et al., eds, *New Politics in the South Pacific* (Suva/Rarotonga: Institute of Pacific Studies, University of the South Pacific, in association with Pacific Islands Political Studies Association).

———— 1997. 'Solomon Islands: Non-Government Organizations', *The Contemporary Pacific* 9, 1:157–66.

200

Runciman, David, 1997. *Pluralism and the Personality of the State* (New York: Cambridge University Press).

Rush, James, 1991. *The Last Tree: Reclaiming the Environment in Tropical Asia* (New York: The Asia Society).

Saadah, Fadia, Peter Heywood and Ian Morris, 1995. 'Health Services in Solomon Islands,' *Pacific Economic Bulletin* 10, 2:23–40.

Saffu, Yaw, 1996. 'Continuity and Change in PNG Electoral Politics', in Yaw Saffu, ed., *The 1992 PNG Election: Change and Continuity in Electoral Politics*, Political and Social Change Monograph 23 (Canberra: Australian National University).

Said, Edward, 1978. *Orientalism* (New York: Vintage Books).

Sansom, Robert, 1970. *Economics of Insurgency in the Mekong Delta of Vietnam* (Cambridge, MA: MIT Press).

Santiago, M. Defensor, 1991. *How to Fight Election Fraud* (Makati, Philippines: Movement for Responsible Public Service, Inc).

Saragosa, Manuela, 1997. 'Indonesia: Forest Fund Boost for Associate of Suharto', *Financial Times* 30 January. Reuters Business Briefing.

Schieffelin, Edward L. and Robert Crittenden, eds, 1991. *Like People You See in a Dream: First Contact in Six Papuan Societies* (Stanford, CA: Stanford University Press).

Schlichte, Klaus, 1997. Why States Decay: A Preliminary Assessment, mimeo.

Schwarz, Adam, 1992. 'Forest Framework', *Far Eastern Economic Review* 12 March:44–5.

——— 1994. *A Nation in Waiting: Indonesia in the 1990s* (Sydney: Allen & Unwin).

Scott, James C., 1976. *The Moral Economy of the Peasant* (New Haven, CT: Yale University Press).

Selvan, T.S., 1990. *Singapore: The Ultimate Island (Lee Kuan Yew's Untold Story)* (Melbourne: Freeway Books).

Sender, Henny, 1996. 'Bambang's Challenge', *Far Eastern Economic Review* 5 September.

Sennett, Richard, 1977. *The Fall of Public Man* (New York: Knopf).

Shapiro, Martin and Alec Stone, 1994. 'The New Constitutional Politics of Europe', *Comparative Political Studies* 26, 4:397–420.

Shapiro, Michael J. and Hayward R. Alker, 1996. *Changing Boundaries: Global Flows, Territorial Identities* (Minneapolis: University of Minnesota Press).

Shils, Edward, 1975. *Center and Periphery: Essays in Macrosociology* (Chicago: University of Chicago Press).

Shiraishi, Takashi, 1996. 'Rewiring the Indonesian State', in Daniel. S. Lev and Ruth McVey, eds, *Making Indonesia: Essays on Modern Indonesia in Honor of George McT. Kahin* (Ithaca, NY: Southeast Asia Program, Cornell University).

Sidel, John Thayer, 1995a. Coercion, Capital and the Post-Colonial State: Bossism in the Postwar Philippines, PhD Dissertation (Ithaca, NY: Cornell University).

———— 1995b. 'The Philippines: The Languages of Legitimation', in Muthiah Alagappa, ed., *Political Legitimacy in Southeast Asia: The Quest for Moral Authority* (Stanford, CA: Stanford University Press).

Singh, Jitendra V., David J. Tucker and Robert J. House, 1994. 'Organizational Legitimacy and the Liability of Newness', in W. Richard Scott, ed., *Organizational Sociology* (Brookfield, VT: Dartmouth).

Sizer, Nigel, 1996. *Profit Without Plunder: Reaping Revenue From Guyana's Tropical Forests Without Destroying Them* (Washington, DC: World Resources Institute).

Skocpol, Theda, 1979. *States and Social Revolution* (Cambridge: Cambridge University Press).

Smith, Anthony, 1995. *Nations and Nationalism in the Global Era* (Cambridge: Polity).

Smith, William, 1995. 'Implementing the 1993 Land Law: The Impact of Land Allocation on Rural Households in Lon La and Ha Tinh Provinces', ActionAid Vietnam, June.

Soriano, J.C., 1987. 'The Return of the Oligarchs', *Conjuncture* 1, 1:6.

South Pacific Regional Environment Programme, 1992. *Solomon Islands: Country Report for UNCED* (Apia, Western Samoa: South Pacific Regional Environment Programme).

Spruyt, Hendrik, 1994. *The Sovereign State and Its Competitors: An Analysis of System Change* (Princeton, NJ: Princeton University Press).

Standish, William A., 1984. 'Melanesian Neighbours: The Politics of Papua New Guinea, the Solomon Islands and the Republic of Vanuatu', Basic Paper No. 9 (Canberra: Commonwealth Parliamentary Library).

———— 1994. 'Papua New Guinea: The Search for Security in a Weak State', in Alan Thompson, ed., *Papua New Guinea: Issues for*

202

Australian Security Planners (Canberra: Australian Defence Studies Centre, Australian Defence Force Academy).

—— 1996. 'Elections in Simbu: Towards Gunpoint Democracy?', in Yaw Saffu, ed., *The 1992 Papua New Guinea Election: Change and Continuity in Electoral Politics*, Political and Social Change Monograph 23 (Canberra: Australian National University).

Steeves, Jeffrey S., 1996. 'Unbounded Politics in the Solomon Islands: Leadership and Party Alignments,' *Pacific Studies* 19, 1:115–38.

Stepan, Alfred, 1978. *The State and Society: Peru in Comparative Perspective* (Princeton, NJ: Princeton University Press).

Stinchcombe, Arthur L., 1965. 'Organizations and Social Structure', in James G. March, ed., *Handbook of Organizations* (Chicago: Rand-McNally).

Strang, David, 1991. 'Anomaly and Commonplace in European Political Expansion: Realist and Institutional Accounts', *International Organization* 45, 2:143–62.

Strathern, Andrew J., 1993. 'Violence and Political Change in Papua New Guinea', *Pacific Studies* 16, 4:41–60.

Strathern, Marilyn, 1972. *Official and Unofficial Courts: Legal Assumptions and Expectations in a Highlands Community*, New Guinea Research Bulletin No. 47 (Port Moresby).

—— 1976. 'Crime and Corrections: The Place of Prisons in Papua New Guinea', *Melanesian Law Journal* 4, 1:67–93.

—— 1988. *The Gender of the Gift: Problems with Women and Problems with Society in Melanesia* (Berkeley, CA: University of California).

Sturdevant, David R., 1976. *Popular Uprisings in the Philippines 1840–1940* (Ithaca, NY: Cornell University Press).

Sundhaussen, Ulf, 1982. *The Road to Power: Indonesian Military Politics 1945–1967* (Kuala Lumpur: Oxford University Press).

Tamney, Joseph B., 1991. 'Confucianism and Democracy', *Asian Profile* 19, 5:399–411.

Tanji, Miyume and Stephanie Lawson, 1997. '"Democratic Peace" and "Asian Democracy": A Universalist–Particularist Tension', *Alternatives* 22, 1:135–55.

Tanter, Richard and Kenneth Young, eds, 1990. *The Politics of Middle Class Indonesia* (Clayton, Victoria: Centre of Southeast Asian Studies, Monash University).

Tapales, Prosperina D., 1993. *Devolution and Empowerment: The Local Government Code of 1991 and Local Autonomy in the Philippines* (Quezon City: UP Center for Integrative and Development Studies in cooperation with the University of the Philippines Press).

Taylor, Michael, 1982. *Community, Anarchy and Liberty* (Cambridge/New York: Cambridge University Press).

Thompson, E.P., 1974. 'Patrician Society, Plebian Culture', *Journal of Social History* 7:382–405.

Thompson, Mark R., 1995. *The Anti-Marcos Struggle* (New Haven, CT: Yale University Press).

Thrift, Nigel and Dean Forbes, 1986. *The Price of War: Urbanization in Vietnam 1954–1985* (London: Allen & Unwin).

'Timber: An Economic Dilemma', 1994. *Economic & Business Review Indonesia* 98, 26 February:9.

Timberman, David G., 1991. *A Changeless Land: Continuity and Change in Philippine Politics* (Singapore/New York: Institute of Southeast Asian Studies/ME Sharpe).

Tordoff, W. and R.L. Watts, 1974. *Report on Central–Provincial Government Relations* (Port Moresby).

Tremewan, Christopher, 1997. 'Singapore in the Asian Human Rights Debate: The Pragmatic Pursuit of Ideology', in Rorden Wilkinson, ed., *Culture, Ethnicity and Human Rights in International Relations* (Wellington: New Zealand Institute of International Affairs).

Truong Quang, 1987. *Agricultural Collectivization and Rural Development in Vietnam: A North/South Study, 1955–1985* (Amsterdam: Academisch Proefschrift).

Tu Wei-Ming, 1984. *Confucian Ethics Today* (Singapore: Federal Publications).

———— 1989. 'The Rise of Industrial East Asia: The Role of Confucian Values', *Copenhagen Papers in East and Southeast Asian Studies: The Modernization Process in East Asia: Economic, Political, and Cultural Perspectives* 4:81–97.

Tuhanuku, Joses, 1995. 'The Reality of Governance in Solomon Islands Today', *Pacific Economic Bulletin* 10, 2:66–84.

Turner, Mark, 1990. *Papua New Guinea: The Challenge of Independence* (Melbourne: Penguin Books).

UNDP, United Nations Development Program, 1994. *Pacific Human Development Report: Putting People First* (Suva: UNDP).

van Dijk, C., 1981. *Rebellion under the Banner of Islam* (The Hague: Martinus Nijhoff).

Van Trease, Howard, 1995. 'The Election', in Howard Van Trease, ed., *Melanesian Politics: Stael Blong Vanuatu* (Christchurch/Suva: Macmillan Brown Centre/Institute of Pacific Studies).

Vasavakul, Thaveeporn, 1995. 'Vietnam: The Changing Models of Legitimation,' in Muthiah Alagappa, ed., *Political Legitimacy in Southeast Asia: The Quest for Moral Authority* (Stanford, CA: Stanford University Press).

Vasil, Raj K., 1984. *Governing Singapore* (Singapore: Eastern Universities Press).

Vietnam, Chu Tich Nuoc, 1993. *Luat Dat Dai* [Land Law] (Hanoi: NXB Chinh Tri Quoc Gia) article 44.

Vietnam, Tong Cuc Thong Ke va Bo Nong Nghiep, 1991. *So Lieu Thong Ke Nong Nghiep: 35 Nam, 1956–1990* [35 years of Agricultural Statistics] (Hanoi: NXB Thong Ke).

Vietnam, Tong Cuc Thong Ke, 1989. *Bao Cao Phan Tich Thong Ke: 30 Nam Hop Tac Hoa Nong Nghiep, 1958–1988* [Statistical analysis: 30 years of Agricultural Cooperativization] (Hanoi: Tong Cuc Thong Ke, July).

Villacorta, Wilfredo V., 1994. 'The Curse of the Weak State: Leadership Imperatives for the Ramos Government', *Contemporary Southeast Asia* 16, 1:67–92.

Villanueva, A.B., 1996. 'Parties and Elections in Philippine Politics', *Contemporary Southeast Asia* 18, 2:175–92.

Waltz, Kenneth, 1979. *Theory of International Politics* Reading, MA: Addison-Wesley).

Wanek, Alexander, 1996. *The State and its Enemies in Papua New Guinea*, Nordic Institute of Asian Studies Monograph Series No 68 (Surrey: Curzon Press).

Wendt, Alexander, 1995. 'Constructing International Politics', *International Security* 20, 1:71–81.

Wesley-Smith, Terence, ed., 1992. 'A Legacy of Development: Three Years of Crisis in Bougainville', Special Issue, *Contemporary Pacific* 4, 2.

White, G., 1994. 'Civil Society, Democratization and Development (I): Clearing the Analytical Ground', *Democratization* 1, 3:375–90.

White, Stephen K., 1994. *Edmund Burke: Modernity, Politics, and Aesthetics* (Thousand Oaks, CA: Sage).

Wilentz, Sean, 1985. 'Introduction—Teufelsdröckh's Dilemma: On Symbolism, Politics, and History', in Sean Wilentz, ed., *Rites of Power: Symbolism, Ritual, and Politics Since the Middle Ages* (Philadelphia: University of Pennsylvania Press).

Winters, Jeffrey, 1996. *Power in Motion: Capital Mobility and the Indonesian State* (Ithaca, NY: Cornell University Press).

Wolfers, E., 1975. *Race Relations and Colonial Rule in Papua New Guinea* (Sydney: Law Book Company).

Woods, D., 1992. 'Civil Society in Europe and Africa: Limiting State Power Through a Public Sphere', *African Studies Review* 35, 2:77–100.

Woodside, Alexander, 1979. 'Nationalism and Poverty in the Breakdown of Sino-Vietnamese Relations', *Pacific Affairs* 52, 3:381–401.

World Bank, 1982. *World Development Report* (New York: Oxford University Press).

—— 1993a. *Pacific Island Economies: Toward Efficient and Sustainable Growth* Volume 1 Overview. Country Department III East Asia and Pacific Region Report 11 351—EAP (Washington, DC: World Bank).

—— 1993b. *The East Asian Miracle: Economic Growth and Public Policy* (New York: Oxford University Press).

—— 1994. *Governance: The World Bank's Experience* (Washington, DC: World Bank).

—— 1995a. *Papua New Guinea: Delivering Public Services*, Volume II The Main Report, Country Department III East Asia and Pacific Region Report No 14414—PNG (Washington, DC: World Bank).

—— 1995b. *World Development Report* (New York: Oxford University Press).

—— 1997. *The State in a Changing World: Development Report* (Washington, DC: World Bank).

Wu Teh Yao, 1979. *Politics East—Politics West* (Singapore: Pan Pacific Book Distributors).

Wurfel, David, 1988. *Filipino Politics: Development and Decay* (Ithaca, NY: Cornell University Press).

Yosef, Roy, 1995. 'The Electoral Process', in Howard Van Trease, ed., *Melanesian Politics: Stael Blong Vanuatu* (Christchurch/Suva: Macmillan Brown Centre/Institute of Pacific Studies).

Index

210

on local strongmen 110
on Sierra Leone 95, 98
on Vietnam 159
reform in states and societies 111
see also states
Mindanao 72n20
minorities 71
missionaries 42, 43
Moerdani, General Benny 104–105
Moro Islamic Liberation Front 68
Moro National Liberation Front 68, 69
Muslims 70

Nacionalista Party 73
Nahdatul Ulama 97
Namaliu, Sir Rabbie 74
Nasser 108
national identity 71, 117
nationalism 89–90
Negara 30
Neo-Confucianism *see* Confucianism,
    in Singapore
nepotism 47n5, 65
Netherlands 95–97
Netherlands East Indies 95
New Caledonia 77
New Guinea 43, 144
New Society Movement see *Kilusang
    Bagong Lipunan* (KBL)
Nigeria 12
Non-governmental organisations
    (NGOs) 66, 85, 140, 141, 142
Non-state organisations 2, 4, 8, 9, 10,
    135–139 *passim*, 142, 154
North Solomons *see* Bougainville

Occidentalism 118, 129
oil 105, 106
Ombudsman Commission 39
opposition
    and Confucian thought 121–125
    and cultural values 132
    and democracy 120–121
    in Singapore 133
order *see* Papua New Guinea
organisational theory 12, 17n3, 21
organisational theorists 17, 19, 36
Orientalism 118

Pakistan 12
Pancasila 102, 103, 139, 140, 141

Papua 42, 43, 48, 49
Papua New Guinea 5
    aid to 3
    and constitutional reform 74–75
    and exchanges with citizens 86, 87
    and international support 84, 85
    and land tenure 80, 82, 90
    and manipulation of meaning 87,
        89, 91
    and nationalism 90
    and society 66
    and state and society 60–61, 68–69,
        70, 83
    and state in 4–5, 64–65, 75–76
    compared to Philippines 5, 61–63
    development in 86
    forestry industry in 78–79
    Highlands 40, 43, 44, 45, 48n6, 49,
        54, 55
    independence of 77
    languages in 42, 61
    order in
        and decolonisation 45–48
        and independence and
            development 48–52
        discussion of 55–59
        in historical perspective 40–45
        introduction 38–40
        state responses to 52–55
    police force 46, 52–56 *passim*, 59
    sexual behaviour in 79
    United Nations Visiting Mission
        (1962) 47
    see also capacity, corruption,
        elections, legitimacy, Melanesia,
        participation, logging
Partai Demokrasi Indonesia 140
Partai Persatuan Pembangunan 140
participation 60, 67, 68, 69, 78, 119–
    120, 161
    in Melanesia 80
    in PNG 47–48, 58
    in Singapore 133
patronage 6, 157
    in Indonesia 6, 7, 100, 101, 102,
        105–113 *passim*, 141
patrons and clients 4, 12, 21–22, 22, 36
    in Indonesia 136, 141–142
    in Melanesia 84
    in Philippines 5
    in Solomon Islands 143, 155

THE DEPARTMENT OF INTERNATIONAL RELATIONS
PUBLICATIONS

STUDIES IN WORLD AFFAIRS

The Department of International Relations produces a series of monographs which are published in association with and distributed by Allen & Unwin Pty Ltd, 9 Atchison St, St Leonards, NSW 2065, Australia, Ph: (02) 9901 4088, Fax: (02) 9906 2218, E-mail: 100252.103@compuserve.com. Titles are:

Ethics and Foreign Policy,
edited by Paul Keal, 272pp, $24.95

Korea Under Roh Tae-woo: Democratisation, Northern Policy, and Inter-Korean Relations,
edited by James Cotton, 367pp, $24.95

Asian–Pacific Security After the Cold War,
edited by T.B. Millar and
James Walter, 152pp, $24.95

The Post-Cold War Order: Diagnoses and Prognoses,
edited by Richard Leaver and James L. Richardson, 288pp, $24.95

Dependent Ally: A Study in Australian Foreign Policy,
by Coral Bell,
205pp, $24.95

A Peaceful Ocean? Maritime Security in the Pacific in the Post-Cold War Era,
edited by Andrew Mack, 232pp, $24.95

Asian Flashpoint: Security and the Korean Peninsula,
edited by Andrew Mack, 188pp, $24.95

Taiwan in the Asia–Pacific in the 1990s,
edited by Gary Klintworth,
300pp, $24.95

Pacific Cooperation: Building Economic and Security Regimes in the Asia–Pacific,
edited by Andrew Mack and John Ravenhill, 275pp, $24.95

The Gulf War: Critical Perspectives,
edited by Michael McKinley, 209pp, $24.95

Search for Security: The Political Economy of Australia's Postwar Foreign and Defence Policy,
by David Lee, 193pp, $24.95

The New Agenda for Global Security: Cooperating for Peace and Beyond,
edited by Stephanie Lawson, 229pp, $24.95

Presumptive Engagement: Australia's Asia–Pacific Security Policy in the 1990s,
by Desmond Ball and Pauline Kerr, 234pp, $24.95

Discourses of Danger and Dread Frontiers: Australian Defence and Security Thinking After the Cold War,
edited by Graeme Cheeseman and Robert Bruce, 327pp, $24.95

Pacific Rim Development: Integration and Globalisation in the Asia–Pacific Economy,
edited by Peter J. Rimmer, 308pp, $24.95

Evatt to Evans: The Labor Tradition in Australian Foreign Policy,
edited by David Lee and Christopher Waters, 253pp, $24.95

Cambodia—From Red to Blue: Australia's Initiative for Peace
by Ken Berry, 387pp, $24.95

Asia–Pacific Security: The Economics–Politics Nexus,
edited by Stuart Harris and Andrew Mack, 311pp. $24.95

China's Ocean Frontier: International Law, Military Force and National Development
by Greg Austin, 447pp, $24.95

Weak and Strong States in Asia–Pacific Societies,
edited by Peter Dauvergne, 220pp, $24.95

These titles may be ordered from good bookshops in most English-speaking countries. In case of difficulty please contact the Export Department of Allen & Unwin (address details as above) for details of local stockists.

CANBERRA STUDIES IN WORLD AFFAIRS

Distributed by: Bibliotech, Reply Paid 440 (no postage required if posted in Australia), ANUTECH Pty Ltd, Canberra, ACT 0200, Australia, Fax order: (06) 257 1433.

THE AUSTRALIAN FOREIGN POLICY PROGRAMME

PUBLICATIONS

Australia's Alliance Options: Prospect and Retrospect in a World of Change,
by Coral Bell, 104pp, $15.00

Selling Mirages: the Politics of Arms Trading,
by Graeme Cheeseman, 85pp, $15.00

Australia's Human Rights Diplomacy,
by Ian Russell, Peter Van Ness and Beng-Huat Chua, 179pp, $15.00

The European Community in Context,
by John Groom, 47pp, $15.00

Coping with Washington: Players, Conventions and Strategies,
by Davis Bobrow, 28pp, $10.00

The Search for Substance: Australia–India Relations into the Nineties and Beyond,
by Sandy Gordon, 107pp, $15.00

Protecting the Antarctic Environment: Australia and the Minerals Convention,
by Lorraine Elliott, 94pp, $15.00

Australia's Taiwan Policy 1942–1992,
by Gary Klintworth, 150pp, $20.00

Australia and the New World Order: Evatt in San Francisco, 1945,
by W.J. Hudson, 160pp, $20.00

The Beijing Massacre: Australian Responses,
by Kim Richard Nossal,
80pp, $15.00

The Pacific Patrol Boat Project: A Case Study of Australian Defence Cooperation,
by Anthony Bergin, 51pp, $10.00

A Select Bibliography of Australia's Foreign Relations, 1975–1992,
compiled by Pauline Kerr, David Sullivan and Robin Ward, 112pp, $20.00

Australia's Evolving American Relationship: Interests, Processes, and Prospects for Australian Influence,
by Henry S. Albinski, 52pp, $10.00

Prices exclude postage and packaging.

Publications can be obtained from Bibliotech, ANUTECH, Canberra ACT 0200 Australia, Fax No: (06) 257 1433